W9-AQM-267

John & Onik,

I hope these success stories make america proud of what you & others have done to make manufacturing great and add to your future success.

Jay J.

HF5386. Jasinowski, Jerry
J383   Hamrin, Robert
   1995   **Making it in America**

HF5386. Jasinowski, Jerry
J383   Hamrin, Robert
   1995   **Making it in America**

DEMCO

JERRY JASINOWSKI

AND

ROBERT HAMRIN

SIMON & SCHUSTER

NEW YORK LONDON TORONTO TOKYO SINGAPORE SYDNEY

MAKINGIT INAMERICA

50

PROVEN PATHS TO SUCCESS FROM

FIFTY TOP COMPANIES

SIMON & SCHUSTER
Rockefeller Center
1230 Avenue of the Americas
New York, New York 10020

Copyright © 1995 by National Association of Manufacturers
All rights reserved,
including the right of reproduction
in whole or in part in any form.

Simon & Schuster and colophon are registered trademarks
of Simon & Schuster Inc.

Designed by Karolina Harris

Manufactured in the United States of America

10 9 8 7 6 5 4 3 2 1

Library of Congress Cataloging-in-Publication Data
Jasinowski, Jerry J.
    Making it in America : proven paths to success from fifty top companies /
Jerry Jasinowski and Robert Hamrin.
        p.   cm.
    Includes index.
        1. Success in business—United States—Case studies.   2. United States—
Manufactures—Case studies.   3. Total quality management—United States—
Case studies.   I. Hamrin, Robert D.   II. Title.
HF5386.J383   1995
658—dc20   94-41724   CIP
ISBN 0-671-50756-7

ACKNOWLEDGMENTS

The people we wish to thank right up front are those who made these fifty success stories happen—the men and women who are the workers, managers, and senior executives at each of the fifty companies. We salute their creativity, courage, and commitment to achieving success. We also want to thank the primary contact persons at each company for providing so much information to us in a prompt and kindly manner and for helping to arrange the interviews. Finally, there are the scores of individuals who were interviewed for the ten case studies, most of whose voices are heard directly in the book.

We also are indebted to a number of senior executives, all of whom are among the nation's top business leaders, for their wonderful insights and their words of front-line wisdom that helped strengthen the book immeasurably. The following individuals took time out from their overloaded schedules to review our opening chapters and the overall structure of the book and then provide their helpful suggestions in lengthy personal and phone interviews: William Adams, CEO (retired), Armstrong World Industries Inc.; Dexter Baker, chairman and CEO (retired) Air Products and Chemicals Inc.; Peter Browning, executive vice president, Sonoco Products Company; Robert Cizik, chairman and CEO, Cooper Industries; Allan Dugan, senior vice president, Xerox Corporation; James Dunlap, president, Texaco USA; George Fisher, CEO, Eastman Kodak Company; Stan Gault, chairman and CEO, The Goodyear Tire and Rubber Company; John Hartley, chairman and CEO, Harris Corporation; Lee Iacocca, CEO (retired), Chrysler Corporation; J. W. Kisling, chairman and CEO, Multiples Co. Inc.; Harvey Mackay, chairman and CEO, Mackay Envelope Corporation; Dana Mead, CEO, Tenneco Inc.; Tracy O'Rourke, CEO, Varian Associates Inc.; Robert Pritzker, president and CEO, The Marmon Group Inc.; John Young, CEO (retired), Hewlett-Packard Company.

Also instrumental in the early shaping of the book, joining in many meetings with us, were Denny Gulino and Peter Hannaford. Laura Brown, Gabe Berg, Angie Fine, and Robb Enright did a variety of organizational and communications tasks that helped make the path smoother for us. And special thanks go to Charles Day, Jr., Editor in Chief of *Industry Week,* whose personal insights and magazine provided valuable information on a number of the success stories.

When it came time to getting the book in the right hands, our literary agent, Jonathon Lazear, acted with swift and courteous dispatch to put us in touch with the nation's finest publisher, Simon & Schuster. Jonathon also gave some valuable advice about the book's focus and structure. We are delighted to have worked with Bob Bender, senior editor and vice president, at Simon & Schuster. We knew from our first phone conversation with him that he is a man who wonderfully combines a keen professionalism with a warm and gracious spirit.

Our wives, Isabel Jasinowski and Carol Hamrin, not only were always enthusiastically supporting the project right throughout its two-year lifespan, but they also provided invaluable editorial assistance and advice about the book title and companies to consider, to say nothing of a contract-signing party that brought our two families together in a delightful evening of celebration.

And each of us, individually, would like to say to the other, "Thanks for making this such an enjoyable, productive, and harmonious collaboration, from beginning to end."

For Isabel, who is a wellspring of support and positive
energy, and my children, Abe, Paul, and Anne Marie, who
have challenged me to look anew at life each day.

J.J.

For Carol and our three children—Eric, Krista, and Kira,
my daily sources of joy—and for John Bernbaum,
a true friend through life's peaks and valleys.

R.H.

CONTENTS

FOREWORD BY LEE IACOCCA   13

INTRODUCTION   15

1: SUNRISE FOR MANUFACTURING   24

2: TEN PATHS TO SUCCESS   33

I: RELEASING THE CREATIVITY AND POWER OF WORKERS

3: EMPOWER EMPLOYEES   51

Grassroots Empowerment—LORD CORP.
Do the Right Thing—HERMAN MILLER
Employee Involvement Works at New and Old Plants—GOODYEAR TIRE & RUBBER
The Boss Has Got to Let Go—JOHNSONVILLE FOODS
Empower the Unions Too—USX

4: TRAIN AND RETRAIN WORKERS   80

The Magic That Happens with Education—WILL-BURT
85 Percent Always in Training—CHAPARRAL STEEL
Training at No Additional Cost—CR INDUSTRIES
Apprenticeship Is Alive and Well—REMMELE ENGINEERING
A Training Partnership with the Union—FORD MOTOR CO.

5: REWARD GOOD PERFORMANCE   103

Money Motivates People—LINCOLN ELECTRIC
You Help Create Gains, You Share in Them—WHIRLPOOL
Hardworking Millionaire Steel Workers—OREGON STEEL MILLS
Another ESOP to the Rescue—REFLEXITE
Everyone Gets an Equal Share of the Pie—NUCOR

II: PLEASING CUSTOMERS AND FINDING NEW MARKETS

6: EXCEED CUSTOMER EXPECTATIONS   127

Know, and Care for, Every Customer—GREAT PLAINS SOFTWARE
Unprecedented Service—DELL COMPUTER
The CEO Meets with the Customers—PREMIER INDUSTRIAL
Hop on Your Harleys and Find the Customers—HARLEY-DAVIDSON
A Direct Line of Sight to the Customer—XEROX

7: ENVISION NEW PRODUCTS AND MARKETS   154

A New-Product-Generating Machine—RUBBERMAID
Good Products—That's It—MICROSOFT
Spin Out Rather Than Spin Off—THERMO ELECTRON
Wackiness and Reinvention—ODETICS
166 Companies to Create Products—JOHNSON & JOHNSON

8: GO GLOBAL   178

Break the Mold and Sell to the World—SUN MICROSYSTEMS
Just Get Out There and Sell—CANNONDALE
Invest Abroad, Invest Again, and Invest Some More—AIR PRODUCTS AND CHEMICALS
Going Global Before Going Domestic—WADIA DIGITAL
The Small Can Span the Globe—RUST EVADER

III: FOCUSING ON CONTINUOUS IMPROVEMENT

9: PURSUE TOTAL QUALITY   205

Toward the Perfect Company—MOTOROLA
Total Employee Involvement Is Fundamental to Quality Improvement—AMP
Being Best-Cost in Whatever We Do—EMERSON ELECTRIC
Total Transformation from a Little Book—UNITED ELECTRIC CONTROLS
TQM Is Something You Are—HARDINGE BROTHERS

10: ACHIEVE ENVIRONMENTAL EXCELLENCE   235

Pollution Prevention Really Pays—3M
Quick Results—COOPER TIRE & RUBBER
Innovate to Meet Impossible Standards—SEARLE
Tying Environmental and Quality Improvements Together—DOW CHEMICAL
Investing in Environmental R&D—EASTMAN CHEMICAL

11: INCREASE SPEED AND AGILITY   258

The Factory of the Future Today—ALLEN-BRADLEY
Selling "Virtual Products" to Customers—ROSS CONTROLS
The Power of Continuous Flow Manufacturing—BADGER METER
The Closest Thing to a Virtual Corporation—KINGSTON TECHNOLOGY
CIM Provides the Competitive Edge—PEAVEY ELECTRONICS

12: SHAKE UP THE ORGANIZATION   285

The Paranoid Survive, and Thrive—INTEL
Shake Out the Complacency—COMPAQ
Reinventing Auto Making—CHRYSLER
Perpetual Revolution—VARIAN ASSOCIATES
Strike Quickly/Strike Boldly—TENNECO

NOTES   327

INDEX   337

FOREWORD

The comeback of American industry over the past decade is one of the great stories of this century.

And I like comebacks. I like them so much that I presided over two of them at Chrysler.

American industry regrouped in the mid-1980s, staged a mighty rally, and is once again the clear leader in the world economy. It leads the world in productivity, in exports, and in low-cost, high-quality products.

Making It in America gives us fifty real-life company success stories to thoroughly document American industry's comeback. It's a book about the challenges these companies faced, how they responded to them, and the remarkable results they have enjoyed.

The stories themselves do most of the teaching. The people talk who should do the talking—the workers, managers, and CEOs of the companies. The human drama of achieving success comes alive. After all, it's *people* who create success—*not companies.*

You live and you die by your people. The executive suite cannot create success if the minds of the workers are shut off. Release those minds, listen to your people, act on what they suggest, and it's absolutely amazing what will result.

I learned this clearly and unmistakably at Chrysler during the toughest years of my career. We didn't just listen to our employees; we let them tell us how to cut $4 billion in costs from the company in just three years.

Chrysler's overall results far exceeded our expectations. And, I'm proud to say, it is now the acknowledged world leader in new car development, and is the world's leading low-cost auto producer.

Chrysler's story is only one of fifty success stories that will give you a strong, positive feeling about America again, and a new hope for the future. And these fifty stories are just a fraction of the business success stories that are occurring throughout America.

There will be many more success stories to come *if* other companies —those in services as well as manufacturing—follow the paths to success that Jasinowski and Hamrin outline. As this business comeback spreads to tens of thousands of companies, America will almost certainly retain its position as global economic leader for many years to come.

What it boils down to is a simple, yet profound, "back-to-basics" movement on the part of corporate America. Use the full talents, energies, and creative juices of your workers. Treat your customers right and get to know them well. Shape and reshape all your processes until they run as efficiently and flexibly as possible.

Sounds simple? Take it from me—it hasn't been!

But this book is the best way I know to make achieving success simpler. It is the complete report on real business success stories I have seen, and it is interesting and fun to read.

Lee Iacocca

INTRODUCTION

To most people, it is a surprising discovery: America is in the midst of a business renaissance and economic comeback that have profound and promising implications for businesses, consumers, workers, and the country's economic future. The renaissance, steadily gaining momentum over the past decade in hundreds of manufacturing companies across America, is the fundamental reason why America's economic sun is rising.

This new dynamism of American industry is a historic development. American industry has not just caught up to the competition; it has *gone beyond the competition*. American manufacturing is again becoming the industrial powerhouse of the world, making enormous contributions to the quality of American life. But most of the American public, and even many American business leaders and workers, are unaware of this important news.

This book's purpose is to let the news out—to tell fifty extraordinary, real-life business success stories that are shining examples of the full sweep of corporate changes that are powering the renaissance. The stories clearly show how any company—really any organization and individuals within those organizations—can achieve success and be part of the spreading renaissance.

Making it in America means several things: making high-quality products in America that add value and variety to people's lives, achieving individual and company success stories under challenging conditions, and American manufacturing continuing to serve as a primary source of wealth and higher living standards in America.

FINDING YOUR PATH TO SUCCESS

These success stories will help you discover your own path to success —whether you are a business leader, a worker, or a student about to enter the workforce. Our success stories come from the manufacturing arena, but the ten paths to success are applicable to service companies as well as government and nonprofit organizations. Large and small, high-tech and low-tech, young and old—every type of company is covered and that means every kind can achieve success.

Success—and how to achieve it—is infused through each page of this book. You'll see bottom-line success highlighted in the closing section titled "The Results" of each company's success story. We think you will agree with us that remarkable results such as these deserve to be celebrated and sought after.

- AMP's quality efforts led to a tenfold improvement in product and service quality in just five years.
- Johnsonville Foods' worker empowerment helped productivity take a gigantic 300 percent leap from 1984 to 1992 while sales increased fifteenfold.

Such real results fire the imagination for what's possible at your company.

The "how to" part of achieving success is seen in "The Response" section of each success story. Then to help you identify the key to how each company achieved success and the specific ways you, too, can achieve success that beats the competition, we highlight a succinct "Lesson" at the end of each story. For instance, learn how to act fast and become a world-class company from Tenneco:

[
LESSON: When trouble abounds, strike quickly and boldly—then stress leadership, quality, and results in order to become a world-class company over the long haul.
]

Often the lessons are counterintuitive, such as this one from CR Industries:

[
LESSON: Training can be expanded to every corner of the corporation without adding training costs by using your own employees as trainers.
]

Lessons for success can also be found in the numerous direct quotes of CEOs, managers, and production workers that bring each success story to life, such as these from Intel CEO Andrew Grove: "We have shot several projects in the head . . . I'm very proud of that." "Ultimately, speed is the only weapon we have." "The more people nip at our heels, the faster we go. One by one, these mosquitos will be swept away by the wind." "Only the paranoid survive."

Overall, a counterintuitive yet profound lesson from the CEOs helping to lead America's business comeback is this: *If it ain't broke, break it.* The old way of doing things—even many former successes—is just not good enough to meet today's competition.

BALANCING BASIC VALUES AND CHANGE

The business renaissance that is unfolding in America is the greatest business change in a century. Why is it occurring now? What is driving it?

What's at work in the American business community today is a dynamic tension between two powerful forces—a back to the basics and to fundamental values aimed at achieving a clear focus and stability *and* an open and eager spirit to constantly innovate and improve in order to deal with explosive change. The truly successful company is the one that can balance both. It will build upon a foundation of long-held values such as honesty, integrity, fairness, and trust while also doing all it can to boldly innovate, be entrepreneurial, and, yes, at times, to really shake up the organization as it welcomes and even embraces change.

That's a tough tension to balance, but as the fifty companies in this book demonstrate, it is possible and the rewards for doing so are great.

The tension is actually great news for America, for it gives it a distinct competitive advantage in today's global economy. Two facts explain why. Fact one: the new economy is based on information and knowledge, thus making a company's success depend most directly on the twin assets of intellect and imagination. Fact two: the distinguishing hallmarks of the American people are ingenuity, flexibility, a competitive spirit, and a drive to constantly change and improve. What we are seeing in America's business renaissance is nothing less than the reawakening of the historical strengths of the American people as they assert themselves with a power unsurpassed in recent American business history.

Thus, at its core, the business renaissance involves companies releasing the full creative power of individuals. This means everything associated with the extraordinary capability of the American people, such as their flexibility, imagination and creativity as well as their willingness to change, build on ideas, challenge the system, and be entrepreneurial. Employing this "people power," companies are constantly learning and continuously improving.

Please note that this emphasis on people—their ideas and learning —differs fundamentally from America's industrial revolution in the mid-1800s, where machine power was central and workers were viewed as adjuncts to the machines. Thus, the nineteenth-century industrial revolution in America has given way to the late-twentieth-century business renaissance where people are central and machines are the helpful adjuncts.

THE DRAMA OF HUMAN ACHIEVEMENT

The closer one looks at what is happening the more fascinating it becomes, for as you focus on people, you see real-life human drama played out with a wide sweep of human emotions: anger, hope, pride, and passion. Yes, *passion*. A sizable majority of the creative changes highlighted in this book occurred because of the passion for improvement on the part of one or more individuals in the company.

Often that person was the CEO. Though we discovered no single magic formula for success, there is in fact something that comes mighty close—a CEO with vision plus passion. Step one for major transformation in a company is for a leader to develop a clear vision of the company he or she wants in the future and the changes needed to get there, taking full advantage of the opportunities for improvement. It involves a willingness to look at the world differently. Step two is to have the passion to make certain that vision is fulfilled. It's thinking plus action. It's dreaming and dogged perseverance.

Jack Welch, chairman of General Electric, a behemoth company long known for its lumbering bureaucracy, displayed both qualities in driving the major transformation of GE through the decade of the 1980s: "If your change isn't big enough, revolutionary enough, the bureaucracy can beat you. When you get leaders who confuse popularity with leadership, who just nibble away at things, nothing changes." That's big thinking and deep passion. That's also a leader, not a mere manager talking.

While corporate transformations are often born from the vision of a CEO, they ultimately succeed or fail because of the workers' attitudes and behavior. For change to really begin, the workers must accept it. For change to really succeed in transforming a plant or company, the workers must embrace it. They must become passionate about making it work.

> It's like I want to beat them all. I want to do it because management has given us their trust and their respect and I want to earn that. I want to let them know that I don't want to lose that. I like it and I want to keep it that way. Whatever it takes, I'm willing to do that.
> —Debbie Phillips, operator at Lord Corp.'s Dayton plant

THE REMARKABLE COMEBACK OF AMERICAN MANUFACTURERS

It is truly amazing how so much can change so swiftly. In the mid-1980s, many in America were lamenting the "death of manufacturing." Obituaries on the Rust Belt were being written.

Japan would "bury us." The decline of America was at hand.

But in the mid-1990s, there are unmistakable signs that America's manufacturers have made a comeback—a comeback so strong that it has once again firmly put them in a global leadership position. As we show in Chapter 1, there has been a tremendous resurgence of American exports such that America became the number one exporter again in 1992. Further, productivity growth in manufacturing has been very strong over the past decade, helping America retain its number one position in overall level of manufacturing productivity.

There are many other indications of a manufacturers' comeback. The quality of American products is once again very high—a recent poll by Peter Hart showed that 66 percent of Americans felt that quality had improved in the past five years. By most performance criteria, U.S. manufacturers are the world leaders in many high-tech industries, including computers, chemicals, pharmaceuticals, data processing and reproduction, computer software, and electronic components and instruments. And major industries in the U.S. have come back smartly to achieve world preeminence, led by autos, steel, and semiconductors. The overall result is a highly competitive economy—indeed, America's economy was ranked number one in the world in terms of competitiveness by the World Economic Forum in 1994.

The comeback of American manufacturers has in turn powered the comeback of whole regions of the United States, the most dramatic example being the Midwest. The infamous Rust Belt of the 1980s is now a booming region—one where most states can trace one in six manufacturing jobs to export-related work. The mountain states' comeback also owes a great deal to manufacturing companies. It comes as a great surprise to most that Utah led the nation in industrial growth in 1993, followed closely by New Mexico, Nevada, Idaho, Colorado, and Arizona.

We want to emphasize that the forging of the business renaissance has had some considerable costs associated with it. Chief among these is the downsizing by U.S. companies over the past decade, which has cost millions of American workers their jobs. But alongside the downsizing have come benefits that accrue not only to the broad economy but also to workers, an issue explored more fully in Chapter 1. Among these benefits are that downsizing played an instrumental role in making America competitive again and often paves the way for upsizing as newly efficient companies learn how to do things smarter and begin to grow and provide new jobs. Another critical point is that not all the jobs lost from manufacturing were actually lost, as many are now found in service companies that directly serve and provide input to manufacturers. The final point that must be understood is this: the manufacturing sector is the catalyst for new service industry development and the overall growth of the economy.

CHOOSING THE COMPANIES

We did not set out to write a book about America's business renaissance. Our initial goal was much less ambitious and quite straightforward: to write a book telling success stories of manufacturing companies and inspire others to follow their example.

We also wanted to tackle head-on the pessimism about American manufacturing that became so widespread in the mid-1980s. We are not arguing that the negative stories about manufacturing weren't often true. Serious problems continue to beset many manufacturing companies. Much of American management still operates in the patterns of the past. But we knew that the whole story wasn't getting out and we felt that many of the bold and creative success initiatives needed equal time.

So we came up with a simple but powerful idea for a book: Go to the workers, the managers, and the CEOs of these companies and ask what was working, see what lessons we could learn, and then tell these success stories to other manufacturers and to everyone who desires business success both now and into the twenty-first century.

This book, then, is grounded in what manufacturers know works, and works well, in the real world. No other book presents such a complete documentation of what successful American companies and American workers are doing right: the new perspectives and practices that are making many manufacturers global pacesetters.

Here's how we chose the fifty success stories. First, we surveyed thousands of manufacturers and talked to dozens of experts and industry and state trade associations about their favorite company success stories. We scoured the literature. We came up with roughly 200 strong and interesting candidates. So how did we narrow the field from 200 to fifty?

We diligently reviewed annual reports and financial documents. We consulted experts, labor and business leaders, and workers. We thoroughly evaluated the press record. In choosing the best fifty stories, we looked for interesting angles, new twists, and strong representation of small to midsize companies, for they represent 95 percent of America's 376,000 manufacturers.

From the final fifty, we chose the stellar success story under each Path to Success as our case study. Personal interviews through site visits with the workers, managers, and often the CEO, help portray the full human drama in each company's story.

But in the end, it really came down to this: you know outstanding success when you see it. It's not very scientific, but it's true. You too will see how the successes portrayed in this book leap out at you.

DISCOVERING THE PATHS TO SUCCESS

As we were writing the success stories, we began to search for patterns emerging from the bottom up. Rather than starting with preconceived theories, we asked what "paths to success" emerged from the actual story specifics. The ten paths that emerged show there is no single silver bullet to meet corporate challenges or solve crises. Rather than fads, you will see in each path proven fundamentals for success.

The ten paths to success can be logically grouped into three basic categories that should be the long-term focus of every company desiring success: workers, customers, and process and structure improvement. These broad categories form the three parts of our book: Releasing the Creativity and Power of Workers, Pleasing Customers and Finding New Markets, and Focusing on Continuous Improvement.

Most importantly, these form the basis for our book's three broad themes that explain why American business is so resilient and will remain highly competitive. The first theme is the remarkable capacity of the American people for self-improvement and personal growth: to meet new challenges head-on, to be flexible and open to new ideas and rapid change, and to be creative in solving problems and seizing new opportunities. The second theme reflects the competitive and growth-oriented nature of the American people: serving customers exceedingly well, creating new products, and finding new markets both at home and abroad. The third theme centers on Yankee ingenuity—the ability to innovate, apply new technologies and seek continuous improvement in the way products are made.

The end result is a book that takes you on a Grand Tour of the real stories that make up America's business renaissance. Some books or articles focus on quality. Others focus on employee empowerment or on customers. A very few may talk about improving technologies and processes or shaking up the organization.

Each of these individual success initiatives is important. But viewing the broad range, as this book uniquely does, helps one appreciate the multiple paths to success as well as the positive synergism of pursing several paths simultaneously as many of the fifty companies have done.

Ideally, a company would periodically "shake up the organization" —putting into play all of the first nine paths simultaneously. As the former CEO of Tenneco, Mike Walsh put it: "Push the needle all the way over [because] organizations are capable of taking on more than most of their leaders give them credit for."

TAKING THE ROAD TO CONTINUOUS IMPROVEMENT

As in Robert Frost's famous poem, American companies are now at a clear fork in the road. They can take the familiar, comfortable path, following the practices and policies that they have grown accustomed to. They may be able to trod this first road for a few more years, but that's about it. The likelihood is that they will become stagnant or out of business altogether by the year 2000.

Or they can take "the road less traveled," which involves a fundamental rethinking of what it is they should be doing, the way they organize work, the way they service their customers, seeing new potential customers, and most importantly becoming a continuous learning and continuous improvement organization.

That is the key: all companies that want to become successful—and maintain that success—must continuously learn and improve. This is as true for the fifty companies in this book as anybody else. If they do not maintain the continuous improvement edge, they too will fall behind the competition. Indeed, the biggest challenge these companies face—and any companies that achieve success will face—is maintaining a sense of urgency for continuous improvement.

Our hope is that as these success stories become widely known, they will inspire companies and other institutions, particularly government, across America to embark on the ten paths to success highlighted in this book—paths that are becoming mandatory for companies to survive, and thrive, in the harsh competition of the global economy.

We think it's a sure bet: No company will want to be left out of America's business renaissance.

1: SUNRISE FOR MANUFACTURING

"Not only the wealth but the independence and safety of a country appear to be materially connected with the prosperity of manufactures."
— ALEXANDER HAMILTON, U.S. SECRETARY OF THE TREASURY, 1789-95

The first rays of America's rising economic sun began to appear in the mid-1980s. They were so dim at first that most people missed them altogether; indeed many thought that America's days in the economic sun were gone for good. By the end of the decade, however, these rays were already shining quite brilliantly, signaling a major comeback for American industry.

And make no mistake about it, it was American industry—not government policies or programs—that generated its own comeback and caused the sun to rise again. The American public is increasingly turning to business for solutions to societal problems and improvement in their quality of life.

There was improvement both domestically and internationally. Domestically, there were stellar gains in manufacturing productivity and technology, with America experiencing average yearly manufacturing productivity increases of 3 percent plus in the 1980s, which in turn enabled U.S. industry to continue as the world leader in the overall level of productivity. Internationally, America experienced an extraordinary export boom. Peter Drucker observed: "The most important event in the world economy in the late 1980s was the boom in U.S. manufacturing exports. . . . The export boom was unprecedented in American history, and indeed, in economic history altogether."

Stellar productivity gains in manufacturing. A manufacturing export boom.

It is fascinating that American manufacturing has led the American economy's competitive resurgence in recent years. This should finally put to rest all the talk about a postindustrial society and "deindustrializtion."

Everything has not been bright on the manufacturing front in recent years. In particular, the cutback in employees that has become known as downsizing has been a painful process for companies and, most of all, for the millions of workers who have been laid off. Most of these were good workers that were laid off through no fault of their own but rather due to general economic conditions, stiff foreign competition, and the bloated, inefficient state that so many American companies were in during the mid-1980s. Downsizing is without doubt the greatest cost incurred in the forging of America's business renaissance.

But we must not forget that alongside this cost, significant benefits accrued that far outweigh it. And that's true not only for the broad economy, but on the job front as well.

The first major benefit is that the downsizing helped to make America competitive again. This happened as companies removed much of the inefficient bloat that was keeping them from being globally competitive. And in today's global economy, being noncompetitive globally means your very survival is at stake, to which the stories of many of the fifty companies in this book attest. Remember, too, that companies were not just downsizing the number of employees but they were also empowering, training, and refocusing employees as part of their overall restructuring. The overall result—a highly competitive and productive economy—is going to lead to greater levels of future investment and growth, which will in turn generate many more jobs in coming years than would otherwise exist.

A second benefit definitely lost in all the media laments about downsizing is that downsizing often paves the way for upsizing. Indeed, a September 1994 study showed that two of every three companies that were laying off workers were simultaneously hiring other workers. What often happens is that companies cut in areas that no longer give them a competitive advantage and expand in areas that add value. In 13 percent of downsizing firms, there was actually a net increase in jobs. Also, a newly restructured and downsized company will often begin to experience a new growth that generates jobs. Many of these new jobs came from new export markets. From the start of the export boom in 1986, 2.3 million new jobs have been created because of the rise in exports. Certainly many of the companies in this book have increased their number of employees, some dramatically. The big picture to keep in mind is that the economy did generate 5.5 million new jobs from 1992 to mid-1994. And these new jobs paid more, not less, than the national average of $15.50 per hour.

A final important point is that the degree of downsizing that has occurred has been overstated and, more important, manufacturers are net generators of jobs. Part of the downsizing is due to the fact that a majority of American manufacturers have lost a sizable number of jobs in recent years because they spun off many of the service functions they used to perform in-house. As manufacturers continue to add more services to their product offerings, these spin-off service companies often grow smartly. Further, many new service companies have been created that primarily or exclusively cater to manufacturers. One study showed that 12 percent of America's workers are employed in the production-oriented service sector, the highest percentage of any industrialized country. This points to an absolutely critical fact: it is the manufacturing sector that gives the most powerful thrust to service industries and the economic growth of the nation.

MANUFACTURING'S "MAGIC MULTIPLIER"

Perhaps the most surprising fact to emerge about manufacturing in the 1980s—the decade of "the death of manufacturing"—is that its share of the economy *increased*. There was also a growing awareness that manufacturing has a "magic multiplier" impact on the rest of the economy that is much greater than the service sector's multiplier. The basic facts are succinctly expressed in a 1993 Congressional Research Service study by David Cantor:

A tendency to view manufacturing as a relatively noncompetitive sector in the U.S. economy appears to be incorrect. First, U.S. manufacturing activity increased somewhat as a contributor to Gross Domestic Product (GDP) during the 1980s from about 21.5 percent in 1980 to nearly 23 percent in 1989. Second, and perhaps of greater importance, the stimulus of manufacturing on the economy is greater than virtually all other broadly defined sectors of the economy. In 1987, the most recent year for which official data are available, a change in manufacturing output of $1 resulted in a total increase in output throughout the economy of $2.30. By way of contrast, a change of $1 in the output of the service sector—the largest of the five broadly defined economic sectors—resulted in a total change in the outputs of all sectors of the economy of about $1.60 in 1987. These indicators of the role of manufacturing point to its significance in the economy.

Here's what the magic multiplier means in terms of manufacturing's overall contribution to the economy. Beyond what manufacturing adds directly to the GDP through direct sales, it stimulates a great deal of additional activity through its demand for intermediate products, raw materials, and services. Add up all of this ancillary activity stimulated by manufacturing and you find that manufacturing accounts for roughly 31 percent of total economic activity—significantly greater than its direct contribution.

Cantor found that the impact of manufacturing on the economy is roughly 1.5 times that of services. The evidence is indisputable: the manufacturing sector supplies by far the greatest stimulus to the American economy per dollar of economic activity. Recognition of this magic multiplier for manufacturing is the first step in understanding why manufacturing is the key to America's economic future—its growth, productivity, job creation, and its standard of living.

THE COMEBACK OF MAJOR INDUSTRIES

What is perhaps most surprising about the U.S. manufacturing resurgence is the comeback of key American industries that were once thought to be in jeopardy. Three major American industries—steel, autos, and semiconductors—are the best examples.

Each industry was losing domestic and global market share in the early 1980s and there was great fear that we were losing these vital industries. Today, each has come back strongly, regaining market share in recent years and strongly positioned to compete effectively in coming years.

The steel industry was perhaps in the worst shape of all. It had very high costs, was grossly inefficient, and was a shadow of itself as the symbol of American industrial might in the first half of this century. But thanks to the efficiency-minded minimills and the radical restructuring undertaken by the giant integrated steel producers (steel companies that produce finished steel starting with the basic raw materials), many

American steel companies today are among the most efficient in the world. Man-hours per ton of production has shrunk dramatically, from almost eleven to four. That is well under the 5.4 hour average in Japan and the 5.6 hour average in Germany. Two companies featured in the success stories illustrate the turnaround. USX's sprawling plant in Gary, Indiana, has transformed itself through employee involvement and investment from one of the world's most inefficient plants to one of its most efficient. At the Gary works, it takes 2.7 man-hours to produce a ton of steel compared with 7.1 hours ten years ago. Chaparral Steel, a minimill that has around 85 percent of its 950 employees enrolled in some type of training course at any one time, produces steel with a record 1.4 hours of labor per ton. Overall, productivity in the U.S. steel industry exceeds European and Japanese productivity and U.S. minimills are the world's low-cost producers. Steel exports in 1994 are running more than 4 million tons—quadruple the rate of the mid-1980s. The market share of imports dropped from 26 percent in 1984 to under 20 percent a decade later. Entrepreneurs are racing into steel. Perhaps most amazing is the fact that the steel industry actually added thousands of workers in the 1987–1994 period.

Automakers, another classic symbol of America's industrial might, also faced tough times in the first half of the 1980s. The quality of American cars was ridiculed, and Japanese cars kept increasing their market share. Today, American buyers are returning to American cars because of their high ranking in customer satisfaction and quality surveys. In a recent survey, 80 percent of Americans felt that the quality of U.S. cars had improved in the past five years. And their perception is accurate. In the last J.D. Power quality survey, seven of the ten most improved vehicles were U.S. brands. One of the most vivid examples of the comeback is the Ford Taurus, which became the number-one-selling car in America, grabbing the spot from the Honda Accord, which had occupied it for many years. Chrysler's "Second Comeback" shows how this company virtually reinvented the way autos are made to power its dramatic turnaround. The result is that the Big Three have regained domestic market share, rising from 70 percent to 75 percent in just three years (1991–1994). Bob Eaton, CEO of Chrysler, highlights the amazing transformation: "In 1980 America was the highest-cost place in the world to build a vehicle. Now we are the lowest-cost producer." This was the result of a decade of ruthless cost cutting, major investments in technology, and radical restructuring of the organization by each of the Big Three.

The semiconductor industry showcases most clearly the strength of American companies in high-tech industries generally and their ability to take on global competitors. Again, U.S. companies had surrendered their once commanding lead to the Japanese in the first half of the 1980s. By 1988, Japan controlled half the world semiconductor market while the United States had seen its share shrink to 40 percent from 60 percent as recently as 1980. U.S. companies fought back, pursuing more valuable products such as microprocessors and custom-made circuits, which exploited American strengths in design and software capabilities. By 1992, America had regained the top spot in the $77 billion global semiconductor business. U.S. chip makers in 1993 expanded their lead to a 44 percent global market share by growing 35 percent, with nearly every producer earning record profits, led by Intel with an astounding $2.3 billion. Similarly, Intel in 1992 shot ahead of Japanese rivals NEC and Toshiba to become the world's largest semiconductor supplier and padded its lead in 1993 with explosive growth of 50 percent to $8.8 billion in sales.

What's true of these three industries is true of American industry overall. By most criteria of performance, America is the world leader not only in the three industries highlighted above, but also in chemicals, aerospace, paper and forest products, electronic equipment, electrical components, drugs and medical products, computers, computer software, food production, and many others. A study by Morgan Stanley of globally competitive industries says it all: in the period 1987–1992, U.S. companies attained more than 50 percent of global profits in nine industries while the number of industries achieving this in Japan and in "Europe combined" were two and none respectively. Most significant in looking to the future is the fact that the United States is the undisputed leader of the next generation of commercially important computer and communications technologies.

As we now look more closely at the improvement in productivity and exports, we should keep in mind that the business renaissance began in the last half of the 1980s because of the individual business success stories that were cropping up all across the business landscape.

STELLAR GAINS IN MANUFACTURING PRODUCTIVITY AND TECHNOLOGY

We begin with manufacturing productivity growth because it is the *primary* factor that sustains and increases our standard of living and propels economic growth. That is why the truth about manufacturing productivity is so critical and so exciting: manufacturing productivity growth averaged about 3 percent during the 1980s and early 1990s, compared to less than 1 percent growth in the rest of the economy. Even during the "feeble" recovery days of 1992–1993, U.S. manufacturing productivity was growing strongly while manufacturing productivity in Japan and Germany was either flat or falling.

These figures explode the myth that took hold in the 1980s that manufacturing had stagnant productivity growth and had seen its best days. Not only was this not true, but the reality was that American manufacturing was becoming a productive powerhouse, surpassing other parts of the economy and our international competitors. It is highly ironic that at the height of the "death of manufacturing" laments in 1985, American manufacturing was right in the middle of six years (1983–1988) when manufacturing productivity increases exceeded 4 percent every year. Tom Stewart summed it up in a 1992 (October 19) *Fortune* article: "It's true that manufacturing is America's productivity star."

What powered the overall manufacturing productivity improvement? Part of it had to do with companies becoming leaner. In their heady days of ever-increasing growth and little stiff international competition, far too many companies had allowed themselves to become bloated, often with numerous layers of management. Ruthless global competition required not only leanness in personnel, but throughout companies' cost structure. The total quality movement, by eliminating large amounts of waste and redesigning the way we manufacture, also had a major impact on costs.

But the driving force behind the dramatic increases in productivity was technological advances and the widespread application of new technologies and equipment. Most of the major technological breakthroughs in recent years originated in manufactured products and processes: advanced materials, microprocessors, fiber-optic communications, medical instruments, pharmaceuticals, space exploration, and computer hardware and software. This is to be expected when nearly three quarters of all private-sector research and development in America is performed by manufacturers. When productivity is measured in terms of output per unit of labor *and* capital, so that technological contributions are included, we find that manufacturing productivity is six times greater than in the nonfarm business sector overall.

No wonder *The Wall Street Journal* could report on December 14, 1992: "Many U.S. companies that rely on technical and scientific research are stronger today than five years ago. They hold their own or boast a widening lead against foreign competitors in such bellwether industries as computers, software, aerospace, chemicals and pharmaceuticals." Many of the success stories in this book are the result of these technological advances and their widespread application.

The healthy increases in manufacturing productivity from 1982 on helped strengthen America's position as the world's most productive economy. A 1993 study by the highly respected McKinsey consulting firm found that Japanese worker productivity is only 83 percent of that in the United States while German worker productivity is 79 percent of the U.S. level.

AN EXTRAORDINARY EXPORT BOOM

Again, a popular myth of the 1980s—that American manufacturing was no longer globally competitive—has been exploded by one central fact: the volume of U.S. manufacturing exports from 1985 to 1993 grew at nearly 9 percent annually compared with a 2.3 percent rate for Japan and 1.7 percent for Germany. They grew at twice the rate of import growth and continued to far outpace economic growth. The result is that the United States's share of exports among industrialized nations rebounded from a postwar low of 10 percent in the mid-1980s to around 14 percent in 1993.

The problem underlying the huge increase in the U.S. trade deficit in the early 1980s was not that companies themselves were no longer competitive. Rather, it was the unusually high interest rates associated with large federal budget deficits that led to a massive appreciation of the dollar in 1981–1985. As soon as the dollar began to decline in 1985, the improvement in U.S. exports was as dramatic as its earlier deterioration.

But it wasn't just the decline in the value of the dollar that powered the export surge. Equally critical is the fact that because of productivity increases America had become the world's low-cost producer in many industries. (Indeed, American unit-labor costs in manufacturing declined by an average of 6.4 percent a year from 1985 to 1993 compared with a 6.6 percent annual increase in Japan and 4.2 percent in Germany.)

The export growth was so strong that it contributed over 40 percent of the growth in GNP in the United States during this period. Exports also are critical to job creation and saving jobs. Since 1985, export growth has saved more than 4 million jobs in communities across America. All together, exports supported 7.4 percent of U.S. civilian employment in 1990, up from 5.7 percent in 1986.

Al Ehrbar, writing in *The Wall Street Journal* on January 18, 1993, underscores the case for optimism about American industry on the international scene:

> The fact that exports have continually outpaced expectations demonstrates what a competitive powerhouse the United States has become. The U.S. share of exports by all industrial countries has risen to more than 22 percent from 15.3 percent in 1986. Moreover, the sources of export growth . . . bolster the case for optimism. The surge in merchandise exports over the past six years has come entirely in manufactured goods. . . . Clearly, the U.S. is taking back market share in the fierce global economy.

THE CLARITY OF THE RAYS

The evidence is as clear as it could be: American companies can compete effectively in world markets and industry can continue its historical role as the primary engine for economic progress.

Responding to the challenge of global competition, American companies rejected the "death of manufacturing" laments of the mid-1980s and launched a dramatic comeback. This book is about that comeback in terms of what individual companies did in order to become world-class competitors.

2: TEN PATHS TO SUCCESS

"We got better because we stood back and asked ourselves what business are we in and are we doing the basics right."
— ROBERT PRITZKER, PRESIDENT AND CEO,
  THE MARMON GROUP

"Leaders at all levels must accept what the transformational leaders tell us: that the organization can 'take it' (enormous change), that only a bias for constant action and a bold embrace of failure, big as well as small, will move companies forward."
— TOM PETERS, FOUNDER AND CHIEF OF THE
  TOM PETERS GROUP

This book is about business success. After all the research and the interviews—closely examining over 200 success stories, highlighting fifty of them, and providing in-depth case studies of ten companies—we find that it comes down to this: successful companies are back-to-basics companies that know how to creatively and boldly implement these basics in today's rapidly changing business environment and economy.

Thus, if you want to achieve success in your company, you should not look for any special theory or gimmick or formula. You simply do the basics and you do them right. Each of the ten paths to success we highlight is one such basic.

The ten basic paths themselves fit into three broad categories that every company must address: workers, customers, and process and structure improvement. These categories define the three parts of our book, each of which contains closely related basic paths to success: Releasing the Creativity and Power of Workers, Pleasing Customers and Finding New Markets, and Focusing on Continuous Improvement.

The final chapter illustrates a very important truth: these paths to success work best in combination with one another. The more of them you can put into play effectively, the better your chances for significant success. If the leadership and commitment are there to really shake up

the organization—to have a majority of the basics at work simultaneously—success is a virtual certainty.

The good news is that there is a limited number of basics for business success. Know them. Implement them. Stay committed to them.
And keep on improving on them.

RELEASING THE CREATIVITY AND POWER OF WORKERS

Workers today are the key factor of production determining competitive advantage. This is true both because people are less mobile than
capital and technology and because people are *the* creative source for
new ideas and innovation. To fully develop the potential of people,
successful companies empower, train and reward good performance.

Path Number 1: Empower Employees

We begin with this trend, for the real frontline action in America's
business renaissance starts with respect for the individual and his or
her potential. This empowerment of the workers in the workplace is
directly parallel to what occurred in the Renaissance of the fourteenth
to seventeenth centuries when the broad masses of people could for
the first time share in learning and advancement, thereby taking
greater control over their own lives.

While many people now recognize the importance of employee
empowerment, few know precisely what it means. We decided that
our definition should spring from those who have actually empowered
employees. From our five success stories, as well as dozens of others
we researched, three theme words best define empowerment: trust,
teamwork, and communication.

In company after company, we saw that management had to trust
themselves and their workers enough, as well as respect their workers,
to open up a dialogue that led to successfully working together. The
correct way for management to think of empowerment is giving up
control and power in order to increase the potential power of the
workers. To paraphrase one executive who really laid it on the line,
it's much better to employ the brains of thousands of workers than to
rely on just the brains of twelve gray-hairs holed up in the executive
suite. Further, workers who are respected and trusted perform better
—period. Here is how one worker expressed it: "When I first found
out what the words 'you make a difference' really mean, I started to

feel different about my job. To me, empowerment means trust, and I like working for a company that trusts me."

In the vast majority of cases, empowering the workers means teamwork. Indeed, teamwork is the single most prevalent characteristic found in our fifty success stories. And wherever it is applied properly, the performance of the company improves, usually significantly and often quickly. Companies are discovering the truth behind the old adage "two heads are better than one." Today, we call that force synergy, and companies from Lord to Motorola to Chrysler have discovered its transforming power.

Good communication is also essential and can take place in many ways: giving employees full information about the company's performance, a company acting on its values, a CEO meeting frequently with the workers. Sometimes it simply means the boss has to listen instead of talk. As Ralph Stayer, CEO of Johnsonville Foods, puts it, "They saw me keeping my mouth shut."

In the five stories in Chapter 3, and in scores of others we uncovered but could not include, we found that remarkable performance results emerge from the empowerment process. Plants, companies, and people all prosper from it. That doesn't mean it is immediately welcomed. As Norm Garrity at Corning says, "It is not a minor change; it's a true cultural shift, and that challenges people." But what's encouraging about the success stories in Chapter 3 is that most workers eventually embraced empowerment. Having tasted it, they can't imagine work life without it.

Path Number 2: Train and Retrain Workers

Why should a company spend money to educate and train its workers? We found that successful companies invest heavily in training their workers for a wide variety of reasons. They train to empower and release their full potential. They train because it is necessary to achieve a sustained world-class competitive advantage. They train because they want to boost productivity, lower costs, introduce advanced technologies, or restructure work around self-managed work teams. They train because they want to be a high-performance workplace.

Whatever the reason, the five companies in Chapter 4 all recognize one basic fact: training is absolutely required to thrive in the 1990s. It may even be required to survive.

But if you really want to know why many companies take training seriously, it is because they recognize they have a stark choice: they can have workers who do "just enough to get by" and who operate at maybe 60 percent or 80 percent of their potential *or* they can have workers who feel like this woman after they have been trained: "It's about working at a plant for thirty or thirty-five years and choosing to do just enough to get by or leaving a trail of excellence that virtually screams, 'I was there.' "

The essence of training is that it is an investment—an investment aimed at enhancing an individual's capacity to do tasks better. In today's competitive, high-technology world, investing in human capital is even more important than capital investment. Bob Galvin, the former CEO of Motorola, was fond of saying, "Companies must come to understand that the cost of training workers is an investment that is always cheaper than not training them."

Training benefits workers even more than the company. The tangible benefits include saving one's job, increased wages, and moving ahead in the company, while the intangible benefits include higher self-esteem, greater confidence, more satisfaction from their work, greater control over their lives, and a feeling of greater attachment and loyalty to the company.

The "how to" part can be individually scripted by each company. Some companies hire outside trainers. Others train their own workers to be trainers, thus holding costs to essentially zero (as CR Industries did). Some utilize local community colleges. Others stress apprenticeship programs. Some offer up-front training only. Others require all workers to have a certain number of hours each year. This latter course is where all the smart companies are headed, recognizing the critical value of lifelong learning.

Perhaps the most important lesson is that training is for everyone. Chaparral Steel didn't get to its highly productive, low-cost position by training 10 percent, 30 percent, or even 60 percent of its workers. It trained them all—*and* it keeps training them (85 percent are in training at any given time). It's a fact that must be understood: *all* workers, regardless of their initial skills or attitudes, can benefit from training.

Make a serious commitment to education and training and it is likely that you will come to share the feelings of Harry Featherstone, CEO of Will-Burt and a devotee of lifelong education: "There's a magic that happens with education." He adds, "Just get a CEO to think education, and I can assure you they would do it—because it's so logical."

Path Number 3: Reward Good Performance

Many companies have discovered that rewarding good performance leads to even better performance—a self-reinforcing performance and reward cycle that drives corporate performance ever upward. The essence of all such efforts is to let the workers share financially in the success of the enterprise. Chet Russell, a crane operator at Oregon Steel Mills, says the workers put in extra effort, trying hard to satisfy customers, "because it's money in our pockets."

In short, money motivates! And as the five stories in Chapter 5 illustrate, motivated people make productive workers, which makes for a highly productive company. It's simply profound common sense.

The range of rewards and incentive techniques is quite broad and can help a company meet a variety of goals—including survival. A Whirlpool plant needed to increase productivity to survive and did so through implementing a gainsharing plan. Oregon Steel Mills was on the verge of closing when it decided to try employee ownership. Hundreds of companies have bonuses and profit-sharing plans so that everyone gets a piece of the action.

It's not too difficult to see how workers will become extremely motivated when they see results like these: at Lincoln Electric, for nearly fifty years the workers received bonuses that equaled their full year's pay; at Oregon Steel Mills, 20 percent of the 517 workers when it started its employee ownership became millionaires.

Money, however, is not everything. Workers also appreciate and are motivated by receiving recognition for good work. Positive reinforcement is still the most direct and effective way to motivate employees. This can be as simple as managers citing good performance by a worker at meetings, recognition lunches or dinners, and performance awards.

And motivated workers produce results that companies love. Here's what we mean by productive workers. Lincoln Electric workers are three times more productive than workers at comparable plants, and Nucor workers produce more than four times the industry average for tons of steel per employee each year. And dramatic results can come rather quickly. Just five years after establishing its employee stock ownership plan, Relexite found that sales quadrupled, the number of jobs nearly tripled, and profits rose almost sixfold.

PLEASING CUSTOMERS AND FINDING NEW MARKETS

Success starts with customers because they are the people who buy the products and pay the bills that fuel economic growth. For all the importance of cutting costs to improve the bottom line, it is essential to remember that the most important way to improve the bottom line is to increase sales on the top line. In other words, growth is stronger than efficiency.

The challenge is that today's competitive environment is tougher than ever because customers can demand and get more for their money. There are more products chasing customers on the supply side, driving down prices and improving quality. Customers themselves demand products from a much more individual point of view, carving the mass market into dozens of new niches.

Manufacturers have already responded aggressively by reducing prices and improving product quality. We chose however not to include the quality path in Part 2 because the quality emphasis now is on total quality, which means striving for high quality in every part of the organization. Our focus will be on what manufacturers have done for customers through vastly improved service and exciting new product development. We also highlight how they have searched the world for new customers by undertaking an aggressive global marketing strategy.

Path Number 4: Exceed Customer Expectations

That's right—not just meet, but exceed, customer expectations. Having moved beyond listening to customers, leading companies now focus on "pleasing" or "delighting" their customers. Whatever it's called, it is now an absolute necessity because the customer is king—and hence must be served exceedingly well.

Interested in growth? Just listen to James Keyes, chairman and CEO of Johnson Controls, a 111-year-old manufacturer of such traditional products as heating controls, batteries, and plastic bottles: "Most of our growth has come from the fact that we do more for our customers."

Interested in real success? Adopt the attitude toward customers of Premier Industrial, expressed by its chairman of thirty-five years, Mort Mandel: "We have killed ourselves for the customer."

Our five success stories show that a laser-sharp focus on superior customer service can work wonders for a company at any stage of development: as a foundation for start-ups (Great Plains Software and

Dell); for accomplishing turnarounds in large, established companies (Harley-Davidson and Xerox); and simply for sustaining success built on a value of superior customer service long held and practiced (Premier Industrial).

We found five key drivers of success in exceeding customer expectations: (1) getting employees customer-focused; (2) installing great tracking and measurement systems; (3) paying attention to details; (4) having the CEO personally involved; (5) constantly making improvements.

Great Plains Software utilizes an unbeatable combination of system and spirit. Its system is as good as any company's. What everything boils down to at Great Plains Software is that the customers sense that the company cares about them. The company has succeeded in forming an emotional link between the customer and its products and services. It is this emotional link, according to a leading expert on customer satisfaction, that is the key to retaining customers and generating repeat business.

A fundamental factor behind the success of Great Plains, as well as that of Dell and Xerox, is the power of new information technologies and the company's willingness to invest heavily in them to get to know and better serve their customers. Fortunately, companies across America are catching on to the power and importance of these technologies: in 1994 they spent over $1 billion on computers and related technologies for customer service departments.

It's almost a guarantee: please the customer, delight the customer, exceed the customer's expectations, and the rewards will be great. By employing right from day one a long-term strategy of treating the customer right, Great Plains Software never missed growing in any of its first forty-eight quarters.

Path Number 5: Envision New Products and Markets

The mass market of the past decade has largely disintegrated—exploding into dozens of new niches. The leading manufacturers have responded by developing new products with a vengeance in order to grow and to gain market share.

Rubbermaid is a standout example. Under the leadership of Stan Gault, a marketing genius, Rubbermaid in the 1980s transformed itself from a company best known as a maker of dustpans into a new-product-generating machine. By the time Gault passed on the reins in 1991, the company was introducing one new product a day (on average) to the market.

Rubbermaid has an innovative culture. So do the other four companies in Chapter 7. From these companies, we discovered three characteristics that best define an innovative culture: spirit, creative freedom, and getting ideas from everywhere.

Spirit is absolutely fundamental, yet it's hard to capture in words. It almost has to be sensed by a visit to a company that has it in order to understand its true genius and powerful impact. At Rubbermaid, what one senses is an animated, can-do, let's discover, let's reinvent, let's-overwhelm-the-competition type of spirit. It is employees saying "we're all product junkies" and "we look at everybody's product and reinvent it." It is the CEO who just wanders around the R&D department on a Saturday morning to see what products are being thought of, and it is the animated storytelling about new products that virtually all employees love to engage in.

At Microsoft, the company spirit or gestalt takes on a different character and feel. At its heart is the idea, driven home in numerous ways by CEO Bill Gates, that they're out to win and win big. Gates is always scanning the horizon for the next big market to enter, while employees are always examining their products to make them better and different so they too will stand out as so many Microsoft products have.

Another given of highly innovative companies is abundant creative freedom for all their employees. And the innovators back this freedom with abundant resources as these firms invest heavily in research and product development. This is a winning combination. Thermo Electron provides perhaps the most powerful incentive for exercising this freedom: invent a major new product or find a new market for a technology and you may be made head of your own spin-out company. And it was heartening to find that creative freedom often involves a sense of fun. Odetics was created as a company where it would be fun to come to work because its co-founders realized that such an atmosphere would encourage creativity and risk taking.

The final ingredient of an innovative culture is to look for ideas everywhere. Be like Rubbermaid, which loves to get ideas from anywhere and everywhere: customers, consumers, employees, top management, and even grocery store aisles.

One clear fact that emerges from all the success stories in Chapter 7 is that the leading innovators didn't just become that way in a turnaround in the 1980s. They had a track record of relentlessly pursuing new products and markets. The why is best described by George Hatsopoulos, founder and CEO of Thermo Electron: "Every line of business you are currently in may be growing very rapidly, but eventually that growth is bound to stop. If you are seriously committed to growth, the only way you can ensure that your company will continue to grow is to develop new types of businesses to perpetuate that growth."

Path Number 6: Go Global

In today's world, a simple, basic imperative has arisen, often for survival and certainly for growth: you have to be a world player with your eyes on markets outside the United States.

Certainly manufacturers have come a long way in recent years in expanding exports and setting up production abroad. Indeed, one of *the* economic success stories for America in the 1980s was the export boom of American manufacturers. This was fueled by the improvement in exchange rates, dramatic cost reductions, and companies looking abroad for growth opportunities.

Fortunately, as the companies in Chapter 8 clearly demonstrate, almost any company can become a world player. No matter how small you are, or where you are located, or what your product is, the odds are that you can export it and reap handsome rewards. Consider Rust Evader, a maker of electronic corrosion control devices. Just two years into its exporting campaign, 88 percent of its production was going to thirty-five countries.

We see in this chapter that some companies can penetrate the Japanese market successfully. Wadia Digital's top-of-the-line audio components are a real hit there. And Sun Microsystems saw a major niche in the Japanese computer industry and went after it. Within a year, it was number one in Japan's workstation vendor market, making it the only foreign company to lead in a computer segment in Japan.

Some companies find that they can best compete in global markets by putting production facilities abroad. Dexter Baker committed Air Products and Chemicals in the mid-1980s to opportunities in Europe, with the result that European sales doubled from $400 million to over $1 billion between 1986 and 1993, and in Asia, where it established a presence in seven countries between 1986 and 1990. The summary of its overall approach provides a good lesson for many companies investing abroad: invest abroad, invest again, and invest some more.

Another encouraging finding is how remarkable results can be achieved relatively quickly by small companies. Sun Microsystems was a small company in the mid-1980s but that didn't stop it from aggressively pursuing global markets. By the first quarter of 1994 it was deriving an astounding 54.4 percent of sales from exports. These exports were instrumental in propelling it to number 120 on the Fortune 500 list in 1993, just as it completed its first decade. Cannondale, a maker of high-end bicycles, saw its European sales shoot up from $1 million in 1988 to around $25 million in 1992.

FOCUSING ON CONTINUOUS IMPROVEMENT

You treat your workers right. You exceed the expectations of your customers at home and abroad. The third part of the triad is to make sure that your organizational structure and processes turn out top-quality products in the quickest and most efficient manner possible. What started out as quality improvement to better satisfy customers became a real revolution in how companies are organized and the processes they use to make things. Total quality is just that—total—reaching to every nook and cranny of the company.

This is accomplished only through adopting continuous improvement as both a philosophy and an operating practice. You never rest on your laurels. You always look for a better way to improve the quality of your product, to eliminate waste throughout the system, and to employ the most efficiency-enhancing advanced manufacturing technologies to attain speed and agility and add value to your product.

Bob Cizik, the CEO of Cooper Industries, has captured the emphasis in Part 3: "Maybe we need something that talks about the quality corporation, because quality means, what kind of company you are, what you want to become, how you organize to do that, and if you are going to meet the market conditions you face and become the kind of company that adds value for customers."

Path Number 7: Pursue Total Quality

A top-quality product is now a given. This chapter is about pursuing total quality throughout the organization.

If you want to see the closest thing to a total quality company, look at the Motorola story. Motorola can say that they are striving to become the "perfect company" because they have the right quality philosophy, commitment, and range of practices in place. They began with a sharp focus on top-quality products but soon moved to a focus on quality throughout every part of the company: accountants, patent lawyers, software engineers have all become part of their quality crusade.

Motorola and the other four companies in Chapter 9 clearly demonstrate that the key ingredients for success in quality improvement efforts are leadership and focus. Know precisely what you are after and have top leadership in the company champion it with hands-on involvement. There are other ingredients that are also required: remember that your ultimate objective is to meet or exceed customer expectations; benchmark against the top competitors; recognize the power of reducing defects, cycle time, and waste; provide employee involvement throughout the organization; undertake full and accurate measurements; keep the focus on continuous improvement.

What's clear from this fairly lengthy list of ingredients is that a total quality effort often will call for total transformation of a company. This was true at Motorola, United Electric Controls, and Hardinge Brothers.

In other cases, companies choose to have a central driver to their quality program. AMP chose extensive employee involvement as its initial driver. Its integrated approach with customer satisfaction is described by former Chairman Harold McInnes: "If you really believe as we do, that total employee involvement is fundamental to quality improvement, and that quality improvement is essential to total customer satisfaction, then you have to find a way to get everybody involved." Emerson Electric has made continuous cost reduction a "religion" or "way of life" through its Best-Cost Producer strategy, which it says is its quality program.

Bob Agan, president and CEO of Hardinge Brothers, provides not only the greatest definition of TQM (total quality management) we have seen but also a great reason for adopting TQM:

TQM works because it is not something you do. It's something you are. TQM is not an event; it is a process that drives every activity in a company. We had to turn the culture of our company in a new direction. It meant re-forming work groups; finding ways to create stakeholders instead of just employees; learning how to create a process of shared decision making; and reeducating everybody about how to earn a living in our place of business. TQM is not an overlay; it's a foundation.

Path Number 8: Achieve Environmental Excellence

Successful companies have often looked at environmental demands and, instead of viewing them as enemies to be fought, they view them as opportunities that are similar to quality improvement. The real pacesetter companies have already grasped the point that will eventually permeate corporate thinking: environmental protection makes good business sense.

There is a small but steadily growing number of companies that are discovering an exciting win-win type of situation in preventing pollution and removing waste from their system: a company's bottom line can benefit at the same time the environment is being protected or improved.

The company that most powerfully illustrates this principle is 3M with its 3P (Pollution Prevention Pays) program. Started in 1975, 4,100 projects through 1993 had made substantial reductions in many of the company's pollutants while at the same time saving 3M over $710 million. This two-decade-old program provides the encouraging lesson that both economic and environmental benefits can continue to be realized year after year.

Searle demonstrates how to successfully meet multiple environmental and economic goals. It faced a tough challenge that no pharmaceutical manufacturer had been able to figure out: to develop a cleaning method that would reduce downtime and related expenses, eliminate toxic air emissions and hazardous waste, and provide a safer work environment for employees. Employing a combination of tenacious commitment and creativity, a project team developed Aqueous Clean-In-Place, a system that according to Searle "proves that efficiency and profit improvement need not be sacrificed for environmental protection." Indeed, as pollution was decreased substantially, productivity shot up by 40 percent.

There are many different ways companies can respond to environmental challenges. The two types that most clearly emerged from our five success stories were: (1) making your employees frontline "environmental managers"; and (2) being willing to invest heavily in environmental R&D. 3M shows the way on the employee front, as it has consistently encouraged *all* its employees to be responsible for creative environmental initiatives that would help prevent pollution.

Continuous improvement is a key in the environmental arena as it is elsewhere. Why is it necessary? The CEO of 3M, L.D. DeSimone, sums it up best:

> There's a good chance that what we do today will be judged by the rules of tomorrow. Processes and practices that meet every legal requirement today may fall well short of tomorrow's standards. We're going to have to take the lead on environmental issues. We're going to have to set the pace of improvement ourselves. Let's face it, being environmentally responsible is the right thing to do.

Path Number 9: Increase Speed and Agility

This path encompasses many common phrases of recent years: flexible manufacturing, agile manufacturing, reengineering processes, factory floor modernization. Whatever the wording, this approach focuses on a central feature of the drive to world-class manufacturing: the utilization of one or more of the advanced computer and manufacturing technologies to create the most quick, agile, and efficient production system possible.

The reason for the stress on speed and agility is that very low cycle times are a central mark of excellence for companies today. This idea of driving down cycle time (the time material is in-house, dock to dock) flowed directly out of the quality movement. And all of this is due to the harsh reality of today's highly competitive global marketplace: either respond quickly and correctly the first time to a customer's order or lose the customer. Also, most companies must recognize that lot sizes will have to come down as customers increasingly want products customized.

So how do companies significantly increase speed and agility? First, there must be a willingness to break some molds. The changes the five companies in Chapter 11 underwent are not for the fainthearted. They put into place new models of production, new models of organization, even new corporate forms in one instance. In all the cases but one, some very advanced and sophisticated manufacturing technologies are involved. The "hard" technologies are led by CAD (computer-aided design), which is now used in most manufacturing companies across America. In many cases, the ideal to shoot for is CIM, fully computer-integrated manufacturing. There are not many such "factories of the future" yet, but Allen-Bradley's EMS1 facility in Milwaukee provides a good look at one. Then there are the "soft" technologies, led by JIT (just-in-time) production, with sophisticated computer software playing an increasingly important role. American companies are getting into such technologies in a big way: in 1993, 41 percent of capital spending was on computers and information processing equipment.

Those involved in the process at Allen-Bradley make the important point that EMS1 is not just a CIM facility—a building housing the latest computer-integrated technologies—but a new process capability. In each of these five stories, we are talking about a new, exciting process capability the company has attained that improves its production process and helps it to respond better, and more quickly, to its customers' ever-changing needs and desires.

One lesson that comes through loud and clear in the stories is that it is never technology alone. It is always technology *and* people. Highly skilled and motivated people are required to make all the sophisticated technology work—and that means extensive training and a positive corporate culture.

To lend credence to our theme that major changes are often involved, two of the companies are at the leading edge of what could well be two revolutions in manufacturing. Ross Controls produces "virtual products" and Kingston Technology is the closest thing today to a "virtual company." Their revolutionary paths are quite different: Ross Controls emphasized heavy investment in CAD technology while Kingston Technology chose to create a wholly new type of corporate organization centered on a network of close partnerships with vendors.

Path Number 10: Shake Up the Organization

We're dealing here with a *radical* shaking up of the organization. Massive, immediate cultural change—not incremental tinkering—was deemed necessary for either survival or growth for all the companies described in Chapter 12. This meant that the companies launched people, product, process, and structural initiatives on virtually all fronts described in the previous nine chapters.

Peter Drucker, not easily given to hyperbole, expresses what is required in twelve succinct words: "Every organization has to prepare for the abandonment of everything it does." Note his use of the words "every," "abandonment," and "everything." He's talking total transformation.

What motivated many of the companies was the new and intense foreign competitors they faced who were eating away at their market share. As market share eroded, some saw their very survival at stake while others saw future growth jeopardized.

How did things get so bad? The basic reason, and it deserves emphasis, is *success had gone to their heads*. They relaxed. They lost their focus about how to continually improve their business.

Leadership—that's what this chapter is really about. Leadership involves not just embracing all the good concepts like empowering employees and TQM but doing something about them. Andrew Grove, Eckhard Pfeiffer, Lee Iacocca and Bob Eaton, Tracy O'Rourke, Dana Mead—they are all leaders because they are effective *doers*.

All of these leaders are masters of three critical ingredients for shaking up an organization: achieving focus, setting tough goals, and acting. First, you have to know what the problems are and what the company should focus on. Then you should set some tough goals—shocking your people with "impossible" goals that will stretch them into new ways of thinking. Finally, *act*—the quicker the better. The three CEOs who were brought in to turn things around—Pfeiffer, O'Rourke, and Walsh—wasted no time in putting into place sweeping shake-up plans.

How did they act? There were five main points of attack that stood out in the majority of cases: cut costs, empower employees, exceed customer expectations, create new products, and increase speed and agility.

It all boils down to leadership aimed at achieving results. So we will close this chapter with the words of one such leader, Dana Mead, CEO of Tenneco, highlighting the hallmarks of true leadership:

You are all leaders. So the challenge is:
• Accept world-class as your standard.
• Realize that someone somewhere is doing something better than we are and doing it faster. Search for it. Match it. And then beat it.
• Get others around you to do the same.

RELEASING THE CREATIVITY AND POWER OF WORKERS

3. EMPOWER EMPLOYEES

America's business renaissance is, more than anything else, about respecting the individual and unleashing the full creative power of people. This means people at all levels—production workers, middle managers, senior executives, and the CEO.

But the real frontline action takes place on the production floor, by the workers. They are the ones who make modern manufacturing work. They are the ones who must take full advantage of today's sophisticated and expensive machines. They are the ones who know best where the key problems—and most promising opportunities—lie.

So we begin at the grass roots—with empowering employees, the most widespread and proven way to be a winner in the harshly competitive corporate environment of the 1990s and beyond. The ultimate goal of empowerment is to make every employee an entrepreneur —motivated to do their job in the best manner possible—as true entrepreneurs always are.

We recognize that empowerment has its skeptics. We've seen the magazine articles that claim it is just a passing fad or that teams don't work. We categorically reject this skepticism. Certainly, there have been situations where empowerment or teams have been tried and they "haven't worked." But it was not the fault of the concept. It was the fault of the management that didn't go about it the right way or wasn't willing to stick with it. Naysayers should pay close attention to David Baldwin, then director of training for Abbott-Ashland:

> We're not focusing on empowerment because it's a fad or the flavor of the month. Our philosophy is: to systematically apply the right people, tools, skills, and techniques to continuously improve our products and processes. We're not in business merely to compete; we're in business to win. And empowerment is the way to be a winner.

GIVE WORKERS THE AUTHORITY AND LET THEM GO

Employee empowerment must be seen in action to be fully appreciated. Here's a snapshot to help you see it in action. Just sit back and appreciate what five union hardhats, given real authority, can accomplish:

U.S. Steel (now USX), Gary, Indiana. Once this company and the city were the very symbol of America's industrial pride and might. By 1986, they were anything but. The image was one of rusting and abandoned buildings, angry customers, and financial hemorrhaging. Into this picture walk five union line workers who were asked to visit angry automotive customers to learn firsthand why they were so dissatisfied with their steel. The five were then *given the authority* to do what was necessary to solve the problems and please the customers—change the way the steel was made, stored, shipped, whatever it would take. They did this and their success led to similar initiatives. Their leadoff initiative helped bring about a complete turnaround in the massive, rusty, dispirited facility. Ford Motor went from nearly flunking the plant in 1987 to giving it a Q1 Award for top quality in 1991. But best of all, the initial team members were so well received by their automotive customers that they are now members of the customers' employee-involvement teams.

That's what a team of workers can do. Here's the powerful impact just one worker can have when given authority: David Velte, an employee for Steelcase at their wood furniture business unit's Grand Rapids plant, was frustrated with the amount of damaged vertical cabinets being delivered to trim. He took the initiative to talk to many departments upstream and from these discussions made two major recommendations. They were both readily accepted and the team of three people modified the racks themselves and set up their own work cells. The results of his initiative? Production capacity increased by 150 percent, there was an immediate improvement in quality, product damage due to handling was virtually eliminated, and reduced labor and scrap costs saved Steelcase approximately $84,000 per year.

EMPLOYEE EMPOWERMENT IS TRUST, TEAMWORK, AND COMMUNICATION

Many attempts have been made to provide a concise definition of employee empowerment. We decided that our definition should spring from those companies that have actually empowered employees. In looking through all of the dozens of empowerment success stories, three words appeared over and over again: trust, teamwork, and communication.

We begin with trust because it is so important to workers. Just listen to Samantha Williams, a production stamper with Wilson Sporting Goods:

> When I first found out what the words "you make a difference" really mean, I started to feel different about my job. Knowing that I have a "say" made me like my job more. I don't feel like I am doing it just for the money anymore. To me, empowerment means trust and I like working for a company that trusts me.

Tom Peters has an interesting perspective on trust: "Technique is important. But adding trust is the issue of the decade. . . . Without trust we cannot expect the human imagination to pursue value-added." True "letting go" of employees must be preceded by trust.

Teamwork is a vital part of the empowerment process for the vast majority of the firms. The correct way to think of empowerment is management giving up power and hierarchical control—the "letting go" we just referred to—in order to increase the power and potential of the rest of the team—fellow workers. Managers become more like coaches, with a bit of cheerleading thrown in.

Good communication with the employees often begins with the boss listening instead of talking. Dave Lichtinger, manager of Lord Corps' plant in Dayton, Ohio, spent six months listening to various employee groups—first their anger and frustrations but later their constructive suggestions for improvement. Good communication also

involves giving employees full information on the company's performance, what is often called "open book" management. At Herman
Miller, good communication means that every employee not only
knows the company's values but believes in the values because the
company "walks its talk."

Words such as involvement and trust may look "soft" but they are
producing many "hard" results. Jack Welch, not known for a soft touch,
is one of the most enthusiastic proponents of employee empowerment
through application of these soft values. Worker involvement and trust
would be just platitudes, he explains—except that "our whole organization is, in fact, living them . . . every day."

ENCOURAGING LESSONS IN EMPOWERMENT

For anyone interested in pursuing employee empowerment at their
workplace, the following lessons, which emerged from the experience
of these companies, should prove encouraging.

One lesson is that empowerment can begin simply. At the Lord
plant, it started when the plant manager "got to talking" with the
employees to hear what was on their minds and what they felt was
needed to make it a better place to work.

We also learn from USX and Goodyear that unions can embrace
employee empowerment. This is by no means universally true, but the
positive examples that do exist show the potential that is there.

Empowerment can also lead to a complete turnaround. We've already spotlighted the turnarounds at Lord's Dayton plant and USX's
Gary plant. In many cases the turnaround is not quite as dramatic but
just as significant, as for example when a company goes from solid and
stable performance to excellent performance.

The final lesson is that empowerment can occur through many creative channels. Certainly training and rewarding good performance,
the respective focus of each of the next two chapters, are often major
ways that workers are empowered. The spirit of diversity is well captured in a November 1992 *Inc.* cover story featuring "The Best Small
Companies to Work For," drawing on the magazine's thirteen years of
finding exemplary companies and teasing out their secrets. "But once
you got past the innovation and the marketing and the financial wiz-
ardry, once you looked beyond the rapid growth, the single most
striking fact about the companies we singled out was that, as a group,

they had the damnedst array of people-management programs you'd ever want to see."

IT ALL COMES DOWN TO PEOPLE

We started by saying that employee empowerment is the way to be a winner. And it is. In case after case, remarkable performance results emerge from the empowerment process. So plants and companies prosper from it.

But most fundamentally, people prosper from it. Not all people, and certainly not all people right away. As Norm Garrity at Corning says, "It is not a minor change; it's a true cultural shift, and that challenges people." But what's encouraging about these empowerment success stories is that most workers eventually not only "came around to it" but actually embraced it. Having tasted it, they can't imagine work life without it.

Empowerment produces excited and committed workers. What company, school, or government office wouldn't like to have all its workers have the spirit and commitment of Debbie Phillips, a team leader at Lord's Dayton plant:

> I'd like to see Lord Dayton get to the point where anybody in the industry hears our name and they think quality, the best there is....I want us to get to the point where every part we make is right the first time. And everybody just wants us to do their work. I like coming to work because I know that I'm important. I matter. My opinions matter. It's just a completely different environment. And everybody should give it really serious thought.

We couldn't agree more. Everybody should give employee empowerment really serious thought.

 ## Grassroots Empowerment
LORD CORP.

It's a most unlikely place for a revolution in the making. A nondescript tan metal building sitting a hundred feet off I-75 just a little north of

Dayton, Ohio. It's not a high-tech company like Microsoft or any of the glamorous biotechnology companies that have sprung up over the past decade. It's not a well-known icon of America's industrial past like GM or U.S. Steel. In fact, the parent company itself, Lord Corp., is not flashy, not well known, and it hasn't even had that much growth over the past few years. This particular plant primarily churns out engine mounts for fixed-wing aircraft.

But a revolution it is! Just listen.

Dave Lichtinger, plant manager, describing pre-1986, pre-empowerment days:

> We were losing a lot of money. Losing 1 million bucks a year so we were really bleeding. The quality was just horrible. I felt like people didn't do the best they could and were very selfish. Morale here was horrible because of the way I felt. Nobody on the shop floor trusted us at all. Turnover rate during those periods was horrible. Fifty percent turnover for a little plant like this in 1985. We had a horrible reputation with everyone on the floor for laying people off at the drop a hat. When I walked down the shop floor, honestly, there were times I'd worry people would throw something at me. There was just a horrible animosity.

Mike Smedley, operator for fourteen years, describing what it was like before empowerment:

> When I first came here we had managers, mid-managers, supervisors. I think it was like two to three indirect to one direct laborer. I mean it was really bad. You had to go through a chain of command to even order a tool. Like maybe five people. You really didn't have any control over what you did. Morale was really bad. People weren't working together. They were fighting among shifts. It was discouraging.

Now listen as Dave Lichtinger describes life after empowerment:

> Nine times out of ten people made the dead-on right decision. Sometimes they didn't and we just lived with that. Our plant expansion is solely the result of improved performance. We earned it with our productivity and quality improvements and the attitudes of the people. There's nothing I know that those guys don't know in the shop. I don't like knowing things that are so secret that they can't know. I love working where there are no secrets and everything's aboveboard. Yeah, open-book. It gets better every year.

Mike Smedley reinforces the picture of dramatic change:

I do feel that Dave and Mike [employee relations manager] both respect what I say. They'll come right out and ask. And that makes you feel real good as an individual. If I need help, I go to any member of my team and they'll drop what they're doing and help you. A real bond there. The freedom is the big thing. Most people around here like to be independent. It's a super place to work. If you can control yourself and don't take advantage of it, you're not going to find any place any better. And I feel strongly about that.

How did this happen? How did this small plant accomplish this modern-day industrial miracle?

Here's how it didn't. There was no big push from corporate head-quarters to spark the effort. There was no big EI (employee involvement) or EE (employment empowerment) program at the plant. There was no management consultant to advise them.

Then *how?*

Grassroots empowerment! It's a classic American story of grit and determination. Of wanting something badly enough. And of the true power unleashed under employee empowerment.

It's a fascinating story and it can be everyone's story. Any plant can do it. Indeed, any workplace can do it—be it a manufacturing company, a service company, a nonprofit organization, or a government office.

For we are not primarily talking here about the transformation of a plant as much as we're talking about a transformation in people's attitudes and emotions. For this reason, the story of how the initial fifty-five employees (now seventy) at Lord Dayton got empowered and how it changed their lives and the plant's performance will often be told in their voices—the voices of plant manager Dave Lichtinger and Mike Rogers (employee relations manager) and operators Mike Smedley, Debbie Phillips, Jim Winterbotham, and Jeff Fashner. They should speak, for it is their success story and they are pleased to talk about it.

THE GRIT BEHIND GRASSROOTS EMPOWERMENT

As of January 1986, the plant was in Dave and Mike's hands. Dave Lichtinger had just become plant manager. Together, he and Mike Rogers came to a common realization: "We didn't want to work an-other ten years being as miserable as we had been. We decided that if nothing else, we were going to be happy." It's not in the textbooks or in Harvard case studies but that's probably as good a reason as any to begin the empowerment journey.

Dave was frank about what he termed the "drivers" of change: they were now in a position to do something about what they had been griping about for so long and about the complaints that it was a horrible place to work. "The combination of these two 'drivers' got us talking to people and the talking took it from there."

That's it. That's the secret behind the success of employee empowerment at this plant. They got to "talking to people." And some kind of talking it was.

Dave and Mike would invite six to ten workers to come and let them know what was on their minds. When one group finished, they'd sit and discuss what was said and then they'd host the next group. And the next. Sometimes all day. Sometimes three, four, or five days a week. And this went on for six months. As Dave put it, "Once people started talking, it was like a feeding frenzy." And much of what was said wasn't pleasant to hear as Dave recalls:

> When we started to talk to people, it was clear the problem was the way the place was being managed. It wasn't, "Dave, we need better tools. Dave, we need better machines." It was, "Dave, you got to get off our backs and you don't understand. If you were out there you'd quit making assumptions." It was all, "Dave this and Dave that."

Here's how it affected Dave. "I went to the hospital that year. I don't know how many times I thought I was having a heart attack. Like four or five times. I'd jump in the car, go down sweating. Couldn't breathe. All stress stuff. It was just a horrible year."

So why put yourself through such torture? After all, Dave was the boss. He certainly didn't have to sit and listen to all the gripes and personal attacks. Here's where the grit comes in. "We decided we were going to do it totally, 100 percent, commit ourselves to it and we were not going to back off. Once you do that, things take off like a rocket. People have to know if they're in or they're out." When asked if he was ever tempted to quit during this stressful year, Dave replied, "We started it. We decided we were going to get it turned around."

A lot more than just red faces and sweating emerged from this lengthy series of meetings. Perhaps the key that laid the foundation for the trust that was ultimately to follow was that Dave and Mike began with this question: "How can we make this the best place to work—

someplace we'd all be proud to come to? It wasn't, how do we become more productive or improve our quality."

With this opening, the workers responded and made some suggestions for change very clear. The overall problem they cited was that "they had no power to control anything and we overmanaged this place." It also became clear that a major problem on people's minds was quality—particularly since headquarters was close to not sending them any more work because of their reputation for poor quality.

Dave and Mike may not have had a model for employee empowerment but they had good instincts. They took careful notes, discussed what should be done, and acted right away. For instance, one real gripe the operators had was that the engineers would always tell them what to do and not give them any leeway for saying, "Gee, I think it should be done another way." Dave pointed out just how bad it got. "It actually got into shouting matches on the floor. I mean almost physical fights. People would fly up to my office, 'You get that guy out of my face or I'll punch him.' " The response: "We told the engineers, 'If you're going to fight with the operators, you're going to leave. They aren't. You are.' " The engineering department turned over, with a few leaving and a few really turning around and joining the teams as they formed. Now the operators make the program run.

A small thing? Hardly. Dave emphasizes, "When this change regarding the engineers began to take place, the operators knew we were serious."

Another beginning step was getting the workers to work together. This started with an employee involvement group focused on quality of work life. In rapid succession came employee involvement groups, staffed solely by volunteers, focusing on quick setups (time to set up or reconfigure machinery), quality improvement, and specific functions like housekeeping. These groups gave the workers their first taste of having some say and some decision-making power.

To attack the quality concern, every person in the plant was given 120 hours of training in blueprint reading, geometric dimensioning, reading gauges, and so forth. They were also given 130 hours of training in teamwork and group process skills. When the training was done, quality problems were cut in half.

Soon after that, there was a "huge bridge to cross": everyone had to inspect their own work. Historically, all their work was sent through final inspection. This small plant of fifty-five workers in the mid-1980s had ten final inspectors, "sitting there all day rejecting people's work," according to Dave. A huge queue backed up. The answer: train all operators to be certified inspectors. Within a year, most of the quality problem was solved.

SELF-DIRECTED WORK TEAMS: THE REAL POWER BEHIND EMPOWERMENT

In the old days, there were six layers of management for fifty-five people. By 1990, there was just the plant manager and seven self-directed work teams. As Dave says, "All of our effort is to make sure no one supervises the work teams. The teams make all day-by-day decisions themselves."

But that's getting ahead of the story. The beginning is back in May 1987 when the first work cell was formed. It was formed to produce a major component for Boeing helicopters. That product was chosen because it was high volume and they were having a lot of trouble with it. Out of a 2,000-piece order, 350 were junk or rework. The plant had a Wall of Shame—a rack with 250 of these $5,000 parts, every one of which needed significant rework.

Dave asked for volunteers for this first work team and got three—two for the day shift and one for the night. "They were the guys that would always tell you exactly what you didn't want to hear but what turned out to be right," remembers Dave.

The three went to school. They came back and reprogrammed that job. They chose everything they needed and picked out a tiny corner of the plant to run their cell in. By September, machines were running between shifts unattended. Lot size (the number of units produced in one run) had been cut in half and, along with it, inventory got cut in half. Throughput time doubled and lead time went from nine months to sixty days. Dave calls it "wildly successful."

Soon the other workers got tired of having this cell constantly cited as a wonderful working example. They wanted part of the action. One by one five more work teams were formed. Not everyone, however, was keen on becoming a part of a team. The figures Dave cites are: 20 percent raise their hand for everything; 20 percent want nothing to do with this; and 60 percent participate when asked.

The teams began to address the major issues related to their area of production. But they weren't self-directed yet. That major step came in

September 1989. All supervisors were gone and the team was responsible for everything: planning, scheduling, cleaning their cell area (the whole plant is spotless and orderly), resolving complaints (only two complaints filtered up to Mike in 1992), hiring, and even firing (three workers have been fired based on recommendations from their work teams).

Dave makes an interesting point about letting each team do their own hiring. "In the past, when we did the hiring, you couldn't win. When they choose someone, they work closely with that person to make sure things go well."

This exact same "make it work" spirit was present when the operators for the first time were given authority to research and buy a series of sophisticated and expensive machining centers. After visiting several vendors, a team of three (including Mike Smedley) finally made the choice. After working with the machines for a while, they discovered that they were not all they thought they would be. Dave pointed out how this would have caused "big problems" if the machines had been chosen by the employer. "Now," he says, "they make them work."

But to really understand what teams are all about and what they mean to the individual worker, you have to listen to the workers. Here's a few of their remarks, first in response to the question "What's been the biggest change for you from employee empowerment and the move to teams?"

Jim Winterbotham, operator for sixteen years, member of the first work team:

> I've had five years running the same part. But it's not boring. Something new every day. It's a matter of the responsibility you accept about what needs to be done. I'm as empowered as my mind will let me be.

Debbie Phillips, operator for five years, first team leader for the rubber-bonding team:

> More day-to-day decisions being made by people in the shop. It's all good. It was kind of scary at first. It gives you more a sense of belonging. Working in a team really helped us. We really needed each other to get through it.

What "makes a team a team"?
Jim Winterbotham:

I'm here talking to you now. And what I started doing five minutes ago, Jeff's doing. I don't have to worry about going out there to a cold machine. I was finishing boring a part—the most critical thing on it. He's over there doing it. I know he is. I guess that's what makes you a team.

EMPOWERMENT TRANSFORMS PLANT PERFORMANCE

We've seen the empowerment process unfold since 1986 at Lord Dayton. How did all this impact the plant's performance? Between 1986 and 1990:

- productivity was up 30 percent
- absenteeism was down 75 percent
- typical setup time was down more than 75 percent
- there have been zero lost-time accidents in the last six years
- overall scrap costs fell 85 percent
- manufacturing cycle time for one product was reduced from seventy-five days to seven days
- work in process has been reduced by 75 percent

And here's the real kicker. Dave proudly points to the fact that 80 percent of these results were achieved before any sizable capital investments were made. "It's people's attitudes, understanding of the goals, and effort."

These accomplishments have been duly recognized in recent years. In 1991, the Lord Dayton plant was chosen as one of *Industry Week*'s ten best plants for the year. In 1992, it received the Award for Excellence in Productivity Improvement from the Dayton Chapter of the Industrial Engineers and the Ohio Office of Industrial Training Award. In 1993, it received the prestigious Institute of Industrial Engineers' Award for Excellence in Productivity Improvement. Not bad for a plant with horrible quality, horrible morale, and a horrible reputation in 1985.

EMPOWERMENT TRANSFORMS PEOPLE'S LIVES

An empowered workplace also changes lives—the lives of managers and of workers. I asked Dave how the move to self-directed work teams changed his life at the plant.

I used to do a lot of firefighting. I really did. My day was ringing phones and chasing parts. Trying to find out why orders were late. Now I spend probably 20 percent of my time on higher-level planning—strategic kinds of things which I never had time to spend on. Another 20 percent is working with teams and people to stay close to what people think. Its totally changed the way I do my job. It's made me a more patient person.

The plant manager cannot be allowed to have the last word in an employee empowerment success story. For that, we return to Debbie Phillips. She is what empowerment is all about, for in the end what it comes down to is each worker being committed and excited.

She was asked what she would like to say to the naysayers out there who feel empowerment is a passing fad or that teams don't work:

I'd say they should investigate further. Somebody asked me one time. I used to work for another company and somebody asked me to describe the differences. Well, it was kind of funny because I didn't realize that I didn't like working there until I worked here. I thought everything was fine. I'd go to work. They'd tell what to do. I'd do my job and I'd go home. And that was fine. Until I've been in this type of environment where I'm the one that has control. It makes all the difference in the world. I don't hate coming to work. I like coming to work because I know that I'm important. I matter. My opinions matter. It's just a completely different environment. And everybody should give it really serious thought.

As we said earlier, we couldn't agree more.

LESSON: Empowerment can begin at the grassroots level when a company encourages an environment of greater freedom and individual responsibility. Specifically, grassroots empowerment encompasses:

- workers and management learning to respect and talk to each other about problems and opportunities;
- developing real trust between workers and management;
- shifting the decision-making power to get the job down to the lowest level possible; and
- creating work teams that can drive real change and eventually become self-directed work teams.

 ## Do the Right Thing
HERMAN MILLER

"IT SOUNDS SYRUPY, BUT THE MAJOR THING THAT'S HELPED US IS THAT WE'VE ALWAYS FOCUSED ON WHAT IS MORALLY RIGHT TO DO, NOT WHAT'S EXPEDIENT."

—PHIL MERCORELLA, SENIOR VICE PRESIDENT

THE CHALLENGE

Herman Miller Inc. (HMI) did not have to "begin anew" when tough times came in 1985 with its first earnings decline in fourteen years. Rather, this Michigan-based furniture manufacturer could draw on its over-forty-year commitment to participative management and update it for the new challenges coming from a wave of discounting and its own manufacturing and delivery problems with its then new Ethospace line.

In analyzing his own company's distress, then Chairman and CEO Max DePree came up with an insightful list of warning signs of a company in ill health, which he described in his best-selling book *Leadership Is an Art*. Among them: "dark tension" among key managers; no longer having time for celebration and ritual; leaders who seek to control rather than liberate; people failing to tell or to understand historic company anecdotes, what he calls tribal stories; an excessive number of manuals; a general loss of grace and civility; dry rules rather than a value orientation that takes into account contribution, spirit, excellence, beauty, and joy.

THE RESPONSE

Yes, you read correctly: spirit, beauty, joy. These are not the type of words you find many companies mentioning, much less emphasizing. But they reflect HMI's values, and values are at the heart of its response, for they are at the heart of all that it does.

Look at its vision statement, under "Our Values: Who We Are," and you will find many phrases not normally seen in corporate documents, especially those of a *Fortune 500* company: "diversity is fundamental to success"; "we believe in the integrity, dignity, and potential of every person"; "all work can be rewarding and enjoyable"; "ownership is essential to participation"; "managers best lead by serving"; "we believe in celebration"; "risk and failure is fundamental to our future success"; "there is always room to improve our results and competency through personal growth."

The key point about these values is that HMI "walks its talk": its values are not just found in writing but they are lived out each day in the workplace because its employees know the values and share in them. Being value-led is "not a strategy—it's a belief that for people to identify with an organization they have to believe in its values," says Michele Hunt, vice president of corporate development. It was the company's historic values, particularly its foundational value of participative management, that it drew on in the period 1986 to 1988 to effect a major turnaround.

It was this heritage of values that employees could draw upon in

1986 when they were once again charged with renewing the process, with developing mechanisms that would help the company use its resources more effectively. As had happened just a decade earlier, the company's ability to accommodate radical change was put to the test.

In 1988, the new process was implemented. At its core is a mechanism to make renewal a continuous activity within the organization to enable an even more timely response to change than before. Part of that response to change led the company in 1991 to begin to sharpen its focus on serving customers by commiting to a goal of 100 percent quality in all areas of the business. While HMI found itself able to build this new quality initiative upon its heritage of participative management, it also soon realized the necessity to integrate within it the systematic use of analytical tools to help get customer-related problems solved more efficiently and effectively.

To understand Herman Miller—its value structure and the way it treats its employees—you must get to know its founder, D.J. DePree, and his son Max, for it is they who are responsible for shaping this company's unique philosophy.

D. J. DePree, who founded the company in 1923 in Zeeland, Michigan, did not begin with an enlightened attitude about workers. Indeed, his epiphany did not come until 1949, twenty-six years into his leadership, and it occurred at, of all places, a professor's lecture. The young Michigan State University professor Carl Frost was talking about the Scanlon Plan, a philosophy and process of participative management built on specific principles. DePree went back and held a series of meetings with HMI employees at every level, culminating in his installing a Scanlon Plan in June 1950.

There are four Scanlon principles: identity, participation, equity, and competence. Always the first principle, identity has to do with everyone understanding the business—its history, its values, its goals and objectives, and the critical issues it faces—and how he or she can responsibly take part. Participation—everyone working together responsibly to accomplish shared business goals and objectives—is a matter of the opportunity of ownership, of feeling responsible to join with others as a positive influence to get the necessary work done. A fair return is what equity is about—enjoying that reward for the investment of his or her time and talents in helping meet the organization's goals and objectives. Competence is everyone being capable in his or her area of responsibility, which in essence is a matter of commitment.

Those principles remain consistent with what were then radical assumptions about most people's attitudes toward work—that is, that people by and large find work pleasurable and rewarding and will eagerly become contributing workers—if treated with dignity and respect.

Max learned well from his father. One of his critical and unique contributions was the concept of "covenantal relationships" between top management and all employees. He once defined the company's central mission as "attempting to share values, ideals, goals, respect for each person, the process of our work together." In contrast, he said, many companies settle for contractural relationships, which he maintains "deal only with precedent and status."

One place where covenantal relationships are fleshed out is the hiring process. In hiring key employees, top managers focus more on character and the ability to get along with people than traditional résumé high points.

When relationships with employees are covenantal rather than contractual you practice open communication. Work team members know that they have a right, indeed a responsibility, to challenge managers, and managers have a responsibility to listen and be open to influence. Challenging the status quo is actually encouraged. It sounds extraordinary, but supervisors often cite their own employees' ability to "go over their heads" as one of the major reasons for the company's success.

HMI's values are also fleshed out in such practices as "roving leadership," an Idea Club, and an annual responders recognition celebration. Max DePree came up with the idea of roving leadership, which seeks to counter the notion that all wisdom resides in the CEO or the CEO's work team or the officers and directors within an organization. In short, it is not just managers who lead. Instead, from time to time many others find themselves with the particular talent or knowledge or opportunity to move work forward. In such cases, they too are called upon to be leaders.

If someone—anyone—in the company sees something wrong or an opportunity for doing better, they should speak up. Hence the Idea Club to recognize those employees who play an active role in the company's suggestion system. In 1992, eighty-one individuals and 116 teams were inducted into the club's ranks, which meant that they had to have either eight or more accepted suggestions, at least $80,000 in implemented cost savings, or at least $208,000 in implemented avoidances, or savings and avoidances combined. Recognizing the fact that a suggestion system is only as good as those who respond to suggestions, Herman Miller holds an annual responders recognition celebration. At the one in 1992, the top twenty-five responders were cited as good models of "covenantal" relationships versus "contractual" ones.

Empowerment based on long-standing values is certainly one key factor for Herman Miller's success over the years. CEO Kerm Campbell points to one other key factor: a focus on innovative design. In early 1994, he excitedly described a chair they would be introducing in the fall as "the most important chair in the history of the world."

THE RESULTS

Growth—spectacular growth—is the major result as Herman Miller has gone from 1976 sales of $50 million to $953 million in 1994 and from 600 employees in 1972 to 5,400 today. Both net sales and new orders for the fourth quarter of fiscal 1994 set company quarterly records.

The company can be glad it stuck to its principles in the mid-1980s, for participative management is what pulled it out of the fire. Workers quickly came up with a number of initiatives, including ways to trim $12 million from annual costs, new business markets, and cutting delivery times for Ethospace from twenty-two weeks to six weeks.

There are a number of benefits that flow directly from the participative system. The absenteeism rate of 1 percent to 2 percent is well below the U.S. average of 6 percent. The 7 percent employee turnover rate is less than half of the 15 percent to 20 percent average of U.S. firms. And suggestions coming from employees have led to an estimated cost savings averaging $11.6 million annually during the last five years. In fact, HMI has recently won two National Association of Suggestion Systems awards—in overall suggestion system performance and in the highest ratio of savings for every 100 employees. In 1989, HMI, along with Volvo of Sweden, was honored to receive the prestigious Carl Bertelsmann Prize for its "outstanding ideas and promising initiatives" in promoting greater employee participation in both the management process of the company and profit-sharing programs.

There are numerous individual work team success stories throughout the company. One particularly important one involves the development of the new Geneva furniture line, for it proved that the "impossible" corporatewide challenge of CEO Kerm Campbell—to cut cycle time by 75 percent—could be done. What normally would take three years took just nine months from the May 1992 decision to develop it as a product until the first order was shipped in mid-February 1993. How does Dennis Foley, product champion for the Geneva project, account for this accomplishment? They broke rules, challenged the traditional order, skipped the conventional steps, and individuals within the teams took risks. "The whole process was more direct. Things weren't in the way anymore."

Those "things" were what Kerm Campbell often mentions when he talks about moving to a relational, adaptable organization: steep hierarchies, walls, bureaucracy, barriers. Foley admits that they hit a wall or two along the way. They had to "guard against falling into the old patterns of checking up on people," "lowering expectations," and "blaming." Yet he is quick to add, "But we always felt comfortable making the decisions we had to make in order to keep the project on course. We had a real sense of empowerment."

[
LESSON: Being value-led means encouraging challenges to the status quo to do the right thing, which fosters in workers individual responsibility and pride in the quality of the job they are doing.
]

Employee Involvement Works at New and Old Plants
GOODYEAR TIRE & RUBBER

"I USE THE WORD 'ASSOCIATE' INSTEAD OF THE COMMONLY USED 'EMPLOYEE,' AND IT'S MUCH MORE THAN JUST A SUBSTITUTION OF A WORD. ONE OF THE DEFINITIONS OF THE WORD 'EMPLOYEE' IS 'TO BE USED.' AND I DON'T THINK ANYONE WANTS TO FEEL THEY ARE BEING USED. BUT IF YOU LOOK AT THE DEFINITION OF 'ASSOCIATE,' IT IS A JOINING TOGETHER. AND THERE IS VERY LITTLE WE CAN'T ACCOMPLISH WHEN WE JOIN TOGETHER, WHEN THERE IS A TOTAL TEAM EFFORT, WHEN ALL MEMBERS OF AN ORGANIZATION BELIEVE THEY ARE MAKING A POSITIVE CONTRIBUTION TO THE SUCCESS OF THE ENTERPRISE."
—STANLEY GAULT, CHAIRMAN AND CEO

THE CHALLENGE

The times were not too good for Goodyear in the mid-1970s. Charles Pilliod, Jr., chairman and CEO, was deeply concerned over the effects of the adversarial relationship between tire industry management and its unionized workforce, the growing threat of foreign radial tire imports from Europe and Asia, and the prospects of shrinking cost-selling profit margins.

A decade later, Goodyear again faced difficult challenges. This time, it was under direct attack by an Anglo-French raider, Sir James Goldsmith. To fend him off, Goodyear decided to do its own trimming, choosing three weak plants to close. The choice of the then fifty-seven-year-old plant in Gadsden, Alabama, was easy. After all, its costs were high, waste was high, and its biggest product line, bias tires, was drying up as customers switched to radials.

THE RESPONSE

The response to the 1970s challenge was to build in Lawton, Oklahoma, a revolutionary plant from scratch, what Goodyear called its "incubator of change." Pilliod's announcement in 1977 that Goodyear would spend a then remarkable $216 million to build a new tire plant in the United States was, to say the least, not exactly embraced by the investment community. But Pilliod, and two highly placed in-house manufacturing executives, knew that radical change was called for. Among other changes, the new plant would not be unionized, in the hope that a different power structure might better tap the brainpower and work ethic of employees.

Despite hand-picking the start-up team, traditional mind-sets were hard to overcome. A forty-five-day, consultant-led training program helped to pound home the message that commitment by the work-force, not control of it, was the new model. New educational and personal qualifications were established for employees, including for the first time the willingness to be a team worker—a top priority for plant success.

Progress, however, did not come easily. Then a recession sent the first job security shock waves through the fledgling and newly commit-ted Lawton team. In 1980, the plant was forced to lay off 200 of its people.

Lawton fought back hard. After a "Future Vision" workshop in 1981, action plans and new strategies went into effect. Among the latter were the development of managerial skills and personal leadership characteristics: improved communication and information systems to aid daily decision making; an evolution to semiautonomous work groups; and managers becoming not bosses but resource experts to a committed workforce. By the late 1980s, employees were empowered to make decisions within the scope of their jobs through open sharing of information, and management was practicing an open-door/open-floor policy where anyone could go to any level to resolve a problem or make a suggestion.

Turning to Gadsden, the immediate fix that saved the plant from closing in 1986 was plant and union negotiators agreeing to changes that would slash costs, accounting for the bulk of a $30 million savings package that kept the plant alive. But alive doesn't mean healthy. Be-cause demand for bias tires kept declining, the plant laid off more than 1,000 workers from 1986 to 1989. And with recession bearing down in 1989, the plant's initial efforts to involve workers were barely crawling.

In stepped J.R. Countryman, the newly elected president of the union local. At a highly emotional union hall meeting, he convinced the members that despite wage cuts and layoffs, there was no alterna-tive but to embrace the joint process. Otherwise the plant would die.

At the heart of the joint process are problem-solving work groups that meet an hour a week or two hours every other week. During the off-shift meetings, employees are paid to discuss problems and develop solutions. Here's how the United Rubber Workers describes the joint process model:

> The model has a middle ground commonly called the "shadow structure." The shadow structure is the common ground mutually identified and agreed upon by labor-management which determines the basis for formulating common vision, goals, objectives and strategies *(how to get there)*. This common ground must be well defined and worked out carefully. It is the key to the whole process.... The common ground is thought of as an *inverted* triangle—which demonstrates empowerment of floor level employees.... We must remember, the real key is the *philosophy and commitment* from the top management of the company if the cooperative endeavor is to be successful.

The "shadow structure" has the commitment of CEO Stan Gault. "The Gadsden plant has been the springboard of a new style of cooperation, which we call here 'Joint Process.' It's a cooperative effort involving plant management, union leadership, and all Goodyear associates in Gadsden. I'm convinced that type of relationship and partnership is going to be the major key to success."

But Lawton and Gadsden were not the whole company. And the company was performing poorly again in 1991 when Stan Gault was asked to defer his retirement plans and help turn the company around. The numbers were indeed bleak: market share had dropped steadily since 1986, there was a heavy debt load of $3.7 billion, operating costs were high, sales forecasts showed a downward trend, personnel had been cut by 15,000, and the morale of Goodyear employees was at an all-time low.

Gault saw that tremendous change was necessary and that all "associates" (not "employees" anymore when he arrived) must understand this, be involved, and pull together. Here is Gault's description of his response:

> We needed a tremendous cultural change involving everyone in the organization. You have to do many things simultaneously. When you're in this kind of jam, time is not on your side. After I was there about thirty days, I thought I owed it to our people to develop the future objectives for the corporation. For lack of a better title, I wrote "The Twelve Objectives for Managing Goodyear Successfully in the '90s." They include having a leadership position in costs, quality, customer service, and innovation. We used video presentations around

the world. I presented and explained the objectives to all our people. I wanted everyone in the organization to know why these were our objectives, what they meant to each individual position, and how everyone fit into the picture—with no one excluded.

That's Gault's view of the role of employee involvement in the transformation of Goodyear. Number ten of the twelve objectives is called "Maximize Human Resource Capabilities," which sounds kind of dry until Gault brings it to life:

The significant achievement within the manufacturing and materials management organizations that I mentioned earlier was not possible based on the edicts of one or two individuals. They were achieved as the result of opening the door to suggestions and team problem solving that are only possible when we move to maximize the limitless resource of people power. The days of the dictatorial manager at any level of an organization are over if a department, a facility, or a corporation expects to prosper and succeed.

THE RESULTS

Plant manager K. B. Kleckner thinks that Lawton's results are pretty special: "Lawton has without a doubt been the most successful plant in the history of Goodyear and probably in the history of the tire business." A benchmark year for Lawton was 1987 when it was the first recipient of Goodyear's World Class Competitor Award. The award recognizes Lawton associates for quality, productivity, and cost achievements not just with Goodyear plants, but with any competitor anywhere in the world. But perhaps most important to it are the customers' plaudits. Associates of the Lawton plant have been honored with Chrysler, Ford, and GM's top supplier awards, including many quality awards. GM's multicategory Mark of Excellence Award recognizes continuous, outstanding efforts in all aspects of business: quality, cost, delivery, management, and technology.

At Gadsden, union members and managers like to stress the intangible results of the joint process—the trust and the improved relations. Grievances have tumbled from 276 in 1988 to seventy-two in 1993. Says one union member, "It used to be whenever we had a problem, the first thing we'd do was file a grievance. Now it's the last thing we do." The company also likes the tangibles. Since joint process took hold in 1989, lost time has dropped 74 percent, productivity has climbed 26 percent, waste is down 39 percent, and energy consumption is down 22 percent. Recognizing Gadsden's improvements, Goodyear has pumped $35 million into the plant since 1991 and about 800 workers have been called back from layoff.

For the company as a whole, Gault's twelve objectives have worked wonders. The total debt load has been cut by nearly two thirds, costs have been trimmed by over $350 million a year, in the process raising operating margins from 6 percent of sales to around 10 percent. In 1993, quarterly percentage increases in earnings exceeded 40 percent, and the $388 million yearly earnings total was the second highest in company history.

All of this pleases Gault. But what also gets him excited is what has happened to his associates.

> During the past year there has been a tremendous change in attitudes. A year ago, Goodyear headquarters was a dark, dismal, discouraging and desperate place. People were not happy about coming to work, but today I have people stopping and telling me that they took forward to coming to work here and how much they enjoy working for Goodyear.

That's not just the CEO talking about people at headquarters. Here's what a representative of the United Rubbers Workers' headquarters had to say about Goodyear:

> We have had some success with several employers—however, our greatest success has been with The Goodyear Tire and Rubber Company. The key factor in the Goodyear experience is that the Company recognizes the importance of cooperation as a way to compete effectively in the global marketplace. It appears that they have genuinely adopted a philosophy and commitment at the corporate level for employee involvement in their plant operations. . . . Goodyear appears to recognize that this is a new era—which demands a different kind of thinking, a different way of production and a different way of doing business.

[
LESSON: Employee involvement can work effectively at both a nonunion, greenfield plant and at an old, unionized plant—creating a cooperative decision-making process—*if* top management and union leadership are committed to doing things differently.
]

The Boss Has Got to Let Go
JOHNSONVILLE FOODS

"IT HAS TO START WITH THE PRESIDENT AND THE WAY YOU RUN THE COMPANY.
IT IS A BASIC CHANGE IN WHO'S RESPONSIBLE AND THE WAY THE WHOLE
BUSINESS IS RUN. YOU DO BUSINESS DIFFERENTLY."
—RALPH STAYER, PRESIDENT

THE CHALLENGE

Ralph Stayer, the president, pulled no punches in describing the challenge facing Johnsonville Sausage (its name through 1986) back in the early 1980s: "Our productivity had to be a heck of a lot better and service to our customers had to be a lot better."

He wasn't talking future growth—he was talking survival. "Our business wasn't going to survive if we didn't get our productivity a lot better." Little wonder that he found himself lying awake nights. He wished his managers could get the employees to lie awake at night as well—to have as much concern for the company as he did. What he saw instead was: "Our people didn't seem to care. Every day I came to work and saw people so bored by their jobs that they made thoughtless, dumb mistakes." But what he desired was impossible under the authoritarian management structure then existing.

THE RESPONSE

"I had to change my management style," continued Stayer. That was step number one. Why? Because he recognized that all kinds of things needed to be changed: "the context in which we operate"; "the performance standards and expectations"; "measurement and feedback systems"; "reward systems"; "personnel systems." "The key," Stayer emphasized, "was that I couldn't change all these."

So he sat down with his managers and workers and they talked. He told his managers, "From now on, you're all responsible for making your own decisions." Disaster followed as the managers could not make the switch from being followers to leaders. Within two years, all had been replaced. But rather than throwing up his hands in frustration at the futility of employee empowerment, Stayer analyzed what had happened and concluded: "Deep down, I was still in love with my own control; I was just making people guess what I wanted instead of telling them."

Over time, one noticeable difference, according to Stayer, was that "they saw me keeping my mouth shut." Employee volunteers began working in teams to attack many of the problems the company faced. Gradually, the workers became responsible for measuring their own performance. Line employees were given control of product quality, which simply meant they were responsible for product tasting. In short, Stayer stopped directing his employees and acted more as a coach—actually letting the employees change the company.

All of this began on the plant floor (actually in three plants), but Stayer knew that it had to spread throughout the company to be truly effective: "Our sales people. Our accounting people. Our marketing people. Our whole company is now run this way."

THE RESULTS

A major result involves Stayer's top concern and what he set out to rectify: the company's poor productivity. Productivity from 1984 to 1992 took a gigantic 300 percent leap.

The company also experienced a fifteenfold increase in sales against intense competition in a flat or declining market. Its return on assets tripled as it spread from being a one-state company to a national one. And it was a job-generating machine. Employment more than tripled, from 200 to 650 workers in 1993.

But here, in Stayer's words, are the results that he is most proud of, for they made all the performance improvements happen:

> Everyone at Johnsonville discovered they could do considerably more than they had imagined. Since they had little trouble meeting the accelerated production goals that they themselves had set, members raised the minimum acceptable performance criteria and began routinely to expect more of themselves and others. Their general level of commitment is as high or higher than my own.

[LESSON: Empowerment must often begin with the president (or CEO) realizing that the workers really do have the best answer, and thus the key to success is to give up some management control and let your workers change what's wrong and decide how to accomplish what's really needed.]

Empower the Unions Too
USX

"THESE ARE LINE WORKERS IN THE STEEL INDUSTRY, SUPPLYING THE AUTO INDUSTRY. I CAN'T THINK OF TWO MORE BATTERED INDUSTRIES. THEY'VE REALLY PUSHED THIS IDEA OF EMPOWERMENT DOWN WHERE IT BELONGS. THAT'S THE SPIRIT OF AMERICAN INDUSTRY THAT'S COMING BACK, AND PEOPLE DON'T KNOW IT."

—MARK GAVOOR, JUDGE FOR RIT/USA TODAY QUALITY CUP

THE CHALLENGE

Challenges don't come much tougher. Once, the Gary Works of USX/ U.S. Steel had been the very symbol of the country's might and pride. The Indiana plant, built in the early 1900s, made more steel than any mill in the world. It was Big Steel at its finest. Sprawling five miles along the shores of Lake Michigan, the company's Gary operations employed nearly 30,000 people and housed everything from a railroad, a hospital, and a cement plant to a factory that made bridges and skyscraper components.

By 1986, employment at Gary Works had shrunk to fewer than 10,000. U.S. Steel found itself embroiled in a six-month strike that lasted into early 1987. Scores of buildings stood empty and many had already been demolished. Gone were the cement plant and bridge-fabricating facility. Its huge new $100 million blast furnace was derided as "the Mistake on the Lake." Gary's big automotive customers were dissatisfied with its steel, threatening to dump it as a supplier. In the midst of so many rusting, idle buildings and angry customers, how can a company possibly respond?

THE RESPONSE

One approach to the challenge, amidst many taken by the company, was almost too simple to be believed. First one, then another, and finally five union hardhats, fresh off the line, were asked to visit automotive customers' plants and learn firsthand the problems they had with Gary Works steel. The team's activities were part of a plantwide quality improvement effort known as APEX (All Product Excellence) aimed at involving all levels of the organization in problem solving, quality improvement, and customer service.

The team of five was given authority to change plant approaches to meeting customer needs and dealing with customer service problems. And they certainly did. They put into effect many changes that did not cost workers any jobs or the company much money. They demanded rubber pads on flatbed trucks to cushion the steel. They created plastic rings to protect the rolls from crane damage. They persuaded workers who package and load each roll or stack to take responsibility for its condition by signing a tag attached to the shipment. Simple, low-cost changes but the results were remarkable.

Seeing their success, the plant manager soon formed a team of three union workers who call on nonautomotive customers. These three workers and the original five-worker team meet with the plant manager each Monday. They then spend the rest of the week at customers' plants helping resolve problems. Here's how the manager of a nearby Ford plant feels about their effectiveness: "We'd have instances of breakage where we'd get the managers, the engineers, the metallurgists working on it. Then the [Gary Works and Ford] hourly guys come in and get their heads together, and the problem would go away."

And the union loves it. Says Cary Kranz, the local president (and son of the former local president), "I would say we've seen a complete turnaround from the way things used to be. They now involve union people and make us feel that we are a part of something. They meet with us and they recognize that we have all the knowledge in the world within these gates."

THE RESULTS

The team's efforts, along with those of other workers at the Gary plant, have helped achieve an enormous improvement in product quality. Automotive customers, who buy almost one third of the Gary Works' steel, now reject just 0.5 percent, down from a high reject rate of 2.6 percent in 1987. Ford, which nearly flunked the plant that year, gave Gary Works its Q1 Award as a high-quality supplier in 1991; Chrysler followed with its QE Award later that year. General Motors, which threatened to drop Gary Works as a supplier in 1987, has increased its purchases from the plant sevenfold. GM also bestowed its Mark of Excellence Award on the Gary plant. As for the team, its members are so well received by customers that they are now members of various customers' employee-involvement teams.

All of this has been accompanied by a quantum improvement in the Gary Works' productivity. The plant, bolstered by a huge $1.3 billion capital infusion since 1980, now takes less than 2.7 man-hours to produce and ship a ton of steel, compared with a USX average of 3.0, a national average for the steel industry of about 4.0 hours, and most significantly 7.1 hours at the Gary plant as recently as 1982. And even the Mistake on the Lake is doing just fine, pouring out an ever-flowing river of molten iron at the rate of 3 million tons per year—a North American record.

[
LESSON: Let the line workers deal directly with the customers and suppliers to straighten things out quickly and effectively. Workers enjoy the challenge of solving problems.
]

4: TRAIN AND RETRAIN WORKERS

Training. It's one of the corporate buzzwords of the 1990s. Should it be? What's really behind it? Is it just the latest passing fad or is there real lasting substance?

The big-picture view is persuasive. The American economy is increasingly becoming an economy based on knowledge. Given this, does it not stand to reason that more and more companies will be creating value by capturing and applying knowledge in new and creative ways? And if this is so, companies must educate and train their workers—not just once but continuously.

The problem—the serious problem—is that far too many workers in the vast majority of companies today are doing "just enough to get by" and thus the companies are getting maybe 60 percent, from its workers, perhaps 80 or 90 percent if they're lucky. Why operate at 60 percent, or even 90 percent, efficiency when this can be boosted through relatively small investments in training? Indeed, 60 percent—90 percent just won't cut it anymore in the ruthlessly competitive global arena. Companies must approach 100 percent from their workers if they want to make it.

The workers are often doing just enough to get by not because they are lazy or stupid but often because they haven't received enough training. A recent Price-Waterhouse survey found that only 58 percent of employers had a structured training program. And because most of the training that does take place goes to white-collar workers, just one in twenty-five nonuniversity graduates receives any training. Further, only 3 percent of young men and less than 1 percent of young women in the United States enter apprenticeship programs, compared, for example, to seventy-five percent in Germany. All together, employers spent $44 billion, or 1.8 percent of total compensation paid by all U.S. employers in 1989.

Most companies just don't have the great insight that Fred Remmele —a German-born tool-and-die maker and founder of Remmele Engineering—has: "Like good tools, craftsmen are fashioned with care." The "care" that Remmele provides is one of the country's best apprenticeship programs and training that for many workers runs between 6,000 to 10,000 hours.

Fortunately, there are a number of signs of change. There's an "extraordinary outpouring" of interest in building a youth-apprenticeship system according to Hillary Pennington, president of Jobs for the Future. Many companies have teamed with local community colleges and universities to upgrade workers' technical skills. All companies should take heed to a clear conclusion that emerged in an article in *Inc.* (Dec. 1992) titled "The Hottest Entrepreneurs in America":

> What's striking is that these companies are all fashioning training programs in-house to suit their own needs. Moreover, none of them view training as a luxury for small entrepreneurial companies. Instead, it's seen as a necessity to build the kind of workforce they need.

Thus, there are many answers to the question "why train?": You train to release the full potential of workers. You train because it is a fundamental requirement to achieve world-class manufacturing status. You train, as the success stories in this chapter demonstrate, if you want to boost productivity, lower costs, introduce advanced manufacturing technologies, save the company, or restructure work around self-managed work teams.

Training is absolutely required to thrive in the 1990s. It may even be required to survive.

ACHIEVING BASIC CORPORATE GOALS THROUGH TRAINING

A principal goal of many companies is to lower costs. One of the best ways is to spend more money on training. It sounds counterintuitive —spend more to lower costs. But take a look at the mind-set, actions, and results of Will-Burt and Chaparral Steel. Harry Featherstone, CEO of Will-Burt, says, "There's not a single factor of cost that has not been heavily influenced in the right way with our education system. Not one single cost factor." The goal set before Gordon Forward when he was asked in 1975 to found a steel minimill was to become the world's lowest-cost steel producer. An extraordinary commitment to training was one of the principal means employed to achieve this goal.

Everyone wants to boost productivity. Chaparral's highly trained workers have enabled it to produce steel with a record 1.4 hours of labor per ton versus 2.4 hours for other minimills and 4.9 hours for integrated producers.

Pursuing total quality is also a widespread goal. CR Industries, which took training "out of the closet" and involved every employee without spending one extra dollar, discovered that training has gone hand in hand with first-class quality.

Or perhaps the main objective is to empower employees through work teams. These teams are valuable (as the previous chapter documented) but they require special training of workers for them to function effectively. Ford discovered this at its Sharonville, Ohio, plant, which undertook one of the most extensive retraining efforts in the country when self-managed work teams were introduced in 1985. The training helped them more than double their targeted goal for cumulative improvement by 1988.

Advanced manufacturing technologies are also valuable and sorely needed in many manufacturing plants. But automation alone—even the best—is not usually enough. As Dale Evans, president of EVCO Plastics has emphasized, you have to hire good people and train them well—"otherwise, you'll just make bad parts faster."

Remmele Engineering, which stressed training as a core value from its founding, demonstrates two other often neglected but important benefits to companies that come from a serious commitment to training. The first is that great training helps a company attract great people, while the second is that training helps make "times get better" for the company.

GREAT BENEFITS FOR WORKERS AS WELL

Workers receive both tangible as well as intangible benefits from training. Leading the list is increased wages. Training can also help workers move ahead in the company. Then there's the most important tangible benefit of all: the training may actually save a person's job. Harry Featherstone credits Will-Burt's extensive education program as instrumental to the company's survival. Ford's plant in Sharonville was scheduled to close in the early 1980s, but an employee-involvement program, leading to self-managed work teams and relying on extensive training, helped save the plant.

To many employees, the intangible benefits are just as important. Higher self-esteem and greater confidence, more satisfaction from their work, and a feeling of greater attachment and loyalty to the company are among the most important.

One of the most fundamental benefits of all to workers is that training becomes a way of life.

TRAINING IS FOR EVERYONE

Some key lessons have emerged from corporate training programs. Training can be extremely beneficial to the company, and it also benefits workers in tangible as well as intangible ways.

The third lesson to be learned from these stories is that training is for everyone. Many companies don't train because they feel they are too small. Others feel that just top managers need to be trained and they can then pass on whatever they've learned. Still others don't bother because they feel their workers aren't smart enough to benefit.

What's clear from this chapter's success stories is that all workers can benefit from training. Just ask the workers at Will-Burt, many of whom had very low reading and math skills, some being illiterate. Their initial suspicious, sometimes hostile attitude toward testing and basic skills training turned very positive when they experienced new-found competencies and corresponding confidence.

The smart companies—and the ones that really benefit from training—train everyone. Chaparral didn't get to its highly productive, low-cost position by training 10 percent, 30 percent, or even 50 percent of its workers. It trained them all—*and* it keeps training them (85 percent are in training at any given time).

Can education and training really help anyone? Ask Shelly Erickson. When she joined Remmele Engineering in the mid-1980s, she didn't even know what a machine shop was. After taking company-sponsored courses in basic math, statistical process control, computer programming, and blueprint reading, Erickson can now handle every aspect of the manufacturing process in her work cell. And she greatly enjoyed seeing her wages double in her first five years with the company.

Or talk to Harry Featherstone, who has seen it all. Great hostility to mandatory tests and initial classes. Great participation in follow-on voluntary courses. Eventual development of an in-house business school that offers graduates a mini-MBA. Fantastic company results (not the least of which is survival) and excited workers. No wonder that he feels "there's a magic that happens with education" and that he is confident about companies adopting education and training in the future. "Just get a CEO to think education, and I can assure you they would do it—because it's so logical."

The Magic That Happens with Education
WILL-BURT

The year was 1985. Employee morale was bad. The quality of the products was bad. There was the threat of closing down.

It all sounds similar to the situation at the Dayton plant of the Lord Corp., which opened Chapter 3, right down to the same year of crisis. But there are a couple of key differences in the two cases.

The threat of closure at the Dayton plant was just that—a threat that was "out there" but not actively present. The threat of closure at Will-Burt was actively present. In October 1985, the board of directors declared that they had to liquidate the company due to the numerous product liability lawsuits on parts that Will-Burt had supplied to major companies. They gave the new CEO, Harry Featherstone, one and a half months to save the company.

Picture yourself in Harry's shoes. You've just taken over a small machine parts company in a small Rust Belt town in Ohio in 1985 at the height of the "death of manufacturing" drumbeat in the media. Product rejects are running as high as 35 percent, with the average around 10 percent to 15 percent. Employees are often absent or late.

Their morale is really low. You've got six weeks to prevent liquidation. What do you do?

The first thing Harry did was establish an ESOP—a 100 percent employee stock ownership plan. Under this, he borrowed $3.5 million on his name and the company's name. That gave him some capital, but it was a huge risk for a company that up to that time had never made more than $400,000 in a year on the bottom line. Clearly there was no way this amount could be repaid without the company improving— and doing so quickly and dramatically.

So now what? Harry Featherstone put through some layoffs. But after taking a real hard look at the situation, he could think of only one thing to save the company: education. He found an analogy with the incompatibility in voting ballots that are written at the sixteenth-grade level while the average person reads at the seventh-grade level. "Our engineers and quality control people were using sixteenth- to eighteenth-grade language while the workers were averaging around an eighth- to ninth-grade level. It didn't work." The workers simply needed education and training. Will-Burt's solution was an education mandate from the new CEO.

Can you imagine how this solution was initially received? The company needed to seriously cut costs and the CEO launched a broad education initiative that would *cost* the company 2.5 percent of payroll in the first couple of years. Let's look at the reactions right from the board to the workers. Featherstone said in his interview that the board had recently told him they thought he was "totally insane." The director of human resources at that time thought he was "absolutely batty." As Featherstone recalls, "I had supervisors here and my staff that yelled at me. Portions of the factory hated it." The workers' perspective is provided by Jack Rose, a man in his early thirties who started with Will-Burt fresh out of high school fifteen years ago. "When Harry came in with this education program, a lot of people, and I myself was one of them, felt 'I know how to read blueprints. I know what I'm doing. I don't need this.' " He elaborated: it was "taken kind of poorly at first. The attitude was, 'I came here to work. Let me earn my money and get the heck out of here.' "

Rose became a quick convert and enthusiast for the value of the education as he came to see the benefits in his own life. His dad, who had worked at Will-Burt for thirty-five years, never did see the value of all this education. Here's how Jack described his father's attitude: "My dad's a workaholic. He's a worker. He likes production. 'I ain't got time to take this test. Leave me alone. Let me run. I would have gotten 200 more parts out if I hadn't taken this damn test."

But Harry Featherstone had what every good leader of a company must have: the courage of his conviction. And because he did, he persevered with his education thrust through the initial skepticism and sometimes outright hostility.

FROM BASIC MATH AND READING TO A MINI-MBA

Having made up his mind that education and training were the way to turn the company around, Featherstone didn't pull any punches. All 280 workers were tested on their reading and math skills, revealing that many had very low basic skills, with some workers even being illiterate. This required bold action, not rhetoric. All workers, from welders to secretaries to lathe operators to sales executives were required to participate in the math classes. Further, Featherstone made it clear to the workers that they were going to the math classes to learn, not just to sit.

From there, a course on reading blueprints was offered on a voluntary basis. Eventually, nearly everyone took it. As Jack Rose put it, "Some definitely needed to take it. And it helped them. Now they have self-confidence. They feel, 'I know what's going on. I don't have to feel stupid.'"

Flush with success from the initial courses, Featherstone launched an ambitious new education program. He actually established, in his small company in the middle of Ohio, an in-house business school that offers graduates a mini-MBA. No company, regardless of size, had a similar program.

The classes are held right at Plant Number 1's classroom beginning at 3:30 P.M., the end of the first shift. There are two twenty-week sessions over a two-year period. Of the sixty-five who enrolled in the first two-year group, less than half graduated. Although Featherstone winced at the dropout rate, he knew that those who made it through could help the others understand the business. All in all, 170 of Will-Burt's 330 employees have graduated with mini-MBAs.

Here's a few of the things, according to Jack Rose, that those workers have learned: marketing, sales, plant layout, production, insurance, management structures, and the company's culture. "A clean-cut course on business from the ground level on up to top management," is how Jack describes it. Practically speaking, "It really gives you a better understanding why some things happen across the street in the upper offices that didn't make any sense to you." His overall feelings: "I've just been amazed. It's well worthwhile."

THE MAGIC WORKED BY EDUCATION

When you talk to Harry Featherstone about education and the value of it, you know you're talking to a true believer. There's a sparkle in his eye and his voice becomes animated. It's clear that Harry would prefer to talk about the impact of education on the individual person's life, but he wasn't shy about pointing out the many companywide benefits his education thrust has led to in its first seven years.

First and foremost, it did save the company. In Harry's words, "I did it to get money. And in 1987, we paid back $1 million to the bank and put zero on the bottom line. In 1988, $900,000 went to the bank." Remember, the most the company had ever made prior to that was $400,000. In 1993, sales reached $24 million and the company paid off the 1985 ESOP loan.

Quality has greatly improved. In the mid-1980s, rejects were so high that 2,000 to 4,000 hours per month were spent just on rework. By January 1994, the figure was twenty-five hours per month, on a much higher sales base. In 1994, it passed ISO 9001 and received a seven-year flag from Caterpillar for superb quality. Best of all, it attained Six-Sigma status—just 3.4 rejections per million parts manufactured.

Another result of training was a reduction in payroll errors. "Our payroll errors went from 33 percent to just .04 percent. We used to have people just track errors. That's a cost. That's efficiency and it's money on the bottom line."

Those are great results for the company. How do the workers now feel?

Jack Rose, for one, is a happy man. "I didn't want to stay on the floor all my life. It's a rough life. I want to better myself." Jack took all the initial courses and now he's mostly through the mini-MBA. Has it helped? "I'm in a position now where I probably wouldn't have been if I hadn't been going through these courses." Incidentally, this young man who started as a janitor fresh out of high school is now a cost reduction auditor who studies jobs to determine ways to increase productivity and different methods of machining to cut costs.

And, oh yes, employee morale is a whole lot better. One good measure of morale is the number of times workers are late to work. In this firm of under 300 employees, the number was running at 100 to 200 a week. In one recent six-month period, there was a total of two employees late. Absenteeism is way down. Sick days are down. And safety couldn't be better. According to Harry Featherstone, they've achieved a "perfect workplace" for the second or third year: no major accidents. And employee turnover had dropped from 35 percent in 1986 to just 1 percent by 1994.

THE VISION PRESSES ON

Needless to say, Harry Featherstone is not a man to rest on his laurels. Two weeks before his interview, he was testifying before the Senate Education Committee on behalf of his idea for an Associate's Degree in Manufacturing. This degree would be recognized by all manufacturing firms, so if employees had to move, they could walk into a plant at the new location, present the degree showing all their skills, and get a good job.

Locally, Featherstone has more immediate plans. He hopes to offer Swedish language classes because Volvo recently moved in nearby. He also said it was his "dying ambition" to try teaching sign language. He pointed out that just in Wayne County, Ohio, alone there were 200 hearing-impaired. He wanted to hire some of them at Will-Burt, but first he wanted a number of his employees with sign language ability so everyone would feel comfortable having them.

So the education bandwagon rolls on at Will-Burt. One who is happy about that is plant manager Larry Murgatroyd. He's got his mini-MBA, a key factor in his becoming plant manager well before his thirtieth birthday. He sees no end in sight. "As technology keeps changing, we must keep up with education. We're on a road here that's not going to stop. It's just going to keep going and going and going. That's what we need to do."

And according to Featherstone, that's what companies all across America need to do. And he's confident they eventually will.

LESSON: A comprehensive education and training thrust may meet stiff resistance at first, but the CEO and top management must persevere. Such a comprehensive initiative, by changing the lives of individuals, can:

- change the whole culture of a company
- greatly improve quality
- reduce costs across the board
- save the company

85 Percent Always in Training
CHAPARRAL STEEL

"EDUCATING EMPLOYEES IS A MUST FOR A COMPANY THAT WANTS TO BE COMPETITIVE IN A RAPIDLY CHANGING GLOBAL ECONOMY."
—GORDON FORWARD, CEO

THE CHALLENGE

Gordon Forward was asked in 1975 to leave his job at a Canadian steel company to help found a steel minimill in Texas. His challenge: become the world's lowest-cost steel producer. To do this, he focused on these ideas among others: the classless corporation, the freedom to act, and universal education.

THE RESPONSE

Chaparral has a lot of employee-friendly practices—like free coffee, informal dress, no reserved parking spaces, a spotless locker room, no time clocks, freedom to pick your lunch hour and break time. Forward felt that if they could tap the egos of everyone in the company, "we could move mountains."

But beyond tapping egos, the company goes to extraordinary lengths to educate its employees. Whereas many companies are pleased with having 20 percent, or even 10 percent, of their workers enrolled in some training, Chaparral has a policy of making sure that about 85 percent of its 950 employees are enrolled in some type of training course at any one time. These courses may range from electronics and metallurgy to credit history. Learning and staying up-to-date is a large part of the organizational culture at Chaparral, and an expectation of senior management. For example, the company makes a practice of providing industrial sabbaticals and travel money so that employees can travel to universities, other companies, and even across the world to learn about new processes and technologies.

THE RESULTS

All of this lowers costs in scores of ways. When Chaparral was designing its new mill for making wide-flange steel beams used in bridges and buildings, the employees developed patent-pending technology that manufactures a final product with just eight to twelve passes through the system as opposed to traditional methods requiring up to fifty passes. Two maintenance workers invented a machine for strapping bundles of steel rods together that costs only $60,000 rather than $250,000 for the old machines, and it did the job faster and with more flexibility.

Certainly, such examples are a major reason why Chaparral produces steel with a record 1.4 hours of labor per ton versus 2.4 hours for other minimills and 4.9 hours for integrated producers.

[
LESSON: Training almost all your workers at any given time is a good investment because it can reduce costs, improve quality, and increase your market share. Training almost always pays back more than it costs.
]

Training at No Additional Cost
CR INDUSTRIES

"WE HAVE EXPANDED TRAINING TO EVERY CORNER OF THE CORPORATION WITHOUT ADDING TRAINING COSTS. IN FACT, WE'RE ACTUALLY SPENDING LESS AND IMPROVING QUALITY AT THE SAME TIME. HOW? IT'S ALL DONE BY EMPLOYEES, FOR EMPLOYEES."
—DAVID CHURCHILL, MANAGER OF EMPLOYEE RELATIONS, AND BILL BURZYNSKI, DIRECTOR OF TOTAL QUALITY SYSTEMS

THE CHALLENGE

Competition from U.S., European, and Asian manufacturers, along with more customers demanding just-in-time delivery, put increasing cost-cutting pressure on this company just west of Chicago. Fortunately, CR Industries, a maker of sealing systems for a variety of automotive, industrial, and aerospace application, was already doing a number of things right. It had instituted quality improvement programs, such as statistical process control; it recognized training and participative management as vital ingredients of quality; and it knew it had to improve communications from managers and supervisors to employees.

But to achieve its stated corporate objectives of exceeding customer expectations and retaining its leading role in seal manufacturing, even these programs were not enough.

THE RESPONSE

Training had to be taken companywide—right to the assembly floor. Under traditional training structures, this would have taken a considerable investment in additional training staff and consultants. CR had a different idea. It believed it already had a reservoir of talent and potential that could improve the company's business processes.

Here's how David Churchill and Bill Burzynski described the CR training way:

CR industries has simply taken training out of the closet—just like corporations learned to do with quality control over the last few years. The idea of taking

quality control from the quality control department and putting it on every line
and at every desk is what CR Industries has done with training. CR has structured a companywide training program that involves every employee—from the
assembly line to the sales force, from engineers to the administrative support
staff, all the way to the executive offices. All this is done without spending an
extra dollar to hire outside trainers, adding full-time training professionals, or
investing in elaborate workbooks and materials.

Learning from its own quality program, the company created a new
training "attitude." As an extension of CR's total quality commitment,
training became a continuous, problem-solving adventure. Many areas
of manufacturing have been restructured to allow the new training
process to work. At the heart of the training program is a work process
standards (WPS) initiative that enables teams of managers, line supervisors, and employees to standardize and improve their companywide
processes.

THE RESULTS

Training has gone hand in hand with first-class quality. From 1987 to
1991, CR's six manufacturing facilities have earned over fifty supplier
certification and quality awards from their customers, including John
Deere's Supplier Quality Certification and Commitment Awards, the
General Motors Mark of Excellence, and Ford Motor Company's Q1
Award.

Though there was resistance at first to the "employees train employees" strategy because it added to the workload, both employees and
line managers now say it has aided in their development. In fact, both
line managers and executives have acknowledged that the strategy
expanded their skills and company perspective.

Early findings also show that involved employees have already been
responsible for two measurable improvements: a reduction both in
cycle time and in costs for many manufacturing and nonmanufacturing
processes.

[LESSON: Training can be expanded to every corner
of the corporation without adding training costs by
using your own employees as trainers.]

Apprenticeship Is Alive and Well
REMMELE ENGINEERING

"AS A BUSINESS WE CONSCIOUSLY, CONSISTENTLY, AND CONTINUOUSLY RAISE
QUESTIONS ABOUT EMPLOYEE SKILLS. THESE QUESTIONS PERMEATE EVERY
DISCUSSION ABOUT MISSION, STRATEGY, STRUCTURE, SYSTEMS, AND THE LIKE.
WE REMIND OURSELVES THAT WE ARE AN INTELLIGENCE-INTENSIVE
ORGANIZATION THAT INVESTS IN SKILLS—JUST LIKE WE INVEST IN CAPITAL
EQUIPMENT.
—MICHAEL BATES, DIRECTOR OF HUMAN RESOURCES

THE CHALLENGE

Training is not something that Remmele Engineering has just picked up in the last decade to help it become more competitive. Indeed, this machine shop headquartered in St. Paul is one of America's standout examples of a company that has emphasized training as a core value and practice from its founding.

The main challenge that caused the company to focus on a formal, comprehensive training program occurred in the early 1960s when the company conducted an extended assessment of its future. What it found was that a major impediment to continued growth would be an inability to find enough skilled people.

THE RESPONSE

Remmele's response was right to the point: if skilled people were going to be a constraint, then let's grow them ourselves. It began its apprenticeship program in 1968. Apprenticeship remains at the core of Remmele's vast training program.

To help it find suitable apprentice candidates, Remmele in 1973 opened its own off-site training center. The center operated for about eleven years, at which time the company decided to rely on regular vocational schools as the feeders for its apprenticeship program. At its zenith, there were seventy machinist apprentices at Remmele, more than in all the rest of Minnesota.

Today, all of the people who enter its formal apprenticeship program are graduates of a two-year machine trades program. And, as Director of Human Resources Michael Bates emphasizes, "We tend to be really fussy about whom we employ." They test the candidates for various competencies, interview them, and take them on a tour through their facilities before they make their selection. To Bates, the reason for the fussiness is simple: "If we continue to get the right people, two things will happen. Remmele will continue to be success-ful, and those people will be successful. It's not one or the other. It's got to be both." In recent years, they have chosen eight to twenty fortunate people each year.

The program moves the people throughout the company. In the early 1990s the company recognized an opportunity to provide differ-ent kinds of skill training in different parts of the business, so it restruc-tured the apprenticeship program so that people spend a roughly equal amount of time in each of Remmele's five plants over a two- to four-year period.

And we're talking about serious training. For boring-mill specialists, training time totals 6,000 hours. For journeyman machinists and preci-sion machinists toolmakers, the total hours are 8,000 and 10,000 hours respectively. That's a lot of time and a lot of money. So the obvious question is, why spend all that time and money training someone you may well lose?

Remmele has two responses. First, they don't lose many people. The retention rate for their apprentices is over 90 percent, which speaks to the quality of the program. Adds Bates: "Do we worry that they're going to go off to one of our competitors? No. If they do, they do. They might get hit by a truck tomorrow too. Does that mean it was a bad investment? We have an investment mentality."

But what about the costs of having a person in training for four years? Chairman Bill Saul likes to take that objection on: "Apprentice-ship doesn't cost you in the long run. We feel that our apprentices, certainly after the first year, are paying their own way. They're provid-ing good work."

Tom Dolezal, vice president of the General Machining Division, sums up an ultimate value of the apprenticeship program: "As people go through the apprenticeship program, they learn that training is a way of life."

The other major training program began in conjunction with Remmele's focused factory initiative, in 1988. The company decided the Production Division needed to be restructured to become a focused factory. They wanted self-managed teams that would take full responsibility for operating "work cells." That type of increased responsibility requires a lot of new skills and that requires training. The broad range of new skills required ranged from the technical, such as measuring and calculating, to interpersonal, such as interacting in teams, with customers, and with vendors.

Absolutely critical to the success of this effort was that employees were involved in the process from the beginning. Says the former human resources manager for the division: "We took their feedback into consideration. We knew they had an investment in the company. We have a mission to be the best, and employees took ownership of that idea from the start."

The training is a combination of required courses and voluntary ones. Everyone in the focused factory is required to complete eight core courses that are delivered during work hours. These courses, which take employees between 90 and 109 hours to complete, develop threshold skills. The challenge is that some workers need help getting to a level where they can really benefit from the required courses. For them, the company provides six review courses, such as basic math and basic manufacturing. These are offered after hours but at the site, which Remmele has found is important to its employees.

Won't employees back away from such basic courses, leaving some big gaps? Mike Bates has a simple response to such skepticism. Trust them. Adam Bowling, when he was manager at Plant 30, showed how that trust worked. When Plant 30 was moving to the focused factory concept, the workers were briefed on what level of understanding would be necessary to do the work. Then the company made proficiency tests available, but not mandatory. The result? Everyone who should have taken the test, did. And they all got the math training they needed. The following is a typical comment of a worker who has taken the math refresher course: "Math refresher has been very useful to me. When I'm doing SPC (Statistical Process Control) and plotting charts, I understand what I'm actually doing. I'm not afraid of an algebraic equation anymore."

This comment depicts the end result of this trust relationship. "We have a very supportive culture here. The employees know that, and they just thrive on the training. When I put up a posting for classes that are limited to ten or fifteen employees, half the time I end up with a long waiting list. They are very enthusiastic."

The seriousness of Remmele's commitment to training is seen in these figures. The company spends an amount equal to 3.3 percent of its annual payroll for training, more than twice the average for all U.S. companies. Production employees typically engage in some form of training (apprenticeship, on-the-job, classroom) for as much as 25 percent of their total work time.

Still, Mike Bates cautions that training should not be viewed as the main driver of change. That role, he maintains, belongs to management, which must do two important things. First, it must provide employees with the tools and skills they need to run their jobs successfully. And it must give up their control of the decision-making process, transferring ownership to the employees. Interestingly, former plant manager Bowling felt that the hardest part of the whole transition to a focused factory was for the managers to let go.

THE RESULTS

Remmele has experienced excellent results, but the most significant ones are qualitative. A few hard numbers will help set the stage for these.

First there is growth. Two decades ago, Remmele was doing $5 million in sales a year. In 1993, sales were around $70 million and in 1994 were expected to be about $80 million. A survey is conducted every two years and the results show that about 90 percent of its customers are satisfied with most aspects of their relationship.

The first two years' performance of the focused factory was impressive:

- customer price reductions of up to 22 percent
- scrap and rework reduction of 25 percent
- daily shipments instead of weekly (JIT)
- levels of six Sigma (3.4 defects per million) production, up from three Sigma (Note: Sigma refers to the number of standard deviations from the mean in any given statistically measurable process. Three Sigma, the quality level for many U.S. manufacturers, is 66,810 defects per million.)

Mike Koppy, an instructor at Duluth Technical College, helps explain why training yields such high impact: "Remmele is the Cadillac of machine shops. They have a real top-notch apprentice program, but the nice thing is they don't settle for that. They keep improving it."

All of the great company results relate in one way or another to excited, commited workers. To see why training works such magic at Remmele, just look at what it has done for Shelly Erickson. When she joined Remmele in 1987, she didn't even know what a machine shop was. After extensive training, she now runs computer-numeric-controlled machinery. In addition to running the machine, she constantly checks for quality, is responsible for tool setting, and she orders bar stock in JIT quantities from the supplier. She also orders tooling, handles routine preventive maintenance, and coordinates shipments to customers. This thirty-two-year-old mother of one says, "I feel like I own a part of the business." She certainly must be pleased with the fact that her compensation doubled in her first five years.

Most Remmele employees are pleased with their compensation. One reason is that apprentices who remain as journeyman machinists often end up making more than $50,000 a year. In addition, many apprentices become managers.

For the company, good training is definitely an excellent way to attract good people. As Mike Bates puts it: "The fact that relatively few places have formal apprenticeship programs gives us something of a recruiting advantage. When we are looking for good people to enter our company, that's a pretty strong sales tool." Training also helps them retain good employees. Bill Saul point out why: "My experience has been that talented people aren't looking for a job very often, provided they're reasonably content where they are. They're too busy doing things they're interested in doing."

Says Bates, "The goal is to get the highest level of what I call psychological ownership. By that, I'm talking about people, in a very real sense, owning their jobs."

Perhaps the greatest benefit of all, according to Bates, is that serious, ongoing training helps make "times get better": "Training and development activities are viewed as an investment, not as an expense item, so you continue to do them whether times are good or bad. My belief is that times get better because you have good people in the right place at the right time."

[LESSON: Apprenticeships can be the core of a training program for highly skilled workers, and they
don't cost you in the long run. When major new initiatives are launched, like focused factories, a broad
training program covering the full range of required
new skills will be needed.]

A Training Partnership with the Union
FORD MOTOR CO.

"I HAD TO BE CONVINCED TO COME BECAUSE I HAVE BEEN DISAPPOINTED TOO
MANY TIMES IN THE PAST, BUT THIS WORKSHOP HAS GIVEN ME A WHOLE NEW
ATTITUDE. THIS WAS REALLY INFORMATIVE. I'M HYPED UP."
**—HARRY PITTMAN, PRESIDENT OF UAW LOCAL 600/DEARBORN
ENGINE PLANT**

THE CHALLENGE

In the early 1980s, the company was in its usual number two slot
among U.S. automakers, but it was losing a billion dollars a year, and
it seemed to be out of touch with its workforce and its customers.
From 1978 to 1982, Ford's annual vehicle sales dropped 47 percent.
During this period, Ford laid off half of its workforce because of aggressive Japanese competition and a deep domestic recession.

The autocratic management style featured frequent battles among
the top leaders with victims falling by the wayside. Little attention was
paid to the followers—the tens of thousands of employees actually
producing the products.

THE RESPONSE

A major cultural shift was required, one that would center on extensive
employee involvement. As Philip Caldwell, Ford's chairman in the early

1980s said, "It's stupid to deny yourself the intellectual capability and constructive attitude of tens of thousands of workers." But how do you begin to meaningfully "involve" tens of thousands of employees?

Training—extensive training—played a major role for Ford. It received special impetus when the 1982 collective bargaining agreement established the Education, Development and Training Program (EDTP). The program's principal objectives are to provide education, training, retraining, and developmental opportunities for both active and displaced UAW-represented Ford hourly workers; support various other UAW–Ford Motor Co. joint activities; and provide opportunities for an exchange of ideas and innovations with respect to employee education, development, and training.

A major part of the EDTP has been seven programs that Ford identified as the "Avenues for Growth." These seven programs serve as the cornerstones for a systematic approach to lifelong learning. Through mid-1994, over 78,000 employees participated in at least one of the Avenues for Growth programs. Due to space constraints, we'll feature just two of the seven programs. The other five programs (with number of participants through June 1994 in parentheses) are:

- Skills Enhancement Program. Provides classes and services in adult education, high school completion, GED, educational enrichment, English as a second language, and math enrichment, in addition to a technical readiness program (83,000); begun in 1983.
- Successful Retirement Planning Program. Provides information and instruction in benefits, health awareness, Social Security, legal and financial matters, and retirement life-style issues (26,800); begun in 1984.
- College and University Option Program. Provides on-site college registration, classes, and services in conjunction with partner institutions (77,100, with 1,800 graduates); begun in 1985.
- Financial Education Program. Provides practical information on financial and investment topics (7,500); begun in 1988.
- Automotive Technology Program. Provides an overview of major automotive systems (1,100); begun in 1991.

The first of the two programs we'll take a closer look at is the Education and Training Assistance Plan (ETAP). Begun in 1984, this plan provides prepaid tuition for both active and laid-off employees engaging in a wide range of education, training, and development opportunities provided by approved educational institutions. Participants are eligible for $3,100 per calendar year for credit or degree courses at approved colleges and universities. Up to $1,800 of this amount may be applied to Personal Development Assistance (PDA), a special feature of the program that covers certain nondegree, noncollege educational and training courses and activities that enhance an individual's personal development and growth. Since 1984, around 25,000 employees have used ETAP and 45,000 employees have used PDA.

Employees say that they would not have pursued educational experiences without ETAP/PDA. Mike Rodgers, Local 900, states, "For the younger seniority workers, these programs give us hope." Helen Wiley, Local 849, adds, "I'm glad I didn't wait any longer to get started! First I finished my high school diploma and then, with the help of ETAP, I just finished my Associate's Degree through Wayne County Community College."

The Life/Education Planning Program, begun in 1985, has a central role in all UAW–Ford Avenues for Growth. It was developed to assist employees in meeting their goals for personal growth and development. Specifically, it helps employees to:

- assess their lives—work, training, and education—in relation to their personal goals
- identify methods, avenues, and resources to achieve their personal goals
- use the UAW–Ford EDTP and community resources to reach their goals

In an initial evaluation of the program, about half of the respondents noted that they had changed plans or developed new plans as a result of the Life/Education Planning Program. With the assistance of life education advisers at all locations, 66,000 workers have become aware of educational opportunities and identified personal goals and action plans. The program even excites older workers, as attested to by one senior worker planning to take both computer awareness and the Successful Retirement Planning Program who was also "looking at returning to school and even earning my GED before I retire."

While most UAW–Ford joint training programs have been established since 1982, there is one that is as old as the relationship between the company and the union. The Ford–UAW National Joint Apprenticeship Committee was established in 1941 as part of the very first collective bargaining agreement. Since that time, well over 22,000 employees have graduated from the program. The tough times of the early 1980s had a dramatic effect on the overall size of the apprenticeship program. In 1983, the number of apprentices "on course" working toward journeyman status was less than 400. In the 1987, 1990, and 1993 national negotiations, the company and the union set program size objectives. By the early 1990s, the number on course had climbed to well over 1,000—an increase of more than 150 percent.

It should be noted that training has not just been for hourly workers. Top executives, who a study had shown were isolated from one another, took training in teamwork strategy at the Executive Development Center. By 1992, the center had successfully trained over 2,000 managers in understanding the benefits of team versus individual activity.

Training literally helped to save Ford's automatic transmission plant located in Sharonville, Ohio. Scheduled to close in the early 1980s, the 2,000 hourly and salaried employees decided to save it. The first step was to officially launch an Employee Involvement program in 1981. The EI idea caught on so well that by 1985 the plant was beginning a program of self-managed work teams, a transition to requiring the most extensive retraining effort in the country. A Launch Training Team consisting of ten hourly and six salaried members developed two training programs: 120 hours of both technical and soft skills training plus forty hours of team-building training. All union leaders and zone superintendents are required to take one forty-hour course in team building. Also, all supervisors attended two courses designed to help them make the change from a traditional to a participative style of leadership.

At first, two rooms at the plant were dedicated to the training. This has grown to more than 17,000 square feet of training area with numerous training rooms, computer labs, and meeting rooms. Since 1987, employees have spent almost 300,000 hours on company time taking the 478 different courses offered—an average of more than forty-two hours per employee per year.

THE RESULTS

Overall, training and employee involvement were at the heart of Ford's dramatic turnaround and comeback in the 1980s. They helped it move to a top earnings position among the Big Three automakers (it out-earned General Motors in 1986 for the first time since 1924). They helped in its successful drive for top-quality products. They helped it achieve tremendous productivity gains (the company sold nearly as many vehicles in 1988 as in 1978 with half as many production workers). And teamwork was the backbone in the development of the very successful and innovative Taurus model introduced in 1985.

Certainly the results at the Sharonville plant speak loud and clear. At the outset of its retraining program, the plant was looking for a 2.3 percent improvement per year and a cumulative improvement of 18.4 percent by 1988. The actual cumulative improvement by 1988 was 45.1 percent. Along the way, the plant took a number of best-in-class awards, won Ford's Q1 Quality Award, and in 1990 won Ford's Preventive Maintenance Excellence Award. And the joint training programs with the UAW show labor and management cooperation at its best.

The final word on the Education, Development and Training Program should be given to Dr. Gary Hansen of Utah State University, who has extensively studied corporate training programs: "I believe the creation of the joint UAW–Ford EDTP represents one of the more creative and farsighted cooperative approaches to human resource development in the private sector in the past two decades. This venture also represents one of the more comprehensive and exciting efforts in employee development and training currently underway in America."

LESSON: A comprehensive training program, developed cooperatively between the company and union, can contribute greatly to improved productivity, quality, employee involvement, and ultimately profitability. In Ford's case, this involved developing seven programs, known as the "Avenues for Growth," that serve as the cornerstones for a systematic approach to lifelong learning.

5: REWARD GOOD PERFORMANCE

Why should a company reward good performance? Because rewarding good performance helps lead to good performance, which is then rewarded, which leads to even better performance, and so forth—a self-reinforcing cycle that drives productivity ever upward.

Chet Russell, a crane operator at Oregon Steel Mills, says the workers put in extra effort, trying hard to satisfy customers, "because it's money in our pockets." And to anyone that has any doubts that money motivates workers, all they have to do is spend a few minutes with Ann Blaise, a tester on an assembly line at Lincoln Electric. She'll tell it to you straight:

> Lincoln people are greedy. They like to call it incentive because it's a nicer word but it's greed. You want money. I've gone to seminars where you're told that people want to be told how good a worker they are. And yeah, that's true. It does feel good. But the bottom line is money. It boils down to money. To get that big chunk at the end of the year.

Motivated employees make productive workers, which makes for a highly productive company. The workers at Lincoln Electric are three times more productive than workers at comparable plants. The employees at Nucor produce more than four times the industry average for tons of steel per employee each year. And employee owners helped turn Oregon Steel Mills from being one of the industry's highest-cost companies to today's lowest-cost producer of steel plate, with overall productivity double the industry average.

The causal relationships—motivated people make productive workers make a productive company—are simply profound common sense.

ALL KINDS OF WAYS TO MOTIVATE

Companies begin to reward good performance for different reasons and they follow a variety of pathways. The five companies in this chapter illustrate the full gamut, from Lincoln Electric's piecework through profit sharing and gainsharing at Nucor and Whirlpool to employee ownership at Reflexite and Oregon Steel Mills.

We should point out that while we chose Lincoln Electric as our case study, its Incentive Management system, built around piecework, is unusual. Nucor is more representative of the reward structures most commonly in place today. It rewards good performance based on the efforts of the whole group. Each worker gets an identical bonus, the size determined by how much steel is produced above the set standard. Nucor went to this system because it was viewed as a critical component of employee empowerment.

Whirlpool's plan was born out of crisis. The plant would survive only if both output and quality improved dramatically and quickly. A tough challenge, particularly in a situation where "management and workers were traditional adversaries." The two sides got together and decided on an approach that would support and highlight improved worker and plant performance: gainsharing. Once again, the premise behind it is pretty simple: "You help create gains, you share in them." They structured the plan around their objectives: increased output determines the size of the gainsharing pool, and improved quality determines the employee's share of the pool.

Finally, there is employee ownership, which is moving toward big-time status: in 1994, around 9,500 companies with about 10 percent of the total workforce had ESOPs and another 5,000 companies had other kinds of workforcewide ownership plans, such as stock option plans. In some ways, it's the most radical pathway and in other respects it's the most basic. Tom Boklund, chairman and CEO of Oregon Steel Mills, saw it as basic. He wanted to run a steel mill with people who actually owned it. So in 1985, as president, he helped orchestrate a management buyout that gave employees 100 percent ownership. And he discovered that workers who are owners make for better workers.

Reflexite also went the ownership route through an employee stock ownership plan (ESOP). The ESOP was formed to prevent the sale of the company and possible closure of its factory in Connecticut. The beginning was extremely modest—just 1 percent ownership by the employees. But from there it took off. A few years later, stock ownership was formally integrated into the compensation system (70 percent fixed and 30 percent variable) and today the employees' share is 70 percent.

WORKERS LOVE THE RESULTS

Workers have to be motivated by results like these. At Lincoln Electric, for all of the plan's first fifty years, bonuses averaged near 100 percent of salary. Joe Sirko saw many of those bonuses in his forty-two years with the company, and he was more than glad to give his opinion of the incentive system:

> I enjoyed every bit of it. From the first year I started forty-two years ago. I've always gotten good points. One hundred points or more. I used to get more bonus than I did wages. For years and years. Worked six days a week, ten hours a day. Got huge bonuses. I used to work for Corning for nine years. Then I said I'd like to work in a place someday where I could spend everything I make all year and then get it all back. And I found such a place. Really.

Employee owners can be equally thrilled. It's a sure thing that 20 percent of the 517 workers at Oregon Steel Mills when it started its employee ownership are downright ecstatic today because these production workers are now all millionaires. And another 50 percent of them have stock holdings that exceed $100,000.

COMPANIES LOVE THE RESULTS TOO

It may be stretching it a bit, but it's essentially true that a company or plant can see great progress toward achieving any goal it may have simply by rewarding good performance. Whirlpool's plant in Benton Harbor, Michigan, had a primary goal: survival. The plant is still there, as are 275 jobs. One big reason is the surge in quality: the number of parts rejected has gone to a world-class ten per million from 837 per million as recently as the late 1980s.

Some of the most dramatic results are found at Reflexite after it established its ESOP. In just a five-year period, between 1986 and 1991, sales quadrupled, the number of jobs nearly tripled, and profits rose almost sixfold.

Money Motivates People
LINCOLN ELECTRIC

Imagine a company like this. No paid holidays. No paid sick days. No paid health insurance. No coffee breaks. No air conditioning in the factory. And the workers' pay is based on piecework.

Sounds almost medieval, or at least early industrial era. You can almost hear the cries from die-hard Marxists, "There's the worker exploitation we've been talking about."

Just one problem: the workers love it!

They especially love the pay, particularly the fact that for many years they received bonuses that equaled their already handsome salaries. This system made Lincoln Electric workers, for years and years, the highest-paid factory workers in the United States, which at that time meant the highest-paid factory workers in the world. And they still are doing well. In 1993, 2,676 qualified employees shared a discretionary bonus of $55 million.

And the system works great for the company. First off, Lincoln Electric is still there, operating in the same location on the eastern edge of Cleveland, still making welding products and industrial motors. This is no small feat, as all around it over the past decade one manufacturing company after another has closed its doors for good—contributors to the Rust Belt image so vividly portrayed in the media in the mid-1980s. Not only is Lincoln Electric still surviving, but it has generally been thriving. Yes, thriving right through the deep recession of 1980–1982 and also through the recession of 1990–1991. Indeed, the U.S. company had never had a loss during its first ninety-seven years. Its only losses were setbacks in 1992–1993 due to some start-up difficulties in overseas operations.

How does Lincoln Electric do it? What accounts for its surviving and thriving? If you ask Don Hastings, CEO since 1991, he will unashamedly point to its incentive reward system, which all starts with piecework. He flat out declares, "The perception of piecework is nineteenth century rather than what we think—it is twenty-first century."

The company also does it because of its total commitment to its vision and principles. Nowhere was this better evidenced than in 1992 when the company's board of directors voted a $48 million bonus for the workers despite the fact that the bonus caused the company's first-ever loss—$45.8 million. No bonus, no loss. But the company thought it was well worth it.

Formally, the compensation system at Lincoln Electric is known as the Incentive Management System. It has two primary components: piecework and bonuses.

Company officials stress that the compensation system is really not a system at all but a comprehensive philosophy. The philosophy is James F. Lincoln's, who along with his brother John C. founded the company in 1895. The philosophy is centered in six precepts: (1) people, (2) Christian ethics, (3) principles, (4) simplicity, (5) competition, (6) the customer. Growing from these fundamental precepts are other tenets of company management philosophy, including honesty, integrity, importance of communication, cooperation, reduction of strife, access to authority, dedication of all participants to the common goal of serving the customer, and sharing the results of success or failure.

The overall impression one gets from these precepts and tenets is that they sound terribly old-fashioned. And they are. But they *work!* To paraphrase the John Houseman TV commercial a bit: "Lincoln Electric does it the old-fashioned way. They earn it."

After a quick tour of the mechanics of the Incentive Management System, we'll get to the hard questions that must be asked of a system grounded in piecework, including its humaneness, how workers view the lack of benefits, potential ruthless competitiveness under such a system, the impact on quality of work, and how older workers fare. Finally, we'll look at the overall results for both the company and the individual workers.

HOW THE PIECEWORK/BONUS SYSTEM WORKS

Lincoln Electric has always taken its underlying philosophy and values very seriously. This allows them to declare very matter-of-factly that their Incentive Management System springs from this simple concept: "At Lincoln Electric, every worker is a manager, and every manager is a worker." Sounds almost corny, but at Lincoln Electric it means there are no arbitrary distinctions between labor and management. The strength of the system resides in the fact that management and labor operate according to the same rules. Every employee knows that Incentive Management operates according to the three Rs: recognition, responsibility, and reward.

In the words of James Lincoln, "Workers should be paid on the basis of their accomplishments and efficiencies; they should share in the profits their efforts make possible." He made that statement in 1952. But actually, the workers beat him to it nineteen years previously when they came up with the idea for bonuses. It all began with a request by the workers for a pay raise in 1933. Because of hard times in the Depression, the company could not grant their request. The workers suggested that if they could make the company more profitable, perhaps the company could share the rewards with them. Management agreed and the bonus system still in effect today was born.

Here's the way the system is structured. "Wherever possible, jobs are put on a straight piecework basis" (that's a company quote). Each worker has a job rate, a flat base rate. For example, if you were hired to operate a drill press, your job rate may be $.70 an hour. This is what you earn if you work at an average rate of speed and ability. If the worker is energetic, or in the more usual case, learns how to become more efficient at his tasks (learns the shortcuts), the worker may earn $.80 an hour or even $1.00 an hour. The latter is known as the "Lincoln buck," which every worker wants to earn. The base rate is then multiplied by the Lincoln Electric Multiplier. This multiplier changes in response to changes in the wage survey for the Cleveland area, and once each year is adjusted upward or downward to bring it into line with the changes in wages as reported by the U.S. Department of Labor. Currently, the multiplier is 12.93.

There is no limit on the amount of piecework that can be earned. A good pieceworker, and there are many at Lincoln, who has become highly skilled at a particular task, can very often earn at a rate 40 percent or 50 percent above the standard on a consistent basis.

The real excitement comes in the bonus determination. This depends on the employee's merit rating. The department head compares twice a year the performance of individuals in each merit rating group in four categories: ideas and cooperation, output, dependability, and quality. Each group, generally a department, is allocated 100 points per group member, which means that the average employee will receive 100 points. Most employees in a group typically fall between 80 and 120 points. Points beyond 110, awarded for outstanding or unusual performance, are not charged to the group average. They are taken from a special pool of points set aside for this purpose.

The board of directors determines the total amount to be shared in the bonus near the end of each year. The amount reflects the company's overall efficiency for that year. For most years up to the 1980s, bonuses averaged near 100 percent of salaries and wages. The bonuses have been as high as 120 percent and as low as 55 percent of annual salaries. In 1992, the bonus rate was 61.9 percent. This means that a worker who received a merit rating of 100 got a bonus check equal to 61.9 percent of his total wages for the year.

When Don Hastings was asked how the merit rating on report cards worked for nonproduction workers, he responded, "very subjectively." Managers, engineers, researchers all get a report card twice a year. Sales people get one report card. All are rated by their supervisors. Hastings himself rates about forty top officers, largely against goals they have established for themselves. But again he said about his own rating of this group, "Very judgmental. It's all performance."

THE HARD QUESTIONS

Let's run quickly through some hard questions that come to mind. All of these were posed to both Don Hastings and a number of production workers and factory managers.

Hard question number one: *Isn't piecework a movement away from today's thrust for a more humane workplace?*

Hastings responded: "I think the most humane thing to do is pay a person properly, pay them for what they do, and make them feel pride in their jobs for accomplishing something and to give them security." This, he added, was far more important than long coffee breaks. "Productivity is the only thing that's going to save manufacturing. It will save their jobs."

He spelled out the link to productivity as follows. There's an interesting thing about piecework: it eliminates wasted moves, workers don't talk an extra five minutes, and they don't take that cup of coffee. You end up with 50 percent more parts without people looking like they're working harder. Near the end of the interview, he became quite animated. "It's an entrepreneurial spirit out there. They're in business for themselves. That satisfaction is why people stay here."

That's all well and good for the CEO to say sitting in his comfortable office. But what about the pieceworker in the un-air-conditioned factory?

Bob Canapik is a machinist who came to Lincoln Electric fifteen years ago straight out of high school. He's been through every part of the shop and two years ago he went through management training for six months.

> I think it's a good system. You get paid for what you do. It can get a little boring if you're running a machine and get paid by the hour. Where's your incentive? If you do fifty parts or a hundred parts, you get the same amount of money. Piecework makes the day go a lot faster. The key to it is that incentive. You have to have incentive in the system. Otherwise people aren't going to work hard. . . . Some operators don't use their thinking to make things easier. If you're smart, you're learning how to do things faster.

Stress under piecework is a major concern. Ann Blaise, a tester on an assembly line who has worked there four years, was asked about the stress.

> Yeah it's a stressful job. A couple of times, I felt really bad in the morning. It's, "My God, if I don't go in I don't get paid." You make yourself do things that normally maybe you wouldn't. But I don't know if that's such a bad thing either. Do I ever take a fifteen-minute break? No. I get pretzels, working and eating at the same time.
> My third day here, I was almost in tears. I didn't know how I was going to keep up, but once you get used to it, it's so nice because now my day flies. Before I know it, lunch is here. At my old job, eight hours seemed like twelve hours. My eight-hour day here seems like five or six half the time.

Hard question number two: *What about virtually no benefits?*
Don Hastings brought out one interesting feature about the no-sick-

days policy. "Our people don't call in sick very often. They take care of themselves better. Last year, our health insurance went down." How many CEOs would love to be able to say that?

And then he added what he and the workers see as the greatest benefit of all: the company's no-layoff policy established in 1958. The company has lived by it ever since. Even in the harsh 1980–1982 recession, when there was a 40 percent drop in sales, there wasn't a single layoff. The security that comes from this, especially in the current times, is perhaps the company policy of greatest importance. Many workers rank this security even over the great pay they receive.

Another interesting feature of their benefit policy was highlighted by Rick Anderson, manager of Lincoln Electric's large plant in Cleveland. He pointed out that there is a set amount of money in the pot. Sports programs, health insurance, dental insurance, fitness center, tuition rebates—employees can have anything they want. But it will come directly out of their bonus. Because of this, the workers themselves have often been the ones to turn down benefits. (Company health insurance premiums are paid by deductions from employees' year-end bonuses.)

Hard question number three: *Doesn't piecework foster a ruthless competitiveness, harmful to teamwork and cooperation generally?*

The company's own profile document says: "The merit rating system is a logical extension of management's belief that both competition and co-operation are essential to a successful enterprise." Don Hastings clearly articulated how these seeming opposites work well together: "We have a situation where people compete against one another for points, which turns into money, but then realizing they have to cooperate as a team or there won't be anything to split." He also added that 25 percent of an employee's merit rating, one of the four categories, is for cooperation. Additionally, all assembly lines are paid as a group. Thus, the individuals on it are not competing with one another on quantity of output. "It's just like a ballclub." Right at the end of the interview, Hastings said, "The system wouldn't have survived since 1934 without its competitive nature. If everyone gets a slice regardless of how they performed, we wouldn't have survived."

The company's underlying belief that labor and management are all part of the same team came to life in the advisory board meeting held on the day of the interviews. The advisory board is a group of thirty-four employees from all over the company's operations. This was clearly a lively group that did not fear top management in any way. Don Hastings was leading the meeting. The group, meeting in a formal conference room, looked like a slice of a rock concert audience: jeans, purple T-shirts, gold bracelets, hats on backward, muscle shirts. One young man spoke up. "We need experienced people. We don't need new people. Do you understand what I'm saying?" A great deal of concern was expressed about the new European operations losing a lot of money, thus jeopardizing everyone's bonus. "Is it impossible to just cut them loose?" The questions kept coming. "Is our recent plant loss due to the economy or bad management?" "In December, we heard about our problems. We sent people out everywhere and now the problem's worse. Why? What happened?" Through this minefield of tough questions, Don Hastings addressed each concern calmly and seriously, always calling on each employee by first name.

Hard question number four: *With the rush for quantity under piece-work, doesn't quality suffer?*

Don Hastings fielded this question with considerable enthusiasm. First he pointed out that quality also counts for 25 percent in each employee's merit rating. Further, the company makes everything trace-able. Every box of welding electrodes, for example, is stamped with the person's initials. If there is a field complaint, that's an automatic ten-point deduction. It's a very harsh penalty for poor quality. This helps to instill pride in the workers. One line takes great pride in having had no rejects on 75,000 parts.

The Incentive Management System also helps hold down the cost of quality. Hastings pointed out how often companies put through quality at a higher cost. Under Lincoln's system, since that cost increase would come out of their bonus, the workers get very creative and come up with a cost reduction. Besides, he adds, what better SPC (statistical process control) could you have? Each employee evaluates the perfor-mance of the employee who handled the product before them.

Hard question number five: *Doesn't the older worker suffer under piecework as speed and strength slow?*

Here we have to give the floor to Joe Sirko. Joe has worked at Lincoln Electric for forty-two years, running a press each one of those years:

I still have all my fastness. They mainly go on you not making any scrap. Quality means more to them. And suggestions. You can make cost reductions by giving good ideas, and get rewarded. I've maintained my production rate. I have no intentions of retiring. And their pension system is the best in the world. Two and a half percent of wages put in for every year. I had to start drawing mine at sixty-five. All I can say is that I'm totally happy.

Incidentally, because Joe thought our interview got cut off prematurely, and thus there may have been questions that didn't get asked, he was there waiting in the lobby an hour and a half later after the advisory board meeting was over.

LOUD AND CLEAR RESULTS

When you ask the workers and managers at Lincoln Electric about results, they usually point to the outstanding bonuses over the years. But there are some broader impacts on the company that are significant as well.

The overall result that sums it all up is that a number of studies have shown that Lincoln workers are three times more productive than workers at comparable plants. On the quality front, the company is so confident of the quality of its products that it gives warranties of five years for the industrial electric motor line and three years for the welding equipment line. Its absenteeism rate is less than 1½ percent and its turnover (after the first ninety days) is less than 3 percent.

Bonuses are where the real action is. Just listen to these facts. The company has paid a sizable year-end bonus every year since 1934. The total of all bonuses paid since 1934 equals the total of all wages and salaries paid since 1934. Recent individual bonuses have averaged around $20,000 a year. In 1991, ten factory workers and around a dozen nonproduction workers had bonuses that exceeded $50,000.

Bob Canapik, the machinist, says his biggest bonus was $22,000 six years ago. But, he hastens to add, "I worked a lot of overtime that year." He also points to a $9,000 bonus in his first year back in 1977. "That was a lot of money then."

A number of employees were asked about the primary qualities of a high ratings point person. What are the people like who get the big bonuses? Once again, Ann Blaise said it most clearly:

Here every day. Uses time well throughout the day. Concerned about quality. Very observant. Willing to work with others. Good at training. Helping other people fit in when they're new.

She was then asked, "Do you see yourself fitting in that category?" "Yeah. You know, I should be getting a score of 130 any day now," concluding the interview with a big laugh.

> LESSON: The combination of piecework and bo-
> nuses makes a powerfully effective compensation
> system, particularly when:
>
> • the compensation system is based upon a
>   comprehensive philosophy and springs from a
>   simple concept like "every worker is a man-
>   ager and every manager is a worker"
> • piecework is structured fairly so that under it
>   you pay a person properly, pay them for what
>   they do, and make them feel pride in their jobs
>   for accomplishing something
> • the benefits of piecework—boosting produc-
>   tivity and fostering cooperation as well as
>   competition—are recognized
> • top management is firmly committed to the
>   bonus system, earning the trust of the workers

 You Help Create Gains,
You Share in Them
WHIRLPOOL

"PRODUCTIVITY USED TO BE A DIRTY WORD AROUND HERE. PEOPLE THOUGHT
THEY WOULD HAVE TO WORK HARDER WITHOUT GETTING ANYTHING FOR IT.
NOW, THEY'RE STARTING TO UNDERSTAND PRODUCTIVITY PAYS."
—LLOYD SPOONHOLTZ, PRESIDENT OF MACHINIST LOCAL 1918

THE CHALLENGE

The challenge was plainly there for everyone to see in 1987. Employees at the small tooling and plating plant in Benton Harbor, Michigan, watched the wrecking balls take down their 750,000-square-foot next-door sister plant. One thousand jobs disappeared along with the walls of the factory. They knew that their plant could easily be next.

At the time, this knowledge did very little to improve morale. According to Bill Bonfoey, a thirty-one-year veteran, the attitude was that "if your machine broke down you sat down and waited for someone else to repair it. Workers hid inferior parts so inspectors would not find them." The odds of this plant staying open were low, matching employee morale.

The company made it clear that the only opportunity for plant and job survival was improved output and quality. Easy to say, but hard to accomplish in an environment where, according to local union leader Lloyd Spoonholtz, "management and workers were traditional adversaries."

THE RESPONSE

Putting aside the adversarial roles, company and union officials decided in early 1988 that they would enhance their survival chances by designing an approach that would support and highlight improved worker and plant performance. The approach chosen, with the help of an outside consultant, was called gainsharing.

This approach did not require large company investment in new technology or equipment. Instead, it invested in the skills and abilities of the plant personnel. The premise behind gainsharing is simple: "You help create gains, you share in them." This particular plan promotes both increased output and quality: increased output determines the size of the gainsharing pool and quality determines the employee's share of the pool.

Gainsharing flowed from Whirlpool's adoption in 1986 of employee involvement as its core strategy. Substantial investment in training and developing its people followed, with a full 3 percent of payroll devoted to this by 1992. The firm soon recognized that its strategy of empowering its people required a corresponding system of rewards for strong business results. In addition to gainsharing, Whirlpool has also provided an ownership opportunity for every employee, granting in 1991 every employee in the United States stock options at very favorable prices. President and COO Bill Marohn cites what the company expects in return: "We expect that our employees will give us their thoughts, ideas, and improvement suggestions, in addition to their time and physical effort."

THE RESULTS

The most important result is that the plant is still there, as are 275 jobs, and for several good reasons. From 1988 to 1992, productivity jumped more than 19 percent. Quality results are equally impressive. The number of parts rejected by customers has improved from 837 parts per million to a world-class level of ten parts per million. That's right—more than a 98 percent decrease in just four years. No one, looking at that, should ever say that a little incentive doesn't pay.

The Benton Harbor plant has been awarded an Outstanding Supplier Award by its major customer. It has been recognized in trade journals and other national publications. Its gainsharing approach has been used as a model for other Whirlpool locations.

While the results are overwhelmingly positive, this didn't happen without some rough times and periods of doubt. But by relying on the ability and motivations of people, rather than technology and dollars, Whirlpool assured the success of gainsharing.

[LESSON: Gainsharing is a payment system that supports and highlights improved worker and plant performance. Tie gainsharing to improved quality and watch quality increase.]

Hardworking Millionaire Steel Workers
OREGON STEEL MILLS

"IN 1985, WE STILL WERE NOT AS PRODUCTIVE AS WE WANTED TO BE, AND
FUNDS WERE NEEDED TO INSTALL THE MOST ADVANCED STEEL TECHNOLOGY
AVAILABLE. AN ESOP TRUST WAS FORMED, WHICH WAS ABLE TO BORROW THE
MONEY NEEDED TO BUY OUT THE EXISTING OWNERSHIP. THIS MOVE
DRAMATICALLY IMPROVED OUR PRODUCTIVITY WHILE PROVIDING FINANCIAL
RESOURCES FOR THE EQUIPMENT AND TECHNOLOGY WE NEEDED TO BE
COMPETITIVE."

**—MALCOLM PUTNAM, VICE PRESIDENT OF EMPLOYEE RESOURCES
(NOW RETIRED)**

THE CHALLENGE

Tom Boklund must have felt that he was given command of a sinking
ship when he was named president of Oregon Steel Mills in 1982. How
could this producer of steel plate survive with abysmal productivity in
a shrinking market? Plant technology was two decades behind the
times and company owners wanted to unload.

On top of that, the company was involved in a bitter strike that led
to the firing of many of its most experienced workers. Looking back at
the replacements he had to hire at this time, Boklund reflects that it's
difficult to operate a steel mill with people who have never seen
one and when an armed camp mentality reigns. "Mistrust and anger,"
Malcolm Putnam says, "were the emotions that dominated labor-man-
agement relations."

Recognizing he needed drastic change, Boklund went to work fast.
The hourly concept was abolished and all workers became salaried.
Time clocks and reserved parking spaces also disappeared. Still, seri-
ous problems persisted.

THE RESPONSE

Boklund wanted to run a steel mill with people who actually owned
it. So a management-led buyout, using the employees' ESOP, gave
employees 100 percent ownership. Top managers kept less than 5

percent. With that came a critical change of attitude. "Under the old ownership, employees just 'put in our time,' " says crane operator Chet Russell. Now that employees are owners, however, Russell says they put in extra effort, trying hard to satisfy customers "because it's money in our pockets."

Other steps were taken. Profit sharing gave workers 20 percent of pretax earnings, boosting wages by as much as 50 percent in good times. The company also has invested $170 million since 1985 on facility improvements and acquisitions.

The structure of the plan has, however, led to one problem for the company. The company's ESOP rules require workers to leave the company before they sell the bulk of their stock. This has led to high turnover and a talent drain at the company.

THE RESULTS

But this is one case where everyone would agree that the results can only be described as remarkable. Since the buyout, productivity is up 300 percent. Sales and earnings grew on average more than 40 percent annually in the 1989–1992 period. From being one of the industry's highest-cost companies, Oregon Steel Mills is now considered the industry's lowest-cost producer of steel plate. In 1982, it took 9.5 hours of labor to produce a ton of steel. By 1988, just three years after the buyout, it took only three hours. Its overall productivity is double the industry average. Little wonder that the company's profits per ton are among the best in the industry.

But it is the nearly 500 blue-collar workers who are truly rejoicing —over both their pay and their stockholdings, especially the latter. Their average pay of $50,000 before benefits is 25 percent higher than the industry average.

But, incredibly, more than one hundred Oregon Steel employees became millionaires (in the value of their stockholdings) just three years after the company went public in 1988. When it went public, its market value, once $15 million, soared to $400 million. Workers' shares, initially worth just pennies apiece, split 112 to 1, climbing to over $38 in 1992. The benefits were widespread. Seventy percent of the 517 people who worked for the company at the time of its initial public offering had holdings that eventually reached over $100,000.

How can an ESOP affect one person's life? Just ask Jackie Williams.

When she joined the company in 1975, she was a young divorcee raising her son in a mobile home. She was making $12,000 a year as a bookkeeper. She now has 33,000 shares of Oregon Steel worth well over $1 million and she has converted another 17,000 into a $650,000 retirement account. Williams, raised in a three-room house in Texas with no running water, moved out of her trailer in 1991 and into the "dream house" she built overlooking the sixteenth hole at the Club Green Meadows golf course.

[
LESSON: Employee owners put in extra effort and try unusually hard to satisfy customers because "its money in their pockets." Company performance can be transformed by workers who themselves are personally benefiting from the growth and improved profitability.
]

 ## Another ESOP to the Rescue
REFLEXITE

"THIS WAS ALWAYS A FAMILY-TYPE COMPANY, A FRIENDLY PLACE TO WORK. BUT NOW IT TOOK US A WHILE TO UNDERSTAND WE ACTUALLY OWNED PART OF THE COMPANY OURSELVES. BUT THAT PART GETS MORE EXCITING EVERY YEAR, ESPECIALLY FOR LONGER-TERM EMPLOYEES."
—PAT NAPOLITANO, QUALITY CONTROL SUPERVISOR

THE CHALLENGE

In 1983, the Rowland brothers were approached by 3M and asked if they wanted to sell their young company, a manufacturer of retrore-flective products that enhance visibility and safety (such as the material that coats highway signs and barriers). Since they were then in their sixties, it seemed like the logical thing to do. The offering price was very attractive and they personally would profit handsomely. There was only one catch. 3M was primarily interested in the technology and patents of the company and not its factory in New Britain, Connecticut, which they could only promise would remain open for a year.

The Rowlands, believing that a company had a responsibility to its community, politely declined the offer. They brought in Cecil Ursprung as president and the heir apparent. As he soon discovered, the sale issue had not gone away, since the founders needed liquidity. What could he do to ensure the existence and the integrity of the plant's operation?

THE RESPONSE

After thinking about putting together a buyout group himself, Ursprung happened to hear about employee stock ownership plans. It just so happened that Hugh Rowland also began hearing about ESOPs around the same time. It seemed the right solution at the right time, so in 1984 an ESOP was formed.

It was a modest beginning—only 1 percent ownership by the employees. But Ursprung soon discovered that the crux of employee ownership was the way its structure and culture meshed with his own strategies and ambitions for the company. So by 1988, employee ownership had been leveraged to 31 percent. Today, it stands at a hefty 70 percent.

Indeed, it can be said that Reflexite pushes employee stock ownership to the limits. In 1987 the ESOP was formally integrated into the compensation system. Each employee's pay is divided 70 percent fixed and 30 percent flexible, with the 30 percent being divided among the ESOP, dividends, and an owner's bonus. In 1989 the company gave employees the right to vote their ESOP shares.

Reflexite gives its 300 employees complete financial information, a reflection of its general belief that the key behind a successful ESOP is communication. Good communication at Reflexite involves a scoreboard, monthly owner's reports, celebrations, group leader participation, and even an ESOP flag.

THE RESULTS

No one can argue with Reflexite's results and Ursprung would attribute a good portion of them to the company's culture of ownership. Between 1986 and 1991, sales doubled, and then doubled again. The number of jobs Reflexite provided for the community nearly tripled. And profits rose almost sixfold. In FY 1993, sales were up 24 percent over FY 1992 and profits were $3,102,000 above 1992 and a new record for the company. The ESOP structure seems to protect profitability in both good times and bad.

Why? Because employee-owned companies can do things other businesses can't, and because employee ownership feeds profitability in lots of little ways. Reflexite finds that it is able to move faster into new markets. Indeed, it attributes the success of its aggressive entrepreneurial expansion, both at home and abroad, to its ownership culture. This is because everyone is pulling together; R & D people respond immediately when a salesperson sees new opportunities for products or markets. It is also able to run leaner, since the general feeling is that every new person dilutes the equity. Salespeople tend to cut sharper deals, for as one marketer put it, "They're worried about return on investment, not just making this sale." There are also many grassroots efforts to rationalize systems and procedures. Finally, the company doesn't have to incur the costs of high turnover. ESOPs build loyalty, for the longer you stay, the more shares you get and the more your nest egg grows.

The results for the employees are striking. The median ESOP account comes to more than $70,000, and accounts in the six figures can be found among many long-term employees.

> LESSON: The ESOP structure protects profitability in both good times and bad because employee-owners can do things other businesses can't and this feeds profitability across the board. In particular, an ownership culture fuels entrepreneurial expansion and enables a company to move faster into new markets.

Everyone Gets an Equal Share of the Pie
NUCOR

> "IF THE COMPANY MAKES ONLY 8 PERCENT RETURN ON INVESTMENT, THERE'S NO BONUS. AND I MEAN ZERO. BUT IF IT NEARS THE 24 PERCENT MAXIMUM, THEY CAN GET A 100 PERCENT STOCK BONUS AND 200 PERCENT CASH, OR THREE TIMES THEIR SALARY."
>
> **—KEN IVERSON, CHAIRMAN & CEO**

THE CHALLENGE

Nucor, located in Charlotte, North Carolina, was one of America's first minimills. Minimills, which melt scrap for steel, were the upstarts pitted against the older integrated companies that make steel by smelting iron ore, limestone, and processed coal in a furnace. The challenge facing Chairman and CEO Ken Iverson as he developed Nucor was this: should he follow the conventional theory and practice a management style based on union power in an oligopolistic industry or should he break the mold and fashion a new type of steel workforce?

THE RESPONSE

Ken Iverson decided to break the mold. No unions. No restrictive work rules. Self-managed work teams of twenty to forty workers. Specialized training for the workers in Germany, California, and Utah, *before* they began work at the new plant in Crawfordsville, Indiana. Encouraging one hundred newly hired workers to help build the Crawfordsville plant. Iverson and his divisional managers touring the company's seventeen plants regularly to talk to the workers. A no-layoff policy (not one layoff in over twenty years). Everyone knows most of the jobs his team handles. *And* an innovative incentive pay system to encourage productivity.

Nucor believes in rewarding good performance based on the efforts of the whole group. So each worker gets an identical bonus percentage that can run as high as 150 percent to 200 percent of base pay, depending on how much steel is produced above the standard.

General managers and department heads also receive incentive pay based on the overall performance of the company. If the company makes less than an 8 percent return on investment, there is no payment. But for every dollar in pretax earnings over the threshold, 5 cents goes into a bonus plan for the fourteen plant managers and the company's four top executives. Thus, if the ROI (return on investment) reaches the 24 percent maximum, they can get a 180 percent stock bonus and 270 percent cash incentives, or four and one half times their salary. With so much at stake and everything equally shared, each manager is not afraid to bluntly criticize other managers who are spending too much on scrap or earning a low return on assets. This they do at their thrice-yearly meetings in Charlotte, when each manager pores over financial figures for the other plants.

On four different occasions, an unannounced $500 bonus has been paid to all employees when the company had a good year. Shares of stock are also distributed to employees periodically. Nucor also pays a minimum of 10 percent of pretax earnings into a profit-sharing plan every year for all employees, excluding officers.

THE RESULTS

Nucor has demonstrated that American-made steel can be produced efficiently and be cost-competitive with any in the world. These results flow from Nucor's unique employee empowerment and reward system and its constant utilization of the best and most innovative steel-producing technologies.

Just how efficient is Nucor? The Crawfordsville plant can roll out a ton of sheet steel in .75 man-hours versus the three man-hours the best big steel makers have been able to achieve. Overall, Nucor produces 1,800 tons of steel per year per employee compared with an industry average of 420 tons. Its cost is about $40 per ton, compared with the industry's $135 a ton.

All of this has contributed to tremendous growth. This once tiny company has used its minimill strategy to amass a market capitalization of $5.6 billion, roughly that of USX's U.S. Steel and Bethlehem Steel combined. Its net sales from 1983 to 1993 more than quadrupled to $2.25 billion.

As for workers' rewards for good performance, they have been quite handsome. In rural Darlington, North Carolina, the normal average annual pay for a veteran steelworker at Nucor runs over two and a half times the area's average worker income. The members of one team at the Crawfordsville plant earned $50,000 to $59,000 each in 1991, working the equivalent of a forty-two-hour week.

The plant managers are happy as well. In 1992, Nucor's profits of $110 million greatly exceeded the $75 million required for a 10 percent return on equity. As a result, the total incentive compensation was $1.9 million to be divided among the eighteen executives. This meant that plant managers nearly doubled their base salaries. One of these, John Doherty of the Norfolk, Nebraska, mill, took home an extra $75,000 in cash and $50,000 in stock. But according to him, he earned every penny of it: "These bonuses aren't entitlements. We're running our own businesses, and we'd better perform."

[
LESSON: Handsomely rewarding good performance with bonuses and incentive pay, distributed in equal shares, is a critical part of employee empowerment. With everything equally shared, everyone is looking out for good performance in others, and they aren't afraid to point out when performance falls short.
]

PLEASING CUSTOMERS AND FINDING NEW MARKETS

6: EXCEED CUSTOMER EXPECTATIONS

Today, a company must not simply try to satisfy its customers. No, companies today must attempt to "surprise" or "delight" their customers. They must seek customers' affection and ideally an emotional bond with each customer. Today's fundamental customer truism and absolute necessity is this: the customer is king and as such must be served exceedingly well.

A SHARP CUSTOMER FOCUS WORKS IN ALL SITUATIONS

We only highlight five companies, but these five clearly illustrate that a laser-sharp focus on customers works effectively in all types of company situations: start-ups, turnarounds, and long-time successes.

Two young men in the 1980s each had the dream of founding a high-tech company: one in computer hardware, the other in computer software. Each saw superior customer service as the distinction that would enable them to break in, compete, and grow. One was Michael Dell, whose genius did not lie in manufacturing, like Steve Jobs but who was a marketing pioneer.

The other young man was Doug Burgum, who wanted to build a software company, out on the northern plains, on the simple home-spun values he learned growing up in nearby Arthur, North Dakota. The key business principle he learned at his father's grain elevator business was "you served your customers for a lifetime." As Burgum puts it, "When we bought Great Plains I was twenty-seven, and I figured we had a great opportunity to build something where we'd instill in people that long-term mentality."

The turnaround stories belong to Xerox and Harley-Davidson. Xerox actually has undertaken two major reorganizations, both focused on the customer. In 1987, then President Paul Allaire announced: "I am changing the corporate priorities at Xerox Corporation. Effective immediately, the order is number one: customer satisfaction." The new focus helped its market share to rebound, but in 1991 earnings were flat and its share of the U.S. copier market still lagged behind Canon's. So Allaire announced another major reorganization and the driving force was to move the entire company still closer to its customers. In essence, it designed a new horizontal organization by letting sets of customers and customer needs define the new business units. Says Allaire: "We've given everyone in the company a direct line of sight to the customer."

Harley-Davidson in 1981 was losing sizable chunks of market share to much bigger Japanese competitors who had better-quality motorcycles they offered at lower prices. So its executives decided that success (and first survival) depended on making customer satisfaction their ultimate goal. This was a revolutionary change for Harley, from a company that virtually dictated to its customers what they could have to one that looked to customer input before making any major product or marketing move.

Then there are those companies who have known this commonsense truth concerning the customer for decades, and achieved spectacular success by sticking to their core value of superior customer service. Premier Industrial, was founded in 1940 on three core values: superior customer service, respect for the individual, and the pursuit of excellence. It is a good reminder in the midst of all the recent hoopla of recent years over these ideas that they are hardly new—just hardly practiced.

THE DRIVERS OF SUCCESS

We've seen the goal—the vision—the philosophy. But what about the specifics? How did all of these companies exceed customer expectations? Five key ingredients emerge as the drivers of success: getting employees customer-focused, installing excellent tracking and measurement systems, paying attention to details, personally involving the CEO, and constantly making improvements.

1. Getting Employees Customer-Focused

Great Plains Software's near-fanatical commitment to customer service begins in its hiring practices. The head of human resources, Howard Hansen, puts it this way: "We place a high priority on people who demonstrate the values that are important to us, who understand what it means to take care of customers who have high need levels." The company also has an unbeatable combination of system and spirit which is described in some detail in its story.

At Premier Industrial, as much as Mort Mandel stresses superior customer service, customers are not number one. The people at Premier are. Remember that another of its core values was "respect for the individual." And Mandel personally invests himself in his employees, particularly when it comes to instilling the core values in key people throughout the company.

One great idea that Tom Peters espouses is to break your workforce down to small "gotta units." These small groups would operate like the local mom-and-pop grocery store: they will do whatever is necessary to please the customer because that's the only way to stay in business, much less grow. "They do it because they gotta."

2. Installing Excellent Tracking and Measurement Systems

When it comes to measuring customer satisfaction, Xerox's Customer Satisfaction Measurement System may be the best in America. The company sends out 55,000 questionnaires each month to its customers to determine their satisfaction. The system also integrates customer research and benchmarking by using the same process, several times a year, to track its competitors' performance as perceived by their customers. All together, it surveys 200,000 Xerox customers a year to identify major areas of dissatisfaction and address their root causes.

It's not as big or as famous, but the tracking system at Great Plains is equally impressive. The company's customer list was designed to be at the heart of its strategy for listening closely to and responding to customer needs. The company by now has end users that number around 35,000, but it knows exactly who every one of them is and the details of their involvement with them—all sales to them and all support provided (including when and by whom).

The key factor here is the power of the new information technologies. They can help a company literally recreate itself to cater to an individual customer's personalized needs. But companies must be willing to invest in them to get to know and better serve their customers. Fortunately, companies across America are catching on: in 1994 they spent around $1 billion on computers and related technology for customer service departments. One survey showed that some 70 percent of 782 large U.S. and European companies said customer service is now the main focus of their investments in technology.

3. Paying Attention to Details

Xerox believes that customer service *before* the sale is important. Its employees go to the customers' workplace and help them rethink the way they work so they can better use Xerox's products. In this way, Xerox can deliver solutions and not just products.

Dell is a master of sweating the details. If a customer calls Dell's technical support line and doesn't get a staff person within five minutes, the company mails the customer a check for $25.

4. Personally Involving the CEO

You will not find too many CEOs of any corporation, particularly a large one like Premier Industrial, who are as personally committed to spending time with customers as Mort Mandel. He blocks out a certain number of days for customers each month. And they remain blocked.

Michael Dell also likes to learn from his customers directly. One manager of computer operations for a software services provider that uses about one hundred Dell PCs was amazed at Dell's attention. After pointing out that he rarely gets to meet with the CEOs of the companies he deals with, he spoke of his meeting with Michael Dell: "He asked me what I'd like to see in the machines. He actually took notes."

5. Constantly Making Improvements

Ever since Harley-Davidson decided to make customer satisfaction its ultimate goal, it has made a series of decisions all focused on making certain its customers remain highly satisfied. The customers wanted quality bikes, so Harley decided to increase production slowly. The customers wanted the look of "yesteryear," so it introduced "nostalgia" bikes.

Know, and Care for, Every Customer
GREAT PLAINS SOFTWARE

This was not a choice assignment—the kind you just couldn't wait to get to. In fact as the windchill factors of 65 degrees below and 80 degrees below zero kept popping up on the TV screen in January, the temptation was to choose another company to lead off this chapter—preferably one with an address considerably south of Fargo, North Dakota.

But something kept drawing us to this midsize company out on the Northern Great Plains—it had an intrigue factor that we just couldn't escape. Perhaps it was the sheer fact of a fast-growing high-tech company located in North Dakota. Or perhaps it was because it involved a twenty-seven-year old who set out to build a company based on his family's old-fashioned business values of serving your customers well and viewing them as lifelong customers. Or that it was a company growing like crazy that had spent virtually zero on national advertising and doesn't even sell its products directly to customers. Or that it hires only college graduates to answer the phone calls from its customers. The intrigue factor with the most persuasive pull, though, was that Great Plains Software was a company that knows who every single one of its 65,000 customers is and cares deeply about their satisfaction and success.

Thus it was that we alighted in Fargo (in March when it was a balmy 22 degrees) to learn the inside story of this highly successful company built on superior customer service.

AN UNBEATABLE COMBINATION OF SYSTEM AND SPIRIT

How do you provide unbeatable customer service? Sure, you must have a great system in place. Great Plains Software's system is second to none. Not only are its features the best, it pioneered virtually all of them: a richly detailed customer database, charging for service, guaranteed response times, an automatic call distribution system, and a communications package to bring the customer's problem right into Great Plains. Each of these features is examined below.

What needs to be stressed up front is that these "outside" features of the system are only half the story—probably much less than half. The real customer support story only emerges when you look at the "insides" of the system. The inside features that provide the company's real dynamic involve pride, personal belief in the mission statement, training and teamwork, an informal and fun environment, and the company's concern for its employees.

"There can be a fantastic sense of pride. We're doing it the best in the business in terms of meeting those guarantees. We reached almost 250,000 calls without a miss. That's a great sense of pride. Like, 'Wow, I was on the team that did that.' We're just totally killing the stuff here." Darrin Hawley, a young two-year technical support specialist, made that statement with a big smile on his face in response to the question, "Doesn't the guaranteed response time put a lot of pressure on you?" He obviously feels a lot more pride than stress.

Sitting with Darrin at the interview was Brenda Osten, a technical support specialist for the past eight years. When she was asked for the "genius" of their superior customer support, she immediately responded: "Doug [the company's founder and CEO] shares the company mission statement when we first start. It is on everyone's walls. That's our main focus every day." This mission statement, which was indeed on walls everywhere around the company on you-can't-miss-it bright red paper, reads as follows:

> To improve the life and business success of partners and customers by providing superior accounting software, services and tools.

Teamwork is another critical ingredient of the inside mix. You don't see it written up anywhere, but you sure do hear a lot about it. Darrin, Brenda, and Roger Demers, the three people interviewed in the technical support group, all emphasized teamwork as a key factor for their group's success and their own personal satisfaction.

The informal and fun environment is part of the overall company culture and an integral part of its success. Walk in the company's huge new physical facility, affectionately called the FOM (for factory outlet mall, which it was until they converted it) and you see huge signs everywhere, the largest being STAR TREK. The whole place is known as the "Space Factory." Demers, a supervisor in the technical support group, made this unsolicited comment right after introducing himself: "It's one of those companies that just the whole work style, the culture —it's phenomenal. I've never worked at a place like it before where you just have such an open camaraderie."

Finally, there's the company-cares-about-me factor. It's clear that the employees there do not view Great Plains as just a job: "The company does care about my personal development." "It trains me as much as I want." "There are many after-hours events that build the family feeling." Dennis Erdle, director of professional services, said it best over lunch: "It's great to see people grow. Each is a different person after two years" (two years is the time each person commits to the technical support group and the time of most intensive training).

DOUG BURGUM AND HIS VALUES FOUNDATION

To understand Great Plains Software, you have to go back to the beginning and you have to get to know Doug Burgum. He grew up in Arthur, North Dakota, a town of 400 people. He spent a good deal of time at his father's grain elevator business. There he learned that today's customers are the sons and grandsons of the people his grandfather was serving in the business.

He also pointed out another formative experience. He worked two years for McKinsey, around the time that they were developing "The Excellent Company Study" (a forerunner to *In Search of Excellence*), which emphasized the importance of good old-fashioned customer service.

When he bought Great Plains Software at the tender age of twenty-seven, he soon got a rude awakening. He went to a trade show, and there he discovered sixty-three other firms in the accounting software business, rather than the ten he thought were out there. Talk about challenges: how do you survive, much less thrive, in a new industry when you're sitting up in North Dakota and you plan to do no advertising and you have sixty-three competitors?

You do it by going back to the basics. Burgum recognized that his company was in an industry—accounting software—that was steeped in tradition and built on long-term relationships. So he decided to build his company on a very simple homespun type of value: if we take good care of customers, they'll take good care of us. That values are the foundation of the company's great success with customers came out clearly in the interview when he said that much of what Great Plains does for the customer is done because "it's just the right thing to do."

This is not rocket science. It's pure common sense. All anyone has to do is think about the frustration they feel each time they are put on hold for ten, five, or even just three minutes. That's not good business and Burgum recognizes that. As he puts it: "You can't separate the product from support."

THE OUTSIDE SYSTEM

It all began with a system Burgum describes as "a spindle with a stack of pink slips." They had two phone lines and one receptionist (his future wife). But the commitment of the employees showed early. They would not go home until everyone was called back. Finally they realized that pink slips and paper notes on customer problems just weren't going to make it.

Breakthrough Number 1—Forced Registration

To build a comprehensive, detailed customer database, they chose a unique approach. The company wrote into each software module (each module handles a specific task) a code that blocked further use after fifty transactions. Customers then had to register with Great Plains to get "keys," which were ten-digit numerical sequences, to unlock their software. While they were waiting for their keys, they were asked twenty market research questions, including company size, business sector, location and so forth. This forced registration system may seem harsh but it provoked very few complaints. Nor should it, for Great Plains was getting to know its customers in this way and it also wanted to be able to notify them of bugs discovered in the software (a frequent problem in those days). The idea came from some guys in development and Burgum had the courage to run with it against the popular opinion of the day and the derision of competitors. Today, Burgum says it's "a total nonissue," and partners (vendors that sell and service its products) preregister most of their customers.

Breakthrough Number 2—Charge for Service

An even tougher initiative for Burgum was to begin charging for customer service through a variety of support plans. Again, no one else in the PC industry was doing this. So why do it? Because it was the best way to ensure a continuing superior level of service for the customer. Other companies continued to offer free service, but often people would be put on hold for ten to thirty minutes before they spoke to anyone and often their problem would not get fully resolved. The fees Great Plains charged at first were modest—around $150 a year—but as the complexity of the software increased, so has the price of the various plans. The current fees run from $125 for basic maintenance to $4,000 for the comprehensive plan. As Burgum explains it, everyone has come out of an airport and seen the bus line with a long wait, long ride, and low fare and the cab line with a short line, short ride, and higher fare. "You owe it to your customer to give them the option of getting in the cab line."

Breakthrough Number 3—Guaranteed Response Time

This was another first for Great Plains and another big step, initiated in 1987 when it was considered foolhardy in the industry to guarantee response times. But Great Plains was listening to its customers and some of them had to have a quick response. So it began to build into its service plan options of three-hour and one-hour guarantees. Remarkably, they've had a 99.9 percent success rate in meeting those guarantees.

Breakthrough Number 4—Automatic Call Distribution System

In 1989, they launched another innovation: an automatic call distribution system. Under this, a call is automatically routed to a specialist trained to deal with the particular problem. The support person knows who's calling, so they'll often answer, "Hello, David, glad to hear from you. I understand you're having some trouble with . . ." Roger Demers in the technical support group points out: "That's what just kills them. They think, 'I haven't even talked to a person yet and yet they greet me and know my problem.'"

Breakthrough Number 5—Communications Packages

In the early 1990s, they introduced Dynamics which served Macintosh users as well as Windows users. Since this was much more open to the end user, Great Plains realized that to give full service they would have to be able to get into the customer's computer and actually have the technical support person see the customer's screen before them. So they sent each Dynamics customer a sophisticated modem communications package that would allow their support people to do this.

THE INSIDE SYSTEM: JEANS, TEAMS, AND TRAINING

Great Plains' superior customer service is a combination of system and spirit. We've just seen the key elements of the system in place. Now it's time to look inside at the spirit.

The inside heart is its technical support group. This is seventy people who look like they have been plucked right off a college campus—as most of them have. They may be answering phones all day, but as we've seen, Great Plains takes that very seriously. The hiring process is rigorous. Everyone must have a college degree and must be judged to be good in dealing with people by teams of managers and supervisors, all trained in interviewing.

Once selected, each is given six weeks of training at their in-house Great Plains University in three basic modules of Great Plains Accounting. During this time, they will sit in with an experienced support specialist and listen to how they handle calls. After three months on the job, during which time they are frequently monitored by their supervisor and given advice about ways to better serve the customer, they go to further training in another module. Then back to the phones for six to twelve weeks, followed by further training in another three-module inventory series. By the end of the first year, most are highly skilled in nine of the sixteen modules in the Great Plains Accounting product.

Clearly the training is comprehensive, but what the employees really get excited talking about is the teamwork. Darrin Hawley expressed the importance of teamwork to him: "You are never really on your own. That's one of the incredible things up there—that teamwork atmosphere they build. There's a team up there to help you if you get stuck on something. You can never say you're alone on the phones."

Teams were structured in three basic types. The most immediate team consists of the four people in each phone-answering cubicle. Usually there's a senior person in the cube, a rookie, and two in-betweens. Then there's the ten to twelve-person team that may specialize in DOS or Windows applications. Finally, the seventy people in the technical support group are considered one big team.

Demers also pointed to "a lot of little things" that contribute to the high level of customer support. One is the weekly team meeting to catch up on new technologies. Then there's the department meeting every Thursday where the idea is to get everything out in the open that's current. To further communication, minutes are taken and distributed and there's also a conversation wall where people post meeting minutes to spread information on recent solutions provided to customers.

And there is Letter Lane. Running the entire length of the outside cubicle wall (about one hundred feet in length) are the hundreds of letters of thanks for outstanding service received by the technical support specialists. When Darrin was asked if this wall was meaningful to him, he smiled and said, "It'll make your day if you get a letter."

There's no better way to capture the spirit of the technical support specialists than the final point Darrin wanted to make:

> If you make the decision that's in the customer's best interest, then you're not making a bad decision. And we'll stand behind you on that. There are things that may not be in the best interest of the company's bottom line. I've never been reprimanded for doing something that's going to help the customer. That's something very impressive about the organization. It may cost an extra $5 or $10 but if it's going to help the customer and keep the customer satisfied, that's what's important.

"TAKE GOOD CARE OF YOUR CUSTOMERS AND THEY'LL TAKE GOOD CARE OF YOU"

Since dedicating itself to serving its customers, Great Plains has never missed growing in any of its first forty-eight quarters, its revenues skyrocketing at a compounded annual rate of 37 percent. The company has overtaken all its initial competitors, enjoying a number-one market share in the Windows, DOS, and Mac markets in 1994. It adds at least 5,000 customers a year to its current customer base of 65,000 for its basic midrange products.

So just how good is its customer support? For six years in a row Great Plains has swept top honors in surveys of CPAs who evaluate and support PC-based accounting systems. In one major accounting software survey of technical support satisfaction, Great Plains not only finished first but was just one tenth of a point shy of earning a perfect score of ten.

> LESSON: Customers are best served when a superb "outside system" is complemented by a great "inside spirit." The visible outside system can consist of:
>
> - forced registration
> - charging for services
> - guaranteed response times
> - an automatic call distribution system
> - communications packages
>
> The more hidden inside spirit may consist of:
> - pride
> - personal belief in the mission statement
> - teamwork
> - an informal and fun environment
> - a company's concern for its employees

Unprecedented Service
DELL COMPUTER

"WE HAD DELIVERY IN ABOUT TWO DAYS. IF WE HAD A PROBLEM, A GUY WAS HERE THE NEXT DAY. IN FACT, EVERY MONTH WE GET A CALL FROM DELL TO MAKE SURE THAT EVERYTHING IS ALL RIGHT. I'VE NEVER HEARD OF ANYTHING LIKE IT."

—TIM DEMPSEY, DEPUTY COMPUTING MANAGER, INSTITUTE OF DIRECTORS (LONDON)

THE CHALLENGE

It was May 1984 and Michael Dell, a college student, was just starting PCs Limited with his $1,000 in savings, operating out of his apartment. A year later, the company was up to forty employees, but it was really just three guys sitting at a six-foot table assembling the computers. How could this fledgling computer company down in Austin, Texas, get a toehold in a field dominated by the likes of IBM and Apple?

THE RESPONSE

Service. Unprecedented service in the rarified, often haughty, air of the computer industry. Give the customer the exact computer he or she wants. Provide the products quickly and at very reasonable prices. Provide great backup support once the computer is in their hands. Undergo unending scrutiny of customer needs. And get the word out to millions through aggressive, jazzy ads and a huge mail-order business.

It's really pretty simple when you think about it. When you constantly talk with your customers over toll-free phone lines—taking orders, dealing with questions and problems—you find out about their likes and dislikes. All of this information goes into the company's massive customer database, which has well over 1 million entries. Referring to all this customer data, Tom Thomas, chief information officer, emphasizes that information is a valuable competitive weapon and that Dell's whole business system is geared to collect it. All of this information enables Dell Computer (the company name was changed in 1987) to come up with continuous small improvements in product features and service.

Through its mail-order operation, it could provide faster and better service than most retail dealers. It also pioneered many firsts: the first PC maker to offer guaranteed next-day on-site service (1987) and the first to provide replacement machines by overnight delivery (1989). Repairs are handled within twenty-four hours by a contract service firm. Its customized orders, which it specializes in, can be shipped within two to five business days. Now that's agility.

Let's look a little closer at this customizing service. Basically, Dell fits out every PC system it sells to match buyer needs. Customers can choose, for example, a color Mitsubishi monitor, an extra-powerful

Intel microprocessor, or a host of other options. The customer receives a computer notebook or desktop computer already loaded with operating system software like DOS and Windows, and applications programs such as word processors and spreadsheets. Dell doesn't make or even stock these items, but orders them from Merisel, a big distribution company, which often ships directly to the customer. So why do it? Because the service lures customers who like dealing with a single supplier.

To really understand Dell, you have to understand where it puts its money and where it doesn't. It doesn't put its money into hard assets. It owns no plants. Rather, it leases two small factories to assemble computers from outsourced parts. For a multibillion-dollar company, its investment in fixed assets is a minuscule $55 million. This enables Dell to take in $35 of sales of every dollar of fixed assets. For another leading computer maker, the figure is $3.

This frugality allows Dell to lavish money on training salespeople and service technicians and furnishing them with the best computers, databases, and software, spending around $50 million annually on this information technology. Its salespeople are not minimum-wage order takers, but thoroughly trained college graduates. They listen and ask questions, and then tap into the company's computers information about the customers' likes and dislikes, as well as praise and gripes about the look, cost, and configuration of Dell machines and rival offerings. The company's army of sales people and technical support experts sit in 740 cubicles in a room the size of a football field, fielding 35,000 customer calls or E-mail messages each working day.

Behind all of this stellar service is the company's motivating "Dell Vision," the critical concept of which is that a customer "must have a quality experience, and must be pleased, not just satisfied." Michael Dell takes that vision seriously: "People who come here and don't gravitate to that don't last long."

Michael Dell didn't know how to design or manufacture the greatest computers. What he did know was how to market them. Dell Computer grew so rapidly because Michael Dell knew the real advantage was in finding innovative ways of getting to the customer and doing whatever was necessary to please the customer.

Then there's the "Hour of Horror," the nickname given to Dell's weekly Customer Advocate Meeting. There, customer complaints and employee suggestions are carefully scrutinized by everyone, from top managers to assembly-line workers. Whatever problems aren't fixed in a week get reviewed every Friday until they are solved. Such scrutiny to customer needs is the hallmark of Dell's success.

THE RESULTS

In May 1991 J. D. Power ranked Dell number one in its first-ever PC customer satisfaction survey. Dell repeated as the winner in September 1993.

Any way you look at it, Michael Dell's simple strategy of doing whatever it takes to reach and please the customer has paid off in spades: Dell was the youngest CEO to bring a company into the exclusive Fortune 500 club, and he parlayed a $1,000 investment in 1984 into a $3 billion plus company a decade later.

Few companies have attained the pace of growth that Dell experienced between 1985 and 1993. From forty employees, it grew to 7,000 and was hiring dozens of new workers a month. It was number one on the 1993 Fortune 500 list of "Biggest Increase in Sales" with a 126 percent increase.

Although it initially sold modified IBM machines, Dell now designs, manufactures, and markets more than thirty different PCs. From the launch of its first international subsidiary in 1987, it now sells PCs in eighteen countries, entering six new countries in 1992 alone, including Japan, where it generated such enthusiastic response that it overwhelmed the resources Dell had committed.

Having achieved spectacular success by focusing on one primary product—desktop computers—and one main distribution channel—direct sales—Dell now faces a new set of challenges. Its product line is highly concentrated in desktop computers (94 percent,) while servers (high-powered PCs that anchor office networks) (19 percent) and notebooks (15 percent) are coming on strong in the PC industry as a whole. Also, after being the first major computer maker to enter superstores and warehouse clubs in 1989, it abandoned these retail channels in July 1994 after retail sales had sunk to 2 percent of overall revenues. It maintained that it could more profitably reach customers by refocusing efforts on its mail-order business.

There's no better measure of how you please your customers than repeat business and here Dell is also doing well: 70 percent of its buyers are repeat customers.

[
LESSON: Break into the big leagues by providing unprecedented service, which may involve such things
as next day service, overnight replacement, customizing the product, highly trained salespeople and
service technicians, and providing high quality
products at reasonable prices.
]

The CEO Meets with the Customers
PREMIER INDUSTRIAL

"WE CHARGED THEM $14, AND A CUSTOMER OFFICIAL CALLED US BACK
EMBARRASSED AND ASKED US TO ADD $100 TO THE BILL—THAT $14 WASN'T
ENOUGH. WE SAID, 'NO, JUST REMEMBER THAT EVERY TIME YOU NEED US, WE'LL
BE THERE'; NOW HOW MANY TIMES DO YOU THINK THEY'LL COME BACK TO US?"

—MORT MANDEL, CHAIRMAN AND CEO

THE CHALLENGE

Premier's challenge in the 1980s was simply to "keep the faith" in its
core values as it grew larger and larger. But could a $700 million
enterprise with 5,000 employees that supplies more than 100,000 different industrial parts really stick to the three core values that had
guided the company since its founding in 1940—superior customer
service, respect for the individual, and the pursuit of excellence?

Talk about a company ahead of its time. Four decades ahead of the
1980s rush to put the customer first, empower employees, and pursue
total quality management, Cleveland-based Premier Industrial was qui-
etly building its business on these principles and practices.

THE RESPONSE

Has it kept the faith? After 34 years in the chairman's seat, Mort Mandel
is ready to assert in his soft-spoken manner, "throughout our history,

superior customer service has been central to our success. We have killed ourselves for the customer."

But how can such a large company continually "kill" for the customer? One good way is Mandel's example. He blocks out a certain number of days for the field (customers and employees) every month. And they remain blocked. "You can learn a great deal if you listen to your customers. So I dedicate those days to them, and that's it. I have to get everything else that the CEO job demands done in the remaining days."

It also involves a CEO who views the company's most precious asset as the fact that "our customers know they can rely on us," that they can rely on Premier's performance. That's why Premier makes sure it has every item in inventory so that a part is always there when one of its 250,000 customers needs it. It means being willing to make late deliveries and driving a part to a person's place of business.

Or even more, it means being willing to go the long extra mile. The background to the opening anecdote about the $14 bill is that a customer's machine had broken down and the needed part was in Premier's warehouse in Chicago. The part was flown to Florida where a Premier representative met the plane and drove it directly to a mechanic at the customer. Total down time for the machine was just five hours. Such service builds up a tremendous reservoir of good will. Mandel points out that a company only has to go that extra step once or twice a year. "The rest of the time it's just bread-and-butter. And that kind of service just clangs right down to the bottom line."

As much as Mandel stresses superior customer service, customers still aren't number one. The people at Premier are. And he personally invests himself in his people as well, particularly when it comes to instilling the core values. For example, he takes senior managers on business trips with him. "That way we get two days of deep immersion in the business philosophy and culture." When he travels to Premier locations, he will designate a high-potential employee to pick him up at the airport: "That often gives me an opportunity to preach the message." He and other members of top management talk to every new manager about the company's values, culture, philosophies, and objectives. "That's the difference between just having a set of objectives and having them ingrained in the culture." And finally, he gets the word out to the line employees. The corporate values are prominently displayed on the walls of its 350 locations.

Mandel himself is now over seventy and he makes no apologies for keeping the faith in his old values in today's hotly competitive and fast-paced marketplace:

> Our three core values have an infinite life and will never go out of style. Companies that lose sight of justice, fairness, hard work, honesty, and integrity are not going to succeed. In my lifetime, it has been fashionable to be cool and sophisticated, and that has brought shame to anything old on the grounds that it's old-fashioned. But old is not old-fashioned. That is a trap society has fallen into. There is nothing new about basic ethics. What I learned from my parents, the values and ethics I had by the time I was fourteen, have helped me in business more than anything I've learned in business, and that has molded the way I run the business.

THE RESULTS

The old values and attention to customers produce some pretty impressive modern-day results. Over the twenty-year period 1973–1993, Premier's compounded annual revenue growth has averaged 9.4 percent while compounded earnings-per-share growth has been 15.8 percent and dividends' compounded growth 16.8 percent. The dividend record is truly astounding. Premier has paid cash dividends without interruption since becoming a public company in 1960. Furthermore, the dividend has been increased annually for nineteen consecutive years, during which time it has increased over 1,800 percent.

In a survey of companies with strong financial profiles, *CFO,* a magazine for financial executives, ranked Premier as the strongest large company in America. Specifically, the survey of 6,000 public companies used certain key financial data to rank how well management balanced profitability, liquidity, and leverage over one-year and ten-year periods. Premier received the highest rating possible for both short- and long-term performance.

[
LESSON: A CEO needs to block out a few days each month for the customers, invest personal time and energy in instilling the core value of customer service in senior managers, and help all employees understand that one of the company's most precious assets is that "our customers know they can rely on us."
]

 ## Hop on Your Harleys and Find the Customers
HARLEY-DAVIDSON

"WE CREATED A VISION THAT WAS SIMPLE: SURVIVAL. A LOT OF BUSINESSES OUGHT TO FIRST DECIDE HOW THEY'RE GOING TO SURVIVE. THEY SHOULD GET RIGHT DOWN TO THE MEAT OF THE ISSUE—SURVIVAL AND CUSTOMER SATISFACTION."

—RICHARD TEERLINK, PRESIDENT AND CEO

THE CHALLENGE

Harley-Davidson looked like just one more old-line manufacturer being hammered into oblivion by foreign competitors. It was 1981 and Milwaukee-based H-D was losing sizable chunks of market share to much bigger Japanese competitors who had better-quality motorcycles that they offered at lower prices. Its own manufacturing systems and product quality were inadequate to meet such world-class competition. Still, thirteen managers at the company stepped forth and bought the company in an $81.5 million leveraged buyout.

Soon, Harley was losing money for the first time in fifty years and it was laying off more than 40 percent of its workforce as it continued to lose more market share to the Japanese. From 1973 onward, the company saw its market share plummet from 75 percent to less than 25 percent under the impact of relentless Japanese competitors. And it wasn't helping its own cause, as its products were a clear case of "badly made in America." It seemed that yet another American icon—the Harley—would be disappearing from the road.

THE RESPONSE

On the verge of bankruptcy in 1985, Harley-Davidson—the very symbol of macho—had to swallow its pride and become teachable. It had to look at and learn from others about quality, employee involvement, and statistical process control.

If you're going to learn, why not go straight to those that are beating you badly? So Vaughn Beals, its chairman, took a team of managers on a tour around Honda's assembly plant in Marysville, Ohio. It was a real eye-opener to Beals: "We were being wiped out by the Japanese because they were better managers. It wasn't robotics, or culture, or morning calisthenics and company songs, it was professional managers who understood their business and paid attention to detail." Beals returned, told his employees, "We have to play the game the way the Japanese play it or we're dead," and began to lead a strong revival. It was across-the-board, involving design, employee involvement, JIT inventory practices, and statistical process control.

But most of all, it involved learning from its customers. Indeed, H-D executives decided that success—and even survival—depended on making customer satisfaction their ultimate goal. It recognized that the "customer-driven" era had arrived and what the customer wanted, the customer had better get.

It all began with an innovative form of customer research: senior managers were told to hop on their Harleys and take cross-country trips to listen to Harley customers wherever they could find them. What they found was that virtually every Harley motorcycle at the bike rallies had been modified and customized. So if this is what customers liked, why not have Harley do it for them. Many ideas from this vast "R&D field team" were incorporated into later designs. All along, however, the company has been sensitive to their fiercely loyal riders' demand for the legendary Harley look.

In two areas, production growth and exports, Harley has chosen to go slow as a form of quality control in order to keep its major customers in North America happy. Harley got burned by quality problems during a production increase in the mid-1970s while part of AMF. Having fixed the product with a redesigned engine, the company does not want to take any chances. Thus, it has ramped up production only gradually since 1986, from 150 units a day to 380 in March 1994. Harley-Davidson plans to reach a production schedule of 425 units a day (or 100,000 units a year) sometime in 1996.

Also fundamental to continuously improving quality has been its vision of establishing and expanding employee involvement throughout the company. Indeed, observers feel that the company would not have survived without this new involvement by all Harley employees, both blue-collar and white-collar. This required establishing the right climate, a nonthreatening one, more so than any formal technique. To Harley employees, it now boils down to this simple point: management listens to them *and* acts upon what they say. They sense for the first time some ownership in their workplace, for labor and management are now able to sit down and agree on a mutual goal: the long-term success of the company.

Once it had regained its U.S. market share in the late 1980s, Harley focused on overseas markets and began to recruit more dealers in Japan and Europe. Important to attracting foreign customers was customizing its U.S. marketing package for different cultures, abandoning its former clumsy practice of simply translating U.S. ads word-for-word into another language. "One steady constant in an increasingly screwed-up world" just didn't win over Japanese riders.

Looking at its dramatic turnaround, Harley's management ascribes most of it to the company's simple five-point philosophy: tell the truth, keep your promises, be fair, respect the individual, and encourage curiosity. And don't forget the number-one item on the motorcycle division's list of strategic objectives: "be number one in customer satisfaction worldwide."

THE RESULTS

Just two years after being on the verge of bankruptcy, dramatic results were pouring in. By 1987, Harley had recaptured its market-share lead from Honda, its major Japanese rival. Just one year later, its market share in the super-heavyweight class surged to 46.5 percent, almost double the 24.1 percent share of Honda—an almost complete reversal of their relative market positions of just five years earlier. Overall, its market share in heavyweight motorcycles rose fivefold in a decade, from 12.5 percent in 1983 to 63 percent in 1993.

Over the five years from 1988 to 1993, sales in the motorcycle division grew at a 21 percent compounded annual rate. Harley's revenues increased 30 percent from 1991 to 1993, and its profits doubled during these two years to $70 million.

One indication of how quick its comeback occurred is its request in 1987 to the federal government to cancel the protective special tariffs it had established on big imported bikes one year before their expiration date in 1988.

In 1988, it became the first defense contractor to be certified under the U.S. Army's Contractor Performance Certification Program, which recognizes contractors that have reduced the government's procurement costs through a consistent commitment to the quality of the delivered product. Later in 1988, the company and its four unions received the first Union Label Award given by the AFL-CIO in recognition of "the foresight and cooperation shown by unions and management in helping to revitalize the company."

Today it can sell every bike it produces. And a lot more. Its 1994 models, introduced in August 1993, were sold out by September. The quality of its motorcycles is now at an all-time high. And it is a premier success story for the combined impact that total quality control and just-in-time programs can have: it reduced manufacturing cycle time for motorcycle frames from seventy-two days to just two, while increasing final product quality from 50 percent to 99 percent.

Thirty percent of its motorcycles are exported to over thirty countries, including Japan, Australia, and throughout Europe. And it's still basically an American-made bike: the American component content is around 90 percent.

Perhaps it has no better result than the loyalty of its customers. This was attested to in June 1993, when some 100,000 members of the H-D family showed up for its 90th Anniversary Reunion weekend in Milwaukee. CEO Richard Teerlink sums up their comeback this way: "We are living proof that you can win your reputation back."

[
LESSON: You can win your reputation back if you aren't afraid to learn from others, particularly your customers. This can encourage highly focused niche marketing and actually customizing the products to the exact desires of each customer.
]

A Direct Line of Sight to the Customer
XEROX

"WE WANT THE CUSTOMER TO INTEGRATE THE COMPANY. WE DON'T WANT TO INTEGRATE THE COMPANY, AND THEN GO TO THE CUSTOMER."
—PAUL ALLAIRE, CHAIRMAN AND CEO

THE CHALLENGE

It was another case of having it too easy. After introducing its first plain-paper copier in 1959, Xerox, based in Stamford, Connecticut, enjoyed a decade of spectacular growth and commanding market share. As a result, in the 1970s the company neglected the fundamentals of its core business, leaving it vulnerable to intense competition from both U.S. and Japanese competitors.

By the early 1980s, its return on assets had been reduced to less than 8 percent and its market share in copiers had been slashed from a dominant 86 percent of the world market in 1974 to a measly 17 percent in 1984. Nothing less than survival was at stake, according to CEO Paul Allaire. As he puts it: "We realized we had to change dramatically from top to bottom: the way we managed and worked, our reward and recognition systems, the way we communicated, and our entire corporate culture."

THE RESPONSE

To survive, Xerox embarked on a quality journey. Total quality would be the paradigm to reengineer the fundamentals of the business—product development, manufacturing, and customer service.

To get started, Xerox relied on benchmarking—a practice it pioneered in the United States in 1979. Benchmarking is simply finding the companies that are the best with a certain practice and going to them to learn. This time it benchmarked on quality from its own subsidiary Fuji Xerox, which had embraced new quality methods early on, winning Japan's top quality award, the Deming Prize, in 1980. Adapting many of Fuji Xerox's principles and practices to its own culture, Xerox implemented its Leadership Through Quality strategy, which had six elements: tools and processes, reward and recognition, communications, training, employee involvement and empowerment, and senior management behavior.

Quality. And customer satisfaction. You can't think of one without thinking of the other when examining the transformation at Xerox. According to Allaire, "The entire corporation focused on meeting customer requirements. We defined this as our quality process."

In fact, rarely has customer satisfaction been so clearly and emphatically conveyed to a company's employees as it was by Paul Allaire, then president, in 1987: "I am changing the corporate priorities at Xerox Corporation. Effective immediately, the order is number one: customer satisfaction; number two: ROA (return on assets); number three: market share."

To show that this was not just rhetoric, Xerox that same year put into place an incentive compensation system heavily weighted toward customer satisfaction. Sales people are rated and compensated according to customer feedback.

The new priorities already had a powerful tool in place: Xerox's Customer Satisfaction Measurement System, which is perhaps the best in America. One fascinating feature of the system is its integration of customer research and benchmarking. The company sends out 55,000 questionnaires monthly to its customers to determine their satisfaction. Several times a year, it uses the same process to track its competitors' performance as perceived by their customers. It then benchmarks those competitors that have high marks on specific measures of customer satisfaction. All in all, it surveys 200,000 Xerox customers a year to identify major areas of dissatisfaction and address their root causes. It also takes the vast amount of information gathered by the system to develop specific business plans with measurable targets for achieving quality improvements necessary to meet customer needs.

Though Xerox's market share for copiers both domestically and worldwide rebounded in the late 1980s, the company still was not where it wanted to be. Earnings in 1991 stayed flat and its share of the U.S. copier market still lagged considerably behind that of Canon.

So in 1991, the second major reorganization was launched by Allaire, this time a year after he became CEO. He didn't hide from the failure of the reorganizations in the 1980s to accomplish what was needed:

> In the 1980s, we went through a number of reorganizations. But none of them got at the fundamental question of how we run the company. The change we are making now is more profound than anything we've done before. We have embarked on a process to change completely the way we manage the company. In fact, the term "reorganization" doesn't really capture what we are trying to do at Xerox. We are redesigning the "organizational architecture" of the entire company.

The driving force was to move the entire company still closer to its customers. The new architecture was developed by an internal group of managers calling itself the "future-tecture" team. The result is a new three-level organization chart that has corporate staff at the bottom, supporting the business teams and districts at the top.

In essence, Xerox designed a new horizontal organization centered on business units. It did so by letting sets of customers and customer needs define the business units. Gone are the usual functional departments—R&D, manufacturing, sales, and so forth. In their place are nine businesses, each focused on one major end customer—for example, Personal Document Products (home office copiers) and Desktop Document Systems (digital systems network products). Profit-and-loss responsibility was moved out of the chief executive's suite and down to twenty business team general managers within the nine businesses. These teams and units now have complete responsibility for a Xerox product, from its conception to final sale to the customer. Says Allaire: "We've given everyone in the company a direct line of sight to the customer." And quality is tied to the customer once again, as quality is expected to improve as Xerox becomes more responsive to its customers.

At times, Xerox employees follow that line of sight right into their customers' workplace, *before* the sale. The idea is to help customers rethink the way they work so they can use Xerox's products more efficiently when they get them. Analyzing the work in this manner helps Xerox deliver solutions, not just products.

There is one other dimension of the Xerox story that must be understood. Allan Dugan, senior vice president, stresses it: "The Xerox success story was totally dependent on employee involvement. And employee involvement essentially means teams. In addition Xerox's recovery was very much due to the cooperation of our union people."

THE RESULTS

Xerox's focus on customer satisfaction has certainly paid off. The results from its mid-1980s refocusing on the customer were reported in its 1989 Malcolm Baldrige National Quality Award application: highly satisfied customers for its copier/duplicator and printing systems had increased 38 percent and 39 percent respectively; customer complaints to the president's office declined more than 60 percent; customer satisfaction with Xerox sales processes improved 40 percent, service processes, 18 percent, and administrative processes, 21 percent.

Early results are in on the 1990s reorganization. Customer satisfaction improved significantly and was rated at 90 percent or more in 1991. Xerox's customers now rate it number one in the industry in product reliability and service.

The emphasis on quality has also been rewarded. Dataquest rates Xerox's products number one in five out of six of its market segments. And Buyers Laboratory in 1992 named its product line the best in the industry. Xerox also has reduced the amount of time it takes to bring a new product to market by nearly 60 percent.

And in the process of increasing customer satisfaction and improving product quality, Xerox has reduced its average manufacturing costs by over 20 percent and increased its return on assets from 8 percent to 14 percent.

LESSON: A customer focus should be central to restructuring the company. First, meeting customer requirements can define the quality process, which involves extraordinary customer research and benchmarking. You also can restructure the company by allowing sets of customers or customer needs to define business units, thus giving everyone in the company a direct line of sight to the customer.

7: ENVISION NEW PRODUCTS AND MARKETS

Perhaps the most profound statement that has been made about new products and product innovation are two words of Hiroshi Yamauchi, CEO of Nintendo. When one of his game designers, Gunpei Yokai, asked, "What should I make?" he replied, "Something great."

That's the spirit that has been lost in the vast majority of companies. It's the reason there are so few breakthrough products on the market —that so many products are passionless. CEOs and managers aren't challenging their employees to make something great. Imagine what could happen in companies across America if they all did?

Why is product innovation so important? A recent major survey by the Boston Consulting Group of 600 U.S., European, and Japanese manufacturing companies provides the answer. The survey addressed the issue of what practices provide managers the greatest leverage in expanding their revenues and gaining market share. It concluded:

Speed in new product development ranks highest in effect on both market share and growth of market share.... Innovation—that is, competitively distinctive new products—ranks very high in driving growth in market share.

Three factors—getting to market quickly, feel for the market, and innovation—together have the strongest influence on growth in market share, and all relate to the new product development function. All have an especially pronounced effect on changes in market share, a finding that makes sense: all three relate to a company's ability to change and keep changing the competitive battle for customers in its favor.

If there is one clear thing we have learned from looking closely at the top product innovators, it is that there is no single formula for success. Rather, when you read through these stories you will find wackiness, freedom, mystique, paranoia, fun, gestalt, and even a flying coffee pot as the ingredients that go into being a company that can consistently turn out new products—sometimes "great" products— and seeing new markets to enter.

Each of the five companies in this chapter have developed a company culture that fosters innovation. One company that has developed such a culture superbly—3M—is not included in this chapter because we chose to use it as our case study for its pioneering work in improving the environment, just one example of its innovative character.

What goes into a culture fostering innovation? Three characteristics stand out: spirit, creative freedom, and the ability to get ideas from everywhere.

A SPIRIT, A GESTALT

We begin with the best—Rubbermaid—a new-product-generating machine that in recent years has turned out an average of one new product a day. During the day-long set of interviews, there were no signs on the walls encouraging innovation, there were no written materials of any kind that highlighted "the innovation process," there weren't even two or three key ingredients that anyone could point to as driving their innovation.

But what one did clearly sense—the secret to their innovative genius—was a spirit to the place.

- We're all product junkies
- Let ideas come from everywhere
- We look at everybody's product and reinvent it

It could be sensed in the spirited storytelling that everyone engaged in. When you get managers, vice presidents, and the CEO bursting to tell stories about tackleboxes, doghouses, hampers, and Bubbles the Whale, you know there is a special spirit.

What's wonderful—and a real key to Rubbermaid's success—is that the spirited environment translates into spirited products. What companies really need are products that have spirit!

At Microsoft, new product development arises from the corporate gestalt—almost the mystique of being a Microsoft employee. Key to the gestalt is that you're out to win and win big. Insecurity is also important to Microsoft's gestalt. As one worker puts it, "People never believe that they've got the best product. It's always the fear that somebody is going to come up with a better one."

CREATIVE FREEDOM

Creative freedom for all the employees is standard in all these companies. Johnson & Johnson practices decentralization with a vengeance, resulting in 166 companies acting independently, scrambling relentlessly for new products and new markets. CEO Ralph Larsen compares his role to that of an orchestra conductor, giving his players inspiration and direction but above all giving them abundant creative freedom. So you have nimbleness from the decentralized structure, freedom for the individual employees, all backed by sizable resources and inspired leadership.

Similarly, Thermo Electron encourages the entrepreneurial spark and the growth of new businesses through its unique "spin-out" strategy. The incentive for employees to innovate is high: anyone who invents a new product or finds a new market for a technology can be made head of his or her own spin-out company. Since 1983, nine publicly held companies have formed in this manner.

Microsoft has its own straightforward winning combination. You hire the best and the brightest and give them enormous challenges and extraordinary freedom.

Note that the brightest may not always be the best. A company should also hire a few off-the-wall types, people who at least one time in their lives have demonstrated that they had the guts to try something extraordinary; that they were willing to break the mold. After all, that person may just do it again for your company. Remember, you're looking for the breakthrough product and a breakthrough requires creativity and creativity usually doesn't come in nice, tidy packages.

Again, Nintendo CEO Yamauchi provides the brilliant insight into a key driver of new product success: "An ordinary man cannot develop good games no matter how hard he tries. A handful of people in the world can develop games that everyone wants. Those are the people we want at Nintendo."

Creative freedom often involves a sense of fun, and most of the truly innovative companies have a sense of fun that permeates the workplace. Indeed, Odetics was created as a company where it would be fun to come to work because the co-founders believed that in such an atmosphere creativity and risk taking would flourish, resulting in new products. "The wackiest place to work in the United States," declares *Industry Week*. Even though it has grown to 600 employees, there's still a Fun Committee charged with thinking up wild and crazy activities.

True creative freedom implies a willingness—no, a desire—to not be part of the pack. To stand apart. To be different. The co-founder of Sony, Masaru Ibuka, hits it right on the head: "The key to success for Sony and to everything in business, science and technology . . . is never to follow the others."

LOOK FOR IDEAS EVERYWHERE

Most of the innovative companies are happy to get ideas from customers, consumers, competitors, employees, and top management.

Johnson & Johnson moves quickly to license technological and medical advances developed by others. It looks to its customers as prime sources of ideas for new products or ways to improve existing products. It uses consumer innovation groups, which differ from traditional focus groups by encouraging more creativity from the respondents.

NEW PRODUCTS AND NEW MARKETS BRING GREAT REWARDS

If there is any doubt that being a great innovator leads to great rewards, one need only look at these companies. Rubbermaid, one new product a day and ranked number one in innovation by *Fortune* magazine; Microsoft, a whole series of blockbuster products generating annual revenues in the early 1990s that surpassed its seven closest rivals combined; Johnson & Johnson, one third of sales from products introduced in the past five years and never posting a loss in its 106 year history.

A New-Product-Generating Machine
RUBBERMAID

It was not the normal stuff of interviews. There was talk of dustpans, hampers, and tackleboxes. A sophisticated manager spoke enthusiastically of Bubbles the Whale. A vice president talked excitedly about a brainstorming session on doghouses. And the CEO of a $2 billion company threw a coffee pot at the interviewer.

Not exactly the normal points brought up in interviews, but then again Rubbermaid is not your normal company. It may make very normal products, but it cranks out new ones with a vengeance. It is nothing less than a new-product-generating machine—introducing an average of one new product a day in 1993.

Rubbermaid was not like this in 1980 when Stan Gault came to the quiet community of Wooster, Ohio, to become the new CEO of the company. From day one, he began to provide the leadership and inspiration that transformed Rubbermaid into the powerhouse innovator it is today.

Just how did it manage to turn out one new product a day? Throughout the day-long interviews, we heard quite a number of phrases over and over again from many executives and managers, the key ones being: "reinventing," "everyone's encouraged," "trends," "Business Teams," "ideas from everywhere." And stories were told everywhere. Everyone had at least one and many shared two or three about the introduction of a successful product.

But most of all, we came away with a sense that the key ingredient —the secret to their innovative genius—could be found in the spirit of the place. Everyone seemed to have the attitude of "what's next?"

You can come close to experiencing the Rubbermaid spirit and attitude by listening to a variety of Rubbermaid voices talk about what makes the company such an innovation giant:

- "everyone being into products"
- "overwhelm the competition by the sheer number of items"
- "brainstorming sessions"
- "we get new products because we have dozens of Business Teams"

- "unique things like the Internal Product Fair"
- "all sorts of crazy things, like the Competitors' War Fair"
- "a growth formula—that's very fundamental"
- "the genius of the system is let ideas come from anywhere"
- "every team, every year, is charged with reinventing what they have"
- "we encourage everybody, at every level, to innovate"

This spirit is reflected in a recent CEO that hung around hardware stores to see the competition and get new ideas, and the current CEO who just wanders around the R&D department on a Saturday morning to see what products are being thought about. One vice president summed it all up in a classic understatement: "The important thing is we don't sit back and wait for somebody to come up with a concept."

Wolf Schmitt, the current CEO, sets Rubbermaid's contagious spirit:

New products and new markets are always on the agenda here. There's not a day that goes by that in some way we're not thinking about new products, talking about new products, or working on new products. So I think you lead by example. You have to be interested. Be in the game.

I'm probably the biggest pain to our people in sending out notes with ideas and clippings. I'm probably on every mailing list in the world because I buy a lot of products I find in catalogues. I send them to people to stimulate new ideas. It's easy. It's fun. People then recognize that you really want this sort of activity going on. I enjoy new products. I think it's fun. I like color. And I think people understand that. As a result it's contagious—maybe that's what it's all about. You sort of inoculate everybody with that desire to do those things.

Perhaps there's no better testimony to just how well Rubbermaid has succeeded in getting itself known as an innovator than the fact that consumers thought it was the number two maker of dishwasher gloves before it even made any.

ENCOURAGEMENT, REINVENTING, AND SPIRIT

This section was initially going to deal with the history of innovation at Rubbermaid because that's where Wolf Schmitt started in his answer to why Rubbermaid is so innovative. But his big three—history, trends, and organization—seemed too staid as categories to really capture the genius of the place. They're important and we'll deal with them later, but one should instead start with the trio of encouragement, reinventing, and spirit to truly capture what makes Rubbermaid so unique in its innovation success.

"We encourage everybody at every level to innovate," sums up Chuck Carroll, president and COO and former head of the Home Products Division (Rubbermaid's largest). "We constantly feed on that."

One concrete way in which innovation is fostered is supporting people who try but fail—fail in the sense that the product is not introduced or is dropped. As Wolf Schmitt says, "Those are the people that need support the most. Creating a willingness and desire on people's part to participate in the process of risk taking—that's what it's all about."

That encouragement helps people think big. It's the reason Gary Mattison, president and general manager of Rubbermaid Specialty Products, could say, "Every team, every year, is charged with reinventing what they have." This is true for even the most mundane items. A vice president of marketing at Specialty Products said that "we are reinventing our bird feeder line every year."

What's amazing is that this reinventing goes on even in the oldest and largest division: the $1 billion Home Products Division, about half the company. One would think that something that large just couldn't keep up the innovative pace. Think again. In the past year, it introduced three new categories that now include ten lines of products. What's more, as the division president, Chuck Carroll, was quick to point out, it expects to have thirty new lines from these three new categories in a couple of years.

No one can say that the big and the old can't be innovative.

Here's another secret behind Rubbermaid's success: "We enjoy sweating the details better than the other guy." "Sweating the details," a favorite phrase of Wolf Schmitt, is an attitude, a vital part of their can-do spirit and a leading characteristic of a "product junkie," another phrase that has become a favorite of many managers and officers. John Lange, vice president of marketing for the Specialty Products Division at the time of the interview, describes the importance of the company's details obsession:

A common thread learned over the years is: when we are just a "me too," we don't hit the mark. When we bring to the market that thought value, the plus-up feature, when we "sweat the details" as Wolf says, that's when it all starts to work.

Here's an example of what they mean by sweating the details. They discovered that people didn't like toothbrushes to touch one another in toothbrush holders. So they developed one where the toothbrushes were angled out when inserted.

Earl Haines, vice president of R&D for Specialty Products at the time of the interview, expands on the search for the perfect product:

> We keep looking for differentiation, for advantage, for the little add-on we can put in a product. And it's often not major. This isn't rocket science. We know that. But we work very hard at detail. And we try to execute just as many interesting little features in there as we can find.

Schmitt may emphasize sweating the details, but he also conveys an aura of delight in the innovative process. While talking about the growth reviews that he and all the corporate officers hold twice a year with each business team, he exclaimed: "It's a great day. I mean it's the day that's probably the most fun around here because you can really get excited and enthused about the future of the company."

A CEO excited and enthused about growth review meetings. Now that's spirit.

The CEO's spirit is expressed in other unique ways, like his throwing the coffee pot during the interview. It was his way of expressing his enthusiasm for this fantastic brand-new product that would not break (obviously), would not scorch, would never melt, had a dripless spout, and so on and so forth.

TAKE IDEAS FROM EVERYWHERE

Rubbermaid definitely does not suffer from the NIH—not invented here—disease that afflicts so many other companies. In fact, the company loves to get ideas from anywhere and everywhere.

This makes for great frustration when you are trying to discover who was the one that had the initial idea for a new product. Though that question was repeatedly asked, no one volunteered themselves as the "father" or "mother" of a new product, nor could they point to any other single person. Chuck Carroll said that most products have many parents. "A group of people found a great idea and it kind of fed on itself within that group and they kept expanding upon it."

One dramatic example of synergy in a group came from Larry Porcellato, vice president of marketing for the Home Products Division, who emphasized that much comes out of interaction between the Business Teams and Operating Committees. He pointed to one brainstorming session the two groups had: it lasted just forty-five minutes and they came away with one hundred product ideas.

John Lange best captures the spirit of their "look everywhere" approach: "We take ideas from everyone: customers, consumers, competitors, associates, and top management. The key to success is not where the ideas come from but recognizing a good idea."

A HISTORY OF INNOVATION

The first question asked of Wolf Schmitt was, "What are the real keys behind the company's culture of innovation?" His response:

> The company has a great history, a tradition of innovation. It is really new products that define us in many ways. Ambitious goals with respect to new product define our work, the essence of the company—the tone—the pace. We're fortunate. We inherited that. It's institutionalized. The lore of the company.

During Stan Gault's tenure as CEO from 1980 to 1991, he took the ambitious goal of the Home Products Division—30 percent of sales from products introduced in the past five years—and made it a corporate goal. In the early 1990s, the goal was raised to 33 percent of sales. The other major corporate goal is 15 percent annual growth for the business. These two goals combined are the key to innovation.

Chuck Carroll raised an interesting point about the 15 percent growth goal. This has become more of a driver for innovation in the 1990s because of the decline in inflation. To hit that 15 percent target now, they need many more new products. Perhaps this was behind his thinking to establish a very high goal for the divisions: 10 percent of sales from products introduced in the last twelve months.

BEING STUDENTS OF TRENDS

Here are some of Schmitt's thoughts on the critical role of understanding trends:

We have found that all successes in the past were driven by trends, really understanding the trends going on around us: Legal, fashion, global, demographic, governmental, technological. Any kind of trend creates opportunity. We are unique here: no matter how negative the trends may seem, within each trend there is an opportunity. We challenge people to come up with the most negative trend they can think of.

As an example of a "negative" trend, Schmitt talked about the recent environmental trend, feared by so many but welcomed by them.

While everyone is encouraged to be a trend watcher, Larry Porcellato has that as his explicit mandate. The key of course is to link the trend back to the business. As an example, he points to the graying of the population. For the elderly, you need to make a lot of products more user-friendly because many of them suffer from some form of physical impairment, so the company developed an "easy-open" feature to its food storage products. However, they were not marketed as "gray products," and found broad acceptance in the marketplace.

Pat McCabe, vice president of marketing in the Specialty Products Division, offered another trend example based on her experience as a group product manager in the Home Products Division. At Home Products, she dealt with household containers—wastebaskets, laundry bins, hampers, step stools, buckets. Pretty mundane stuff. Her question was a good one: "What do you do with those products to reach that 15 percent growth goal?"

You look at trends, particularly the baby boomlet and rising number of young kids. Kids love to do the same things their parents do. So the Home Products Division developed a kids' line of these same products for kids and called them Little Roughnecks.

BUSINESS TEAMS AS THE KEY ORGANIZATION UNIT

Rubbermaid recognizes that encouragement, spirit, a history of innovation, and trend watching are all important but they would not go very far if the right corporate structure were not in place to foster, sustain, and channel all this creative energy. The Business Teams are the basic business units and the real drivers of innovation.

These teams are the third stage in an evolutionary organizational process. Now, each product line has a Business Team that is managed by a core of four representatives, one each from marketing, R&D, manufacturing, and finance. The team makes the basic decisions about what product areas they want to go into. Only wholly new businesses make it to the corporate level for final decision.

STORIES OF INNOVATIVE SUCCESS

Each of the nine people interviewed at Rubbermaid—the CEO, one division president (who is now president of the company), five division vice presidents, and two managers—had a story or two about a new product at Rubbermaid. There were tales of step stool toolboxes, plastic planters, tackleboxes, the Little Roughneck line (with Bubbles the Whale), food keepers, RTA (ready-to-assemble) furniture, and doghouses. But the one that got the most attention was the litterless lunch kit.

It was the CEO who spoke glowingly of the way the litterless lunch kit was developed. Wolf Schmitt began by talking about the global environmental trend and how many in the plastics industry perceived that as a threat. Rubbermaid, however, sees it as a "phenomenal opportunity" to demonstrate leadership and be part of the solution.

He jumped in with an example. A province in Canada declared one day a week as a "litterless day" for schoolchildren. Rubbermaid's largest Canadian customer challenged them to develop a product for the litterless day. Simultaneously, customers in the United States were looking for value-added products to promote during the recession, which in turn fed a growing trend: people carrying their lunch to work. So they developed the litterless lunch kit, which was beautifully styled and available in many fashion colors. As Schmitt said, "It was a smash hit. Customers were happy. The government was happy. Schoolchildren loved it. And we developed a good reputation for being part of the environmental solution."

ONE NEW PRODUCT A DAY LEADS TO SO MUCH MORE

One new product a day. Meeting the tough goal of 33 percent of sales from products introduced in the past five years year after year. Rated number one in innovation and as the "Most Admired Corporation in America" in 1994 by *Fortune* magazine. You can't get much better than that in new product development.

But perhaps this is the most amazing fact: 90 percent of the new products Rubbermaid introduces are successes, contrasting with the average for American companies of 90 percent flops.

It is little wonder that under Stan Gault's leadership from 1980 to 1991, Rubbermaid enjoyed a record forty-one quarters of earnings growth, going from a faltering little company to a sturdy $1.8 billion giant in 1992. Its return on equity has averaged 20 percent in recent years. And it enjoys a market capitalization of $5 billion—nearly three times revenues.

As Wolf Schmitt says, "For a company that makes dustpans, that's pretty good."

LESSON: Spectacular product innovation requires setting goals for new product development and developing a creative culture (spirit) that encourages everyone to:

- come up with new ideas
- reinvent old products
- take ideas from everywhere
- sweat the details needed to improve products
- see how new trends create opportunities

 Good Products—That's It
MICROSOFT

"OUR SUCCESS IS BASED ON ONLY ONE THING: GOOD PRODUCTS.
IT'S NOT VERY COMPLICATED."
—BILL GATES, CHAIRMAN AND CEO

THE CHALLENGE

Bill Gates, who dropped out of Harvard at nineteen to start a company with his high school buddy Paul Allen, saw only one clear challenge in the 1980s: continue to turn out blockbuster software products that would make Microsoft *the* intelligence that drives computers. In the 1990s, he saw an even more ambitious challenge: develop new software products that would make Microsoft *the* intelligence behind the emerging Information Highway.

THE RESPONSE

How does one go about building a dominant, some would say dominating, position in the computer industry with so many upstarts and such fierce competitors?

Microsoft's approach—which is for all intents and purposes Bill Gates's approach—is you hire the best and the brightest, you give them enormous challenges and extraordinary freedom, and you create a company gestalt that you're out to win and win big (almost as though that's Microsoft's destiny). Oh yes, you also reward your achievers very well (by 1992, at least 3,400 of the 11,000 people who had worked for Microsoft had become millionaires by virtue of their stockholdings).

New product development doesn't derive from any formal program or structure. Quite the contrary, it arises from the corporate gestalt— almost the mystique of being a Microsoft employee. This is best captured in the comments of a Microsoft employee: "There is very little deadwood here. People just care passionately about what they are doing. I think that's because we've done a pretty good job of putting them into small teams and empowering those teams. They feel like they own the product. It's a world of difference from the more hierarchical organization where decisions are filtered down from the top." What better stimulus is there for new product development than to have your employees feeling like they "own the product"?

A second ingredient is insecurity—this drives the desire to always want to do better: "Bill is at the top and he always wants it to be better and everybody has picked that up through the years." This is precisely what occurred with the development of Word. Microsoft funded many versions of Word before it was good enough to grab substantial market share. This finally occurred in 1990 when the Windows 3.0 version appeared.

The third ingredient—the one that has driven Microsoft straight to the top—is Gates's constant scanning of the horizon, first in the personal computer industry and now in the computer/telecommunications industry. He is always looking for where the next opportunities are, and in particular what the big trends are and how to get out in front of them. His major vision in 1994 was for what he calls "information at your fingertips," all centered on making Microsoft a key player in the Information Highway. But he was also looking at a lot of other things, including a wallet PC, natural language programming, and entering completely new businesses, such as on-line services.

In looking to the future, Gates has the proper perspective: he does not expect Microsoft's current dominant position to guarantee it a leading place on the Information Highway. Success, he knows, will depend on Microsoft's ability to hire and manage brilliant technologists.

A chronicle of Microsoft's breathtaking series of new product introductions and initiatives in just a fifteen month period will dramatically illustrate this horizon-scanning thrust:

- In May 1993, it introduced Windows NT, a new-generation operating system. A big chunk of Microsoft's spending the previous three years (around $150 million) had gone into the development of Windows NT, which the company hoped would get to the electronic heart of big business. Specifically, it would enable office PCs, linked together, to handle such complex processes as inventory management, accounting, and transaction processes that had been done previously only on mainframes or minicomputers. Says Gates: "It sort of defines how high the ceilings will be around here."
- In June 1993, it unveiled Microsoft at Work, its blueprint for the office of the future. This is an office software system that can connect computers, phones, copiers, fax machines, and printers into a seamless web. This move brought Microsoft beyond the PC market (a mere $38 billion in 1992) into the markets for copiers, printers, telephones, and fax machines, which combined exceeded $60 billion in 1992. Gates recognized the large risks involved: "We're putting our name and reputation on the line here. If we don't pull this off, it could jeopardize our future initiatives."
- In October 1993, Microsoft announced that it planned to revamp its entire applications-program line with a new version of Microsoft Office. This is a software "suite" that includes a word processor,

spreadsheet, E-mail, and database package—all for one low price. It is based on a communications technology Microsoft calls Object Linking and Embedding (OLE) that breaks down the barriers between programs. With OLE2 introduced that fall, it would be possible to add new features by adding new modules, which in turn could create a whole new business line for Microsoft.

- In December 1993, Microsoft launched a massive media blitz for its two new software packages designed for kids: Creative Writer and Fine Artist. It viewed these two as the opening salvo in an all-out assault on the growing home market, for which it hoped to introduce more than a hundred products within two years. To accomplish this, it did away with business units based on technologies in its consumer division, replacing them with units organized around "usage opportunities." Sales in its Consumer Software Division in June 1994 were running at $300 million per year, triple the rate of a year earlier.

- In March 1994, the company announced its first major Information Highway deals: two projects with cable TV giant Tele-Communication. Again, these were just the first steps of a far more ambitious market-extending agenda—to make Microsoft *the* intelligence managing the Information Highway in the 1990s and beyond. To achieve this, Microsoft established in 1991 a massive research project called Advanced Technology Group (ATG). By 1994, this group had 500 members and a $150 million a year budget (nearly a fourth of its total R&D budget). ATG has two parts: Microsoft Research conducts long-term research into such areas as speech recognition and new user interfaces, and Advanced Consumer Technology, which explores technology for new markets, including pocket computers, set-top boxes, interactive TV interfaces, and services and video programming.

- In late March 1994, Gates commanded a new product–new market blitzkrieg in a stunning week of announcements and activities:
  - He started the week by unveiling plans for Teledesic, a joint venture with McCaw (America's largest cellular phone firm) that would result in a $9 billion wireless global communications network, linked by 840 new satellites.
  - Gates then announced a deal with Japan's Nippon Telegraph and Telephone to design business applications for CD-ROM and fax machines.
  - He threw in a trip to Beijing where the president, Jiang Zemin, asked him to help China, the greatest market of all for the Information Highway, to help develop its information industry.
  - To close out the week, Gates announced a $152 million deal with Mobile Telecommunication Technologies, America's largest paging firm, to develop a nationwide wireless network for sending and receiving data from personal computers and other devices.

- In April 1994, Microsoft introduced a new arsenal of groupware products aimed right at the market lead that Lotus enjoyed in that arena with its Notes product. Groupware is the glue that ties networked PCs together, allowing workers to share information and work closely with one another. Almost immediately following this introduction, Gates announced that Microsoft will develop a new class of products in this area called *Information Exchange*. While Notes held the commanding position with 750,000 users, Gates recognized that there are nearly 30 million other networked computers that could use groupware.
- In May 1994, Microsoft unveiled one of its most ambitious projects, video server software called Tiger. Designed to serve up television shows and digitized movies across phone or cable networks, Tiger is just the "first piece" of an end-to-end interactive video system.
- In July 1994, Microsoft announced its plans to introduce Chicago, a hugely ambitious overhaul of its two major products, the MS DOS operating system and the Windows user interface. Chicago is anticipated to spur new demand by increasing Windows user-friendliness and generate around $1 billion in sales in its first year. Some feel that it will transform the messaging industry as we know it.

THE RESULT

Talk about powerful new products: MS-DOS, Word, Windows, Excel, Windows NT, Microsoft at Work, Microsoft Office. The MS-DOS operating system is used by 81 percent of the 22 million IBM-compatible PCs built every year. And over two thirds of all PCs sold in 1992 had Windows already on board. Just MS-DOS and Windows alone generated revenues of $2.3 billion between 1989 and 1992, with just under $1 billion coming in 1992. This was more than 90 percent of all the revenue growth in the PC software industry that year.

Microsoft's sales rose 36 percent in fiscal 1993, to $3.8 billion. That means that it had more revenues than its seven closest publicly held rivals combined. The $3.8 billion represented a nineteenfold increase in just seven years. It enjoys a net profit margin of around 25 percent, and its net income of nearly $1 billion would be more than twice their combined profits. Powerful products yield powerful profits!

In late 1993, senior U.S. executives affirmed Microsoft's tremendous ability to envision new products and markets when they voted it the country's number one innovative company.

[
LESSON: You hire the best and brightest and give them enormous challenges and extraordinary freedom, create a company gestalt that believes you can always come up with a better product, and constantly scan the horizon for major new product and market opportunities.
]

Spin Out Rather Than Spin Off
THERMO ELECTRON

"WE STRUCTURED THERMO ELECTRON SPECIFICALLY TO STIMULATE GROWTH AND TO PROVIDE THE INCENTIVES THAT ARE MOST IMPORTANT TO ENTREPRENEURIAL MANAGERS. I FIRMLY BELIEVE THAT OUR STRUCTURE IS THE WAVE OF THE FUTURE."

—GEORGE HATSOPOULOS, FOUNDER, CHAIRMAN, PRESIDENT, AND CEO

THE CHALLENGE

Thermo Electron has faced two major challenges since George Hatsopoulos founded it in his garage in 1956 as a company that would identify emerging societal problems and develop technological solutions. First came the challenge of developing new types of businesses to keep growth going. As described by Hatsopoulos, an independent-thinking CEO if there ever was one: "Every line of business you are currently in may be growing very rapidly, but eventually that growth is bound to stop. If you are seriously committed to growth, the only way you can ensure that your company will continue to grow is to develop new types of businesses to perpetuate that growth." Acting on his own advice, Hatsopoulos expanded from the company's original activity—research in energy-conversion technologies—into six major lines of business.

This expanding diversity and the growth that accompanied it caused Hatsopoulos to worry about his Massachusetts-based company's future.

He was concerned that as the company grew larger and broader, its entrepreneurial spirit would fade. "It is very well known that when companies reach a certain size they have great difficulty expanding into new lines of business. The entrepreneurial spirit gets squashed. The bureaucracy, the structure, and the hierarchy get in the way." His second concern was that R&D outlays to get new technologies moving were dragging down earnings. A final challenge was to motivate and retain his best engineers as Thermo grew and diversified.

THE RESPONSE

Being the creative, free-spirited thinker he is, Hatsopoulos saw a single neat and distinctive solution to all three challenges. Recognizing there was tremendous strength associated with small companies, he said, "We came out with the idea of splitting the company into small pieces that would be cobbled together by some common culture." Under this spin-out strategy, he began in 1983 to one by one spin out several divisions of the company as they developed new core technologies, creating by 1993 nine new publicly held companies.

There are three ways that its spin-outs differ from the traditional spin-offs of other companies. One, Thermo retains a majority of the equity in the new company. Second, it offers new stock to the public rather than distributing stock to existing shareholders. Third, it sells its core technologies, not its underperformers.

Certainly the spin-out strategy serves as a major motivator for employees to innovate. If you develop a great idea, rather than just a "nice job" or even a bonus, you may get to run your own company. Or as Hatsopoulos puts it, "There's no better way to stimulate creativity than to see a guy next to you get $500,000 in options for a great idea."

The strategy does indeed foster a constant search for ways to develop a product in new ways. John Wood, the chief executive of Thermedics (the first spin-out), points out that whenever anyone came up with a bright idea, it would ripple through the company, and someone else would find a way to use it in an entirely new way. In short, people are always asking, "What else can we do with this?"

There are some costs to the spin-out strategy. Hatsopolous puts a price tag of $3 million to $4 million a year on the added legal and administrative costs of running so many separate public companies. But the benefits are well worth it.

THE RESULTS

Its distinctive spin-out philosophy has enabled Thermo Electron to succeed with its general strategy of spotting new markets and then innovating like an agile start-up. Its divisions are in hot competition with one another to become the next spin-off. The bar is set quite high: a business must show the potential to grow 30 percent a year before management will cut it loose. The spin-outs, as well as scores of acquisitions, have made Thermo a highly diversified technology factory, with products ranging from artificial hearts to smokestack monitors to bomb detectors.

A major side benefit of this structure is that creative employees, who in many other high-tech companies often leave to start their own business, stick with Thermo Electron because of the lure of a high payoff and the support of the parent.

It's the best of both worlds for the spin-out company. It has the independence to make decisions quickly and seize new opportunities as its smaller competitors do, while enjoying the support of a Fortune 500 parent.

The parent company has certainly thrived under this strategy. From 1983 to 1993, sales soared from around $200 million to well over $1.2 billion. And Thermo stood at the top of the Fortune 500 list for 1993 for greatest growth in earnings per share (over ten years): an astounding 97.1 percent annual rate, more than double the growth rate of the second company on the list.

[
LESSON: Use major new products and technologies to create new companies, thus providing incentives for entrepreneurs within your company to do their best and create more new products.
]

Wackiness and Reinvention
ODETICS

"WE HAVE ADOPTED A POSTURE OF NOT INSTITUTIONALIZING ANYTHING. IF SOMETHING IS A SUCCESS, WE DON'T WANT IT TO GO ON IN PERPETUITY. THERE IS A POINT IN THE SUCCESS CYCLE THAT YOU SAY, 'LET'S QUIT RIGHT NOW.' AND I ALWAYS GET THE RESPONSE, 'HOW COME WE'RE NOT DOING THAT AGAIN? THAT WAS GREAT.' AND I COME UP WITH THE SAME ANSWER EACH TIME: 'LET'S REMEMBER IT AS BEING GREAT BECAUSE THERE IS A POINT WHERE IF IT PERSISTS, IT BECOMES THE OBLIGATORY COMPANY PICNIC OR THAT SORT OF THING, AND IT CARRIES A LIFE OF ITS OWN.' IN A SENSE OUR WAY IS MORE CHALLENGING BECAUSE IT MEANS THAT YOU CAN'T REST ON YOUR SUCCESS."

—KEVIN DALY, CHIEF TECHNICAL OFFICER

THE CHALLENGE

The challenge was to create a company where it would be fun to come to work. A company where creativity and risk taking could flourish because of the fun atmosphere. Yes, this really is true. Listen to Joel Slutzky, co-founder, explain his philosophy:

> We feel that if it's not fun to get up in the morning and go to work, then it doesn't matter what the P&L looks like. You've missed something. Life isn't that long that you can overlook the social aspect of the company as well. And, in fact, we've found that there is a tight linkage between how you feel about the company and how you are going to do as far as growth and profitability and things like that.

THE RESPONSE

Even though the company has grown to 600 employees, there's still a Fun Committee with the sole responsibility of thinking up wild and crazy activities. Many of these activities are led by top corporate officers.

But as the saying goes, there's a method to all this madness. This atmosphere fosters a feeling of freedom and creativity, which leads to constant change and innovation. A fun atmosphere also supports working in teams. Here's how, according to Marti Cassell-Fix, a software engineer: "Everyone works very hard and everyone is very team-oriented. They do their own part, but they support everyone else. If we're working on a deadline or a program, as soon as one person gets their work done, they will go and help the next person to get theirs done."

THE RESULTS

What results from this freewheeling environment is a company that constantly reinvents itself it terms of products. In the early 1980s, the company's main product was digital tape recorders for space vehicles. Today, these account for only a third of its business. Back in 1983, they got into robotics through Odex 1, a six-legged walking robot. This in turn led to a "cart machine," which TV studios use to automatically play commercials and programming as well as automated tape libraries for a complete mass storage market. The latter product line has been spun off into a wholly owned subsidiary, ATZ Products.

Their engineers also dreamed up time-lapse recorders used in ATMs that can record thirty full days of transactions on regular VCR tape. The company's newest product is a digital signal processing system that transmits line-action video over the phone lines.

> LESSON: Creating an unconventional place to work —breaking-the-rules, wacky, spontaneous, and fun —can bring out creativity and risk taking and result in a host of new products.

 166 Companies to Create Products
JOHNSON & JOHNSON

"WE'RE ALWAYS FOLDING SOME COMPANY AND CREATING OTHERS."
—RALPH LARSEN, CHAIRMAN AND CEO

THE CHALLENGE

In the 1980s, Johnson & Johnson's main challenge was to keep decentralization and empowerment fresh and working as effectively as they had for the company since the 1930s. Can a company really keep creating new operating companies well past the one-hundred-company mark, entering new markets all the while, without chaos taking over?

THE RESPONSE

Johnson & Johnson envisions new products and new markets about as well as any other company. But it is not due to any formal product development strategy or program. It all stems from the company's structure and culture.

First, its unique structure. Decentralization is practiced with a vengeance. The president of each of the 166 companies is expected to act independently, deciding who will work for them, what products they'll produce, and who their customers will be. CEO Ralph Larsen compares his role to that of an orchestra conductor, giving his players inspiration and direction but above all giving them abundant creative freedom.

These independent units scramble relentlessly for new products and new markets. With so much risk taking being encouraged, Larsen's attitude toward failure is important: some failures are to be expected and when they occur you might cut those companies loose. At J&J, failure means not attaining or maintaining the first or second leadership position in a market. It's been said that knowing when to let go contributes as much to its success as its flurry of new product introductions.

The decentralized structure is held together, and made to work, by a strong company culture. This culture centers on a set of core values, expressed in a document called "Our Credo," that brings a sense of family to all employees, wherever they are located or whatever their product line may be. J&J emphasizes that "the most important thing we have in this corporation is the value system we live by."

A number of elements of the company's culture contribute to its success with new products and markets. It moves quickly to license technological and medical advances developed by others. They aren't inflicted with the not invented here syndrome of many companies. Nor do they display any arrogance in their willingness to play catch-up with much smaller companies. In the late 1980s, they looked at far-smaller United States Surgical and its newly invented advanced instruments for endoscopic surgery. Seeing a huge market potential, they mounted an all-out effort to catch this nimble and shrewd competitor. It also looks to its customers as prime sources of ideas for new products or ways to improve existing products, using the consumer innovation groups described earlier.

Many of these elements come together in one of its most interesting individual success stories of the past decade. It began in 1983 when a Johnson & Johnson staff person heard of a new Danish technology to produce disposable contact lenses. Managers at the Vistakon division wanted to start a new business of making and selling such lenses, so J&J bought the rights and proceeded to spend hundreds of millions of dollars on the product over the next seven years. All the while, the unit was small enough that its president, Bernard Walsh, could make rapid-fire decisions regarding production or marketing with no interference from headquarters.

Freedom and nimbleness backed by sizable resources—a winning combination for many of J&J's units over the past decade. It's also a winning combination for the entire company, which sees its many new products as "largely the result of our investment in R&D, which reached a record level $1.3 billion in 1994."

THE RESULTS

Let's begin with the results that came from funding the managers back in 1983 who wanted to take a flyer on this very new market for disposable lenses. Vistakon has become the world's largest disposable contact lens company, with sales well in excess of $300 million in 1993.

Numerous examples like this add up to a pretty impressive whole. In 1993, one third of the company's sales came from products introduced in the past five years. New businesses? Of the principal businesses listed in its 1993 annual report, more than half didn't even exist ten years before. And new markets? Nearly half of its sales come from outside the United States—in 155 countries—much of it generated in the past decade.

When J&J has a good product, it stretches it as far as possible. Tylenol not only had to survive the tampering scare in the 1980s but it also had to fend off the fierce challenge of Advil from American Home Products. Today, there are more than twenty shapes and sizes of Tylenol in five categories—all of which generate $1 billion in annual sales.

A number of J&J's subsidiaries have done so well with employee empowerment and training that they could have been featured in Chapters 3 and 4. Ethicon, at its plant in Puerto Rico, emphasized teams and put each employee through the World Class Manufacturing University in the late 1980s. The results were that every operator in the plant was certified to check his or her own quality, allowing an operator-to-quality-assurance-technician ratio of forty-five to one and an operator to supervisor ratio of thirty-eight to one. In addition, the defect rate is only 390 parts per million. At Johnson & Johnson Medical in Sherman, Texas, nearly 99 percent of all plant operators were trained in Integrated Quality Systems and 75 percent of the workers took part in 275 Quality Improvement Teams. The continuous-improvement efforts of these teams resulted in $2.6 million in savings in 1990 alone.

Looking at the big picture, in its 106 years J&J has never posted a loss. Over the past decade, revenue has more than doubled, dividends more than tripled, and earnings per share have risen an average 13.3 percent.

[LESSON: Use decentralization to give your business units abundant creative freedom and resources, and balance centralized culture with a strong structure of core values, and new products will pour forth.]

8 : GO GLOBAL

Perhaps Lee Berlin, chairman of LecTec says it best: "To be competitive, you have to worry about that little company over in Germany or in Japan. He's going to be over in your backyard unless you are in his backyard first."

Go global. For many American companies, that is a simple, basic imperative, often for survival and certainly for growth. Joseph Montgomery, founder of Cannondale, has the right guiding philosophy: if you are going to have a successful consumer product today, you have to be a world player.

Fortunately, almost any company can become a world player. The companies in this chapter demonstrate that no matter how small you are, no matter where you are located, no matter what your product is, you can go global and reap handsome rewards.

What does it take? Bill Raduchel, the COO of Sun Microsystems, summed it up beautifully:

There are two things a global company needs to have: a global network and global people. Companies don't do business with companies. People do business with people. A great global network is important. But it only augments and extends personal relationships. It doesn't let you build a relationship like people do.

One thing is clear: companies go global for a wide variety of reasons and they go global in a variety of ways. Many emphasize exporting (Sun Microsystems, Rust Evader, Wadia Digital, and Cannondale) while others emphasize investing abroad (Air Products and Chemicals). Some rely heavily on overseas distributors (Sun Microsystems and Rust Evader), while others shun such distributors (Cannondale). But one theme unites all five companies: the results of their global efforts are spectacular and are a driving force in the overall growth of the company. The companies in this chapter derive between 40 percent to 90 percent of their total revenues from overseas sales.

Following our practice of featuring companies that undertook major new initiatives in the recent past, such longtime export stalwarts as Boeing, Caterpillar, and many other major exporters will not be covered. In 1993, Boeing and Caterpillar ranked number one and number three respectively among America's fifty largest industrial exporters, in percentage of total sales from exports (57.9 percent and 32.3 percent). Certainly their outstanding example over the years played an important role in alerting a large number of companies to the critical importance of going global. We also wish to acknowledge Gillette as a leader in the investing abroad strategy, as it has successfully entered three huge markets in recent years: China, India, and Russia.

SEEING OPPORTUNITIES AND ESTABLISHING GOALS

What motivates companies to go global? All have to initially see the opportunities and benefits. After doing so, some want to firm up their vision and establish corporate goals for the percentage of revenues to be derived from overseas sales.

Rust Evader is the perfect example of a company that was not in any crisis but simply saw a great opportunity. In 1989, it decided that its product, an electronic corrosion control device for motor vehicles, might have better potential abroad than in the United States. The reason wasn't too profound: overseas, people keep their cars longer.

Air Products and Chemicals is an example of a company constantly on the lookout for big developments, and hence opportunities, overseas. In 1957, it responded to the European Common Market formation, and in the late 1980s it invested heavily to take full advantage of the move toward a single market in Europe under the EC 92 initiative.

Also in the late 1980s, it moved quickly in the world's fastest-growing region, Asia, establishing a presence in seven countries between 1986 and 1990. In the early 1990s, it focused on China, the fastest-growing country in the region.

Some companies are bold enough and confident enough to look to Japan as an opportunity. Sun Microsystems saw a major niche in the Japanese computer industry, while Cannondale recognized that the Japanese would love its high-end bicycles if they could be exposed to them. Interestingly, both Sun Microsystems and Air Products and Chemicals emphasized that making it in Japan was very important to them, for if you can meet their high quality standards, you can compete anywhere.

Two of the companies also set explicit export and overseas sales goals. When Wadia Digital was first established, its initial goal was to derive 28 percent of revenues from export sales. Air Products and Chemicals established its global goal after operating abroad for nearly three decades. In the mid-1980s, it established the goal of increasing the percentage of its sales coming from outside the United States from around 25 percent to 50 percent. Meanwhile, Sun Microsystems has never had global goals, with its CEO Scott McNealy believing that "goals only limit you."

MARCH TO YOUR OWN DRUMMER

The companies in this chapter follow few fixed patterns in going global. Sun Microsystems is a fascinating study, for while it has a definite business model it follows, the model itself has been heretical, and the company has never had global goals or a global plan, it sells only a tiny fraction of its products directly, and it doesn't manufacture in foreign markets. As opposed to the traditional direct model, Sun's approach is to serve specific overseas markets with assistance from local third-party product, service, and distribution companies that have extensive experience with local requirements and cultures.

In sharp contrast, Cannondale chose to ignore the advice it received from old Japan hands and shunned distributors when it entered the Japanese market. It relied on the company's general direct-to-dealer approach.

Rust Evader's drive to big-time export success began with a low-cost ad placed in *Commercial News USA* that generated a flood of responses. Wadia Digital saw the world as its market even before the company was founded and its first major purchases came from six foreign countries because it had targeted key distributors in each. Air Products and Chemicals' overall approach can best be summarized as "invest abroad, invest again, and invest some more."

GOING GLOBAL BIG-TIME

Why go global? The results of these five companies speak for themselves. First, a company often sees opportunities for higher growth markets. Exports or manufacturing overseas can produce the bulk of your sales and profits. Air Products and Chemicals is well on the way to reaching its 50 percent goal, as it already derives over 40 percent of revenues from overseas sales. Cannondale also finds that foreign sales account for 40 percent of its total sales (1992), a sharp increase from only 5 percent in 1988. And Sun Microsystems in early 1994 was deriving 54.4 percent of its revenues from exports alone.

Second, companies want to challenge the best. In recent years, this has often been the Japanese. Companies can do well in the large and lucrative Japanese market. Sales of Cannondale Japan quadrupled in the year after its first bike was shipped, and the company showed profits in its first year. Sun Microsystems is number one in Japan's workstation vendor market, making it the only foreign company to lead in a computer segment in the Japanese market.

Third, companies can often achieve dramatic export results quickly. Perhaps the champ in terms of quick and dramatic results is Rust Evader, which two years into its exporting campaign was exporting 88 percent of its production to thirty-five countries. Wadia Digital is right in the running. Remember its initial goal of 28 percent export sales? In each of its first five years, export sales ranged from 70 percent to 80 percent every year.

Break the Mold and Sell to the World
SUN MICROSYSTEMS

At just twelve years of age, Sun Microsystems is a global giant. It has taken the world by storm since sending its first workstation abroad in 1983. From that humble base of a few isolated workstations sitting in universities in New Zealand and Australia, Sun Microsystems derived an astounding 54.4 percent of its revenues from exports alone in the first quarter of 1994. The list of its global number ones is daunting:

- the number one supplier of RISC workstations and servers worldwide (a 39.8 percent share of the world market in 1993)
- the number one workstation computer maker in Japan, the only foreign company to hold a leading market share in that country
- ranked number one in Hong Kong, China (Mainland), and Korea, and controls over 40 percent of the workstation/server market in Asia
- the number one vendor in Europe in 1992 with 33.5 percent of the market
- the leading vendor in Latin America, ranked number one in Mexico, Brazil, Venezuela, Chile, and Columbia

This international success translated directly into spectacular overall corporate performance in recent years. In the decade 1984–1993, its revenues exploded more than one-hundredfold to $4.3 billion. Revenues per employee were at $352,000 in the first quarter of 1994, and gross profit margins stood at a strong 41 percent, both figures far outstripping its major computer maker rivals. Scott McNealy, its young CEO, ties it all together: "When you diversify your portfolio internationally, you have a much more consistent earnings stream. We've made money every year for the past twelve years in the computer business. I don't know any other computer technology company that can say that."

Fantastic! How did they do it? What was their strategy—their secret for attaining such great global success?

They did it by breaking virtually every rule in the book. They defied, and often turned upside down, conventional wisdom at every turn.

Sun has no global goals. Remember that "goals only limit you" was NcNealy's response to a question about them. Further, it followed a whole series of turn-conventional-wisdom-upside-down moves.

- Sun sells only a tiny fraction of its products abroad directly.
- Sun doesn't establish manufacturing operations in foreign markets it enters.
- Sun's open systems approach made it a maverick in the computer industry.
- It entered Japan by establishing multiple partners.

So which of these accounts for its global success? All the above. It understood the big growth opportunities were outside the United States. Bill Raduchel puts it simply: "It's as Willie Sutton said when he was asked why he robbed banks: 'because that's where the money is.' If you want to sell computers, you've got to sell where the demand is." And Sun recognized, virtually from day one, that the big demand was going to come from overseas markets.

Joe Roebuck, vice president for Worldwide Field Operations, provides the second reason for Sun's success: "I hope it doesn't ruin your chapter that we didn't have this brilliant plan—it was real opportunistic." When he was challenged about there being no detailed corporate strategy for going global, he responded: "All I knew was I'm going to go and set up businesses around this part of the world because there's a lot of business there." Asked if he had complete autonomy, he said: "I would say the idea was as long as we had the U.S. and Europe covered really well, it's fine to do this other stuff."

Vision. Opportunistic. And relationships. Sun Microsystems is very big on close relationships with its partners in each country. And you build these relationships through people. A great global network, which handles 1 million E-mail messages a day from around the world for just 13,000 employees, is important. But the technology only augments and extends personal relationships. It doesn't let you build a relationship like people do. And Sun, as we discovered, has some terrific global people that drove its international success.

THE BOSS'S VISION

We begin with Scott McNealy because, though Sun Microsystems is not Scott McNealy, he does have a lot to do with where Sun is today. So we're going to let him do most of the talking in this section. Important to his insights is the spirit lying behind the words. These were his opening thoughts when he was first asked to reflect on the reasons for Sun's global success.

The first reason has to do with open interfaces, which are more attractive to foreign companies than to U.S. companies. They do not want to be dominated by a foreign company. So when we went to the international arenas, we offered open chip architectures with SPARC, open operating environments with Solaris, open networking with NFS, and they go, 'You mean you won't sue me if we build a clone?' Most of the marketplaces clone manufacturers. The whole strategy is prointernational.

I tell international audiences, "Please keep buying these proprietary technologies and sending your money to us every year because your money makes America a much better place to live. It gets them angry. They want to go open, go SPARC, go Solaris, go network-based computing so they don't get locked in.

Second, I grew up in Detroit. People there had the most Detroit-centric view. My dad only went internationally for automobile dealer trips. I figured I'd much rather go fight the battle in their harbor, not our harbor. So when we got Sun rocking and rolling, I said we're not going to stand around and wait for somebody to build up a workstation business and then use that to go dump offshore and blow us away. We're going to go over there and win. And most important, we said we had to win in Japan. That is the best way to test your level of quality in a world-class way. If we can ship world-class quality products to Japan, I never hear a peep out of U.S. or European customers.

They trained us on quality. They beat us up. They hammered on us. They embarrassed us. They worked with us. They put people in our factories. And they made us world-class suppliers. If we had not been shipping into the Japanese market, we never would have learned how to do that. That is absolutely the most important reason we're trying to sell to the Japanese market—because they will train you up in quality.

When the CEO of Fujitsu sits me down and reads me the defect of every defective machine we've shipped to them in excruciating detail for an hour and a half, you think I don't want to come back here and work the quality issues?

Going international was a requirement from my perspective. The imports can't invade if you've already invaded the domestic sites abroad.

The third reason centers on the fact that we are in the business of establishing global open interfaces. You can't get unit volume just here in the U.S. Can't be a niche player—the U.S. is just too open. You play globally to get the unit volume.

The final reason is that I'm not a believer in the U.S. coming up with every new fad. If you don't have people living abroad, you won't bring back the latest innovations.

OPEN SYSTEMS

Open systems is one of the founding philosophies of Sun Microsystems. For most of the 1980s, Sun was the one champion of this concept in the computer industry. In the 1990s, it is becoming rapidly accepted by many former opponents. Open systems are based on freely available, vendor-neutral interface standards and therefore offer users a wide range of product choices from multiple vendors.

Ultimately, the goal of open systems is to provide the user with choices: the ability to select multiple products from multiple vendors and integrate them seamlessly on powerful networks. Through open systems, companies are able to make every resource on the network available to any authorized user who needs it, from any physical location on the network.

How does this basic business model factor into their export success? Bill Raduchel:

> If you want to have exports, and have other companies support you, you must recognize that they won't want to support you if they feel they are captive. Therefore, we could sign up Fujitsu, Toshiba, and all the other partners because we weren't tying them down to us. They could easily leave us at any time. Most other companies have proprietary systems, but our technology is open, anyone can license it. It's fundamentally counterintuitive: the way to build your technology is to give it away. Fundamentally the way you get people to support your technology is you give away the interfaces. You let people go and build competing products because that makes your interface the winning interface. Thus open systems make us very attractive to partners. From their perspective, if it's an open system, whether my investment succeeds is controlled by my own efforts. Sun wouldn't have gotten anywhere in Japan if we were a closed-system vendor.

Open systems was McNealy's brainchild. Was it well accepted in the company at first? "There was huge opposition. And there still is. It's so counterintuitive. You make it successful by giving it away" repeats Raduchel with a big chuckle. He concluded his excited spiel on open systems with this critical point: "It's always neutral to bad in the near term and always neutral to great in the long term—so depending on your perspective on life, it's smart or stupid. It's very much a time perspective question."

One thing's for certain—Scott McNealy hasn't lost his enthusiasm for the idea. As he was being asked, "So you feel this open interface world is—" he interrupted and shot back, "Inevitable. Unstoppable. A freight train, a tidal wave. We've ridden it from zero to nearly $5 billion in twelve years. Not a lot of other waves are that big."

THE PARTNERSHIP MODEL

Open systems feeds right into Sun's partnership model, the other leg on which it builds all its international business. Indeed, though the partnership approach is not unique to the computer industry, Sun feels that "no other vendor has implemented this strategy so completely and successfully on a worldwide scale." Here's how it works.

As the world's leading supplier of UNIX workstations and open client-server solutions, Sun's core competency is designing and building a leading-edge hardware/operating environment platform. Other suppliers can leverage in creating value-added products. Thus, Sun's business is based on a partnership model where third parties incorporate, complement, or add value to the Sun foundation.

Understanding this business model is crucial to understanding Sun's investment philosophy in Asia and most other parts of the world. Unlike other major computer vendors who do business abroad, Sun's priority is to invest in strategic business relationships rather than dedicated in-country corporate staff and facilities. As opposed to the traditional "direct" model favored by its competitors, Sun's approach is to serve specific markets with assistance from local third-party product, service, and distribution companies that have extensive experience with local requirements and cultures.

What it boils down to is that Sun recognized early on that it alone couldn't reach all its potential customers nor could it alone meet the needs of all its worldwide customers. The solution was to get many people operating together in mutually beneficial partnerships.

Here's the rather simple path they take in each new country they enter. First, they seek out multiple distributors. The chief characteristics they look for are: (1) people who understand the technology, (2) financial stability, (3) vertical expertise they can bring to the market, and (4) ability to bring other products to bear with Sun's products. The latter point is important. This means that the distributor can make money on the Sun piece and sell the other pieces around it. Most companies following the direct approach do it all themselves. But the

Sun way fosters the growth of these businesses. As Tim Dwyer, vice president and general manager of intercontinental operations says, "That makes us very popular. We get known as the company that does good partnering."

After they have located multiple partners, they put in a station manager. This is usually closely followed by a subsidiary being established. The subsidiary is then the front line for securing further distributors and generally running the business. For instance, the Hong Kong subsidiary is responsible for all future activity in Asia outside Japan, which includes generating new activity in China. In virtually all its foreign markets, other than some European countries and fifteen Americans in Japan, Sun hires all nationals of the country. Scott McNealy depicts the commonsense wisdom behind this approach: "It's so much easier to take someone with a lifetime of experience and teach them about Sun than to take Sun people and teach them a lifetime of experiences." He followed with a perfect illustration of the value of nationals. "Dr. Amo [who heads the Japan subsidiary] went to school with everybody in Japan. He actually said so."

HOW SUN IS FLOURISHING IN JAPAN

The story of Sun Microsystems' experience in Japan deserves a book in itself. It would certainly show every naysayer who cites the difficulty of entering the Japanese market how it can be done. Probably the chief reason for Sun's success is their willingness to break the mold, followed closely by great perseverance.

"At first," Joe Roebuck said, "I had a hard time convincing many people there's this big market in Asia." One person he didn't have to convince was Tim Dwyer, who joined Sun in 1987 after spending four years in Japan with PrimeComputer. Dwyer's key role was not only as a global visionary but as a global foot soldier—one of the true global people. In Scott McNealy's words:

> I give Tim Dwyer a lot of credit. He took me over to Japan once every three to four months. We went and visited the top executives every time. Were very stiff at first. Uncomfortable meetings. They were uncomfortable. I was uncomfortable. We were talking through interpreters. They just got used to seeing me. They knew I wasn't going anywhere. They knew I was committed. They knew I was going to continue to come visit them. To this day, they don't come visit me. I've got to constantly go visit them, but that's all right. They're sending me checks, so I'll go see them. Now I actually have eight-year relationships with

some of these people. We're like buddies. That's the way it is—you've got to be
willing to grind it out on this stuff.

Those last dozen words speak volumes: "You've got to be willing to
grind it out on this stuff." Even when you're a high-flying entrepreneur
and rising star in the computer industry. You can't get too proud. You
just can't sit back and expound your vision. You've got to do the work.

The other critical trait that emerges about McNealy is his perseverance. He later added: "I wasn't going to lose the staredown." He knew
that these elderly Japanese chieftains weren't about to instantly embrace a brash young twenty-nine-year old when they first met him. So
he settled in for the long haul.

That gets us back to Tim Dwyer. Anybody who logs 2 million miles
on their frequent flyer account should get a "Global Person of the
Year" award. Tim was hired to get Sun firmly established in Japan and
to grow the business there. He was told that if Sun didn't become a
major player there, the Japanese would be a major player in Sun's U.S.
market. Scott had also said that the firm could never be a successful
company long-term unless they could succeed in Japan.

The first thing Dwyer did was to broaden the channels of distribution there. Sun thought it was limiting to have just two, C. Itoh and
Toshiba. Broadening ran entirely contrary to conventional wisdom,
which said you don't have multiple partners. Nobody had ever gone
this route before. So Dwyer set out to line up all five of Japan's major
banking groups as partners since they controlled around 50 percent of
overall business in Japan. Sun told each banking group to focus on
companies they're closely allied with and compete fiercely elsewhere.

To develop the relationships, Dwyer set up partner meetings with
each company individually. At first, these quarterly meetings took three
days. They were "arduous." They felt Sun wasn't doing that well. So
Sun had its people work with their counterparts until the problems
were ironed out. After one year, the meetings were considerably
shorter and not as many top executives needed to be involved. The
companies were intermeshed through their working-level people.

Dwyer pointed out one immediate and major benefit to Sun from
these Japanese relationships. The standards were now different. It
looked around the world to see who was doing the best. As he put
it, "The company changed forever after that immersion with the
Japanese."

Dwyer emphasized that Sun didn't sell directly against them (except for a small share in the education market). "That was key." But what about the issue of whether this dependence on partners leaves Sun at their mercy? Dwyer responds, "They all saw their self-interest aligned with Sun's. Even if one did bail out, we had a lot more. Nobody quit. They've all grown with us and are now more closely interwoven than ever."

What about the question of attracting Japanese nationals to come work for an upstart American company? No problem according to Dwyer, because "since we were doing it differently [open systems and multiple partners], we attracted some of the best people."

This approach yielded remarkable results. Sun was the number one workstation vendor in Japan within one year, a spot it has held ever since. Japan went from being about 3 percent of Sun's total sales in 1986 to 15 percent by 1990. In 1994, it was around 18 percent, which meant that Japanese sales were approaching $900 million. As McNealy said, "Japan is doing wonders for us now. Without Japan, we'd be having a rough quarter."

THE SAME APPROACH EVERYWHERE

It was Joe Roebuck who said it: "Same old formula: find a local distributor, a really good one, sign them up, get the business started, and when it gets big enough put a station manager in." That's the process that Sun repeats over and over again, resulting in its having partners in nearly fifty countries around the world in just one decade.

We don't have the space to go into all the delightful stories of how they lined up the initial partners. You have to hear Joe Roebuck spin those tales, as he was actively engaged in many of the earliest forays. Within the first ten minutes of the interview, we had heard hilarious tales of how Sun started its operations in Japan, Korea, Singapore, China, and Venezuela. They involved a canceled appointment in Korea which led to paying a bellhop $10 to write down all the companies in the phone book with electronics in their name. In Singapore, it was a flat turndown, a courtesy dinner to give them help, a serendipitous meeting with an Indian professor from the nation's leading university, and a "done deal." In China, which no one knew anything about, their first piece of advice from their newfound expert, conveyed at a bar in Hong Kong, was, "Don't do business there. But if you must, open in

Hong Kong, but with no machines. The Chinese like to go to Hong Kong to play and to California for great per diems."

The company carefully looks at where the growing economies of the world are and what their information technology component is. And Roebuck has settled down a bit and is now one of three individuals to determine the company's allocation of funds for international expansion. Sun's seven guys that oversee the major regions of the world come in with their business plan once a year. They typically say, "I want to open x cities and I need y people to do it." Joe Roebuck, Joe's boss, and the vice president for finance then determine who gets what, based on their firsthand knowledge of these areas, where they have already been and met with the local managers and major customers.

SUN'S VISION FOR THE FUTURE

Sun's vision for the future is clear: it is a ⅓, ⅓, ⅓ vision. There's a slight difference in the breakdown. Scott McNealy says that in a few years, Sun will derive ⅓ of its business from the United States, ⅓ from the Pacific Rim and Latin America, and ⅓ from Eastern and Western Europe. Tim Dwyer sees it as ⅓ U.S.-based, ⅓ from Western Europe and Japan, and ⅓ from emerging new markets. Perhaps this isn't surprising since Dwyer oversees emerging market expansion.

Actually, the two are not that far apart. Under both, Sun is looking for substantial growth in China, India, Russia, Latin America, the Middle East, and many African nations. The main point is that Sun is looking to expanding foreign sales to drive its growth in the years ahead.

To this end, Sun launched in 1993 a series of three New World Tours. The first took Scott McNealy and another seven or eight top executives to Asia. The second was to Latin America. The third is planned for South Africa, some northern African nations, the Middle East, and Eastern Europe. Everyone interviewed at Sun acknowledged the value of these trips, for gaining knowledge of these areas and opening doors, but perhaps most importantly for raising the level of awareness in the company about further global opportunities. McNealy was positively ecstatic about the trips: "I call them my Johnny Appleseed trips. It blew people away that a CEO showed up in Bogotá. It's exciting. It's pioneering. If you don't get in there, immerse yourself, get involved, you're not going to play in the markets."

Whatever future mix you take, in the end what is most impressive is

Sun's vision of securing 67 percent of its business from overseas by the year 2000.

> LESSON: There are two things a global company needs: a global network and global people. Other actions can also be helpful:
>
> • take on foreign competitors abroad in their own backyard
> • have key people live abroad
> • establish a variety of long-term relationships with foreign partners
> • develop and control a host-country distribution system
> • be willing to do the unconventional, such as sharing your technology

 ## Just Get Out There and Sell
CANNONDALE

"MOST PEOPLE WHO SIT BACK AND COMPLAIN ABOUT PROBLEMS IN JAPAN HAVE NEVER TRIED TO BREAK INTO THIS MARKET. JUST GET OUT THERE AND SELL."
—SCOTT MONTGOMERY, FORMER PRESIDENT, CANNONDALE JAPAN

THE CHALLENGE

The company was founded in 1971 by Joseph Montgomery but it didn't produce a bicycle until 1983. While Montgomery's vision was to mass-produce aluminum bicycle frames, he was forced for twelve years because of little investment capital to be content with making bicycle accessories, first above an old pickle factory in Wilton, Connecticut, and later in Stamford and Georgetown, also in Connecticut.

His first bike frame rolled out in 1983, and by 1988 Cannondale, America's premier maker of high-performance mountain bikes and racing bikes, was doing $30 million in sales. But it still was deriving only 5 percent of those revenues from overseas. And no Cannondale bike was sold in Japan, which, after all, had been exporting 888,000 bikes as recently as 1985.

The challenge was this: how does a relatively small company, with high quality, high-priced products, break into foreign markets in order to begin riding a major export wave that's forming? The challenge was a critical one for Cannondale to meet because since the mid-1980s, Japan's bike exports plummeted to 155,000 while U.S. bike exports skyrocketed thirty-fivefold, to 669,000 units.

THE RESPONSE

Scott Montgomery may only have been thirty years old when he headed for Japan, but he knew the right formula: breaking into the Japanese market meant breaking with conventional wisdom. First off, he let go Cannondale's local-firm sales agent and set up a wholly owned sales subsidiary. This ran directly counter to the advice he had received from Japanese experts that he could survive only if he teamed up with a local company. Next, he set up shop in a small community far outside Osaka where rents were relatively cheap.

While Scott had his own hands-on marketing style—keeping in touch with his customers and products by bicycling five miles to work every morning and entering two bike races a month—his key move was hiring two Japanese-speaking American professional bicyclists to head up sales and promotions. Every weekend the two would enter races on Cannondale bikes, garnering lots of free publicity. On weekdays, they would make sales calls on dealers. They found that Japanese retailers were eager to deal directly with Cannondale. This direct-to-dealer approach reflects Joseph Montgomery's philosophy, which he expresses as, "We didn't want too many layers of people touching our product." Echoing his father's credo, Scott says, "They know that with every level of distribution comes a level of service breakdown."

Cannondale's response when it came to selling in Japan boils down to this: "Just get out there and sell."

Looking to the future, it is likely that Cannondale will continue to do well in the export market for the simple reason that Joe Montgomery works extremely hard to keep his bikes from becoming archaic. The company redesigns over 90 percent of its thirty-seven models each year. As Montgomery puts it, "If your reason for living is innovation, making products for a lot of different niche markets, then the name of the game is reinventing your product all the time." To this end, Cannondale's entire manufacturing process is tailored for constant innovation.

THE RESULTS

Joseph Montgomery's guiding philosophy is that if a company is going to have a successful consumer product today, it has to be a world player. And a world player is what Cannondale has quickly become. Cannondale bikes are now found in sixty-two countries, a list of which hangs on Scott Montgomery's office wall back in Georgetown, Connecticut, where he is now vice president for marketing. "I have it up there for inspiration."

He and his father hardly need much inspiration when it comes to going global. From their tiny base of 5 percent of total sales in 1988, foreign sales shot up to 40 percent of total sales of $100 million by 1992. European sales alone went from just over $1 million to over $25 million. These overseas sales were largely responsible for the doubling of the company's overall revenues from 1990 to 1992.

Sales of Cannondale Japan quadrupled in the year after its first bike was shipped. Its unique marketing approach led to a tripling in the number of dealers carrying its high-end bikes (to 260). The truly impressive result is that Cannondale Japan showed profits of $60,000 in its first year, even when all start-up costs were factored in. By 1993, Japanese sales accounted for 5 percent of overall sales, jumping ahead 50 percent that year alone. Cannondale is especially pleased with this market, for since it is competing against American bikes that carry extra distribution costs in Japan, it can charge more and come away with a profit margin 25 percent higher than on U.S. sales.

[
LESSON: Avoid wholesale distributors by going directly to the dealers and retailers, raise your visibility through special events, constantly develop new products and take an aggressive, "just get out there and sell" attitude.
]

 ## Invest Abroad, Invest Again, and Invest Some More
AIR PRODUCTS AND CHEMICALS

> "OUR UNDERLYING STRATEGY IS TO CONTINUE TO INVEST AGGRESSIVELY IN EUROPE, BECAUSE WE FEEL THE FUTURE IS BRIGHT."
> **—HAROLD WAGNER, PRESIDENT AND CEO**

THE CHALLENGE

Since 1957—when Pennsylvania-based Air Products and Chemicals first planted its flag overseas—the company has recognized that the key to corporate growth is greater global market access. Thus, the challenge it faced in the mid-1980s was to solidify its growth prospects up to and through the 1990s by further globalizing the company's operations. Specifically, it set for itself the goal of increasing the percentage of its sales coming from outside the United States from around 25 percent to 50 percent.

THE RESPONSE

The main means for meeting this ambitious goal has been to invest aggressively overseas. Indeed, Dexter Baker, who was CEO in the mid-1980s, crafted a very simple strategy: invest abroad, invest again, and invest some more.

This is not to say that Air Products hasn't sought out global markets to export its products and services. It has, and has done so successfully. But it is the company's example of being a global investor *par excellence* that we wish to highlight.

Europe

Air Products' first overseas venture was in Europe in 1957. The parent company at that time was a fairly small enterprise, with annual sales of around $30 million, almost exclusively in the United States. But it wanted to take advantage of the emerging Common Market and so it followed what was then a nontraditional approach—perhaps the only viable option it had as a small industrial gas company up against firmly entrenched and much larger competitors. Its plan was to embark on a pan-European strategy—seeking out partnerships, wherever possible, with existing European industrial gas firms and companies in related fields to give it footholds and a chance to compete across Europe.

Almost exactly three decades later, Air Products identified another major European movement and corresponding opportunity with the EC 92 initiative, making Europe a giant free trade zone. In the five years leading up to this major development, it invested over a billion dollars in Europe. To put this investment in perspective, it is almost three times the $350 million original cost of all of the company's assets in Europe. These investments enabled it to replace older, less efficient industrial gas plants, add new capacity for existing products, and introduce new products such as ultra-high-purity electronic gases and liquid hydrogen. In the case of chemicals, the investments gave it manufacturing bases in Europe.

What it did in FY 1993 epitomizes investing aggressively abroad. It received orders for its two largest on-site projects ever in Europe to help oil refineries meet new environmental requirements (over $1 billion in future revenues). It began operations at its first gas production plant in Central Europe to supply oxygen to a leading steel company in Poland. It purchased a controlling interest in Ferox, a Czech company that manufactures cryogenic paints. A long-term agreement to purchase helium in Russia strengthened its position as the world's largest helium supplier.

Asia

Air Products also has used the "partnership approach" to expand in Asia. The company first entered the region in 1980 with an industrial gas joint venture in Korea. It has since set up operations in eight other countries—Japan, Thailand, Taiwan, Hong Kong, China, Malaysia, Singapore, and Indonesia. It entered seven of these countries one after another from 1986 to 1990. Teaming with established companies in Asia and hiring top local people were the key strategies that allowed Air Products to become a major player in Asia in its first decade of operations there.

The second Asian country it entered was Japan. As former CEO Dexter Baker puts it:

Our strategic reasoning then, as it is now: Japan is the ultimate test. We used to say, "If you can make it in New York, you can make it anywhere." The slogan now is, "If you can make it in Tokyo, you can make it anywhere."

Air Products had to meet exacting quality standards in manufacturing, process engineering, and service when, in 1988, it won out over five Japanese competitors and supplied Nippon Steel with its first Western air separation plant. Baker adds, "The point is that U.S. companies ready to be evaluated in minute detail by prospective Japanese customers can gain access, win orders, and grow."

The company's recent focus has been on the country that currently affords the greatest potential: China. Its strategy is to become the number one or number two industrial gas company in China. It expects to accomplish this by doing business of up to $300 million there from 1993 to 1997 in major air separation equipment sales by establishing additional regional gas joint ventures and a local manufacturing and project execution capability.

Latin America

Air Products' expansion into Latin America dates back to 1973 when it established an industrial gas subsidiary in Brazil. Further expansion of the industrial gas business occurred in 1980 with the formation of a joint venture with the INFRA Group in Mexico, that country's largest industrial gas supplier. In 1993, it invested well over $100 million to further expand its equity position in the industrial gas businesses of the INFRA Group. This was the company's largest investment ever in the gas business.

THE RESULTS

The company's major investments overseas have paid off handsomely: sales from overseas operations, including exports, now account for over 40 percent of the corporation's revenues—so that it is well on its way to meeting its 50 percent goal.

Europe

- European sales, including U.S. exports to Europe plus its share of joint venture revenues, more than doubled from $400 million in 1987 to over $1 billion in FY 1993.
- It has operations in thirteen European countries at 130 locations. It is the second largest gas company in Europe and has the most balanced geographic portfolio.

Asia

- From 1987 to FY 1993, sales from its joint ventures in Asia grew in excess of 60 percent per year.
- Its pro rata gas sales in Asia today are seven times greater than just five years ago, despite the fact that it got into Asia late and its chief competitors have been there for decades.

Latin America

- Air Products' chemicals are currently sold into every country in Latin America, using an in-house sales force and a network of agents and distributors. Products sold into the region are primarily manufactured in the United States or Europe and sold to many of the same customers and end-use markets that Air Products serves in other parts of the world (such as adhesives, textiles, construction, automotive and agricultural manufacturers).
- In Mexico, it now has the largest position of any of the international suppliers in the $300 million Mexican industrial gas market and has laid the groundwork for doubling its chemical sales by 1996.

Exports

- The company was the winner of Pennsylvania's 1992 Governor's Export Award in the large manufacturing category. It was recognized for its outstanding achievements in developing international trade through the export of giant heat exchangers to the Middle East, Asia,

and Australia. The combined current market value of these exports—
which have taken place over the last twenty-five years—is in excess
of $1 billion.

• In addition to heat exchangers, Air Products exports a variety of other
cryogenic equipment and chemicals to customers in approximately
ninety countries around the world. Exports zoomed in the 1987–1992
period, tripling in value to over $300 million annually.

[LESSON: If you wish to propel future growth through
international activity and get close to your customer
in foreign markets, be willing to invest abroad, invest
again, and then invest some more.]

Going Global Before Going Domestic
WADIA DIGITAL

"THERE IS A BIAS AMONG VENTURE CAPITALISTS THAT FIRST YOU GET A STRONG
FOOTHOLD IN THE DOMESTIC MARKET AND THEN YOU THINK INTERNATIONAL.
BEFORE THE COMPANY WAS EVEN FOUNDED, WE CONSIDERED THAT
TO BE BACKWARD."

—DONALD WADIA MOSES, VICE CHAIRMAN (FIRST CEO)

THE CHALLENGE

Wadia Digital was founded in 1988 with the mission of developing,
manufacturing, and marketing the very finest digital audio and video
products in the world. In their original business plan, the co-founders
put a goal of 28 percent of sales from exports. They actually believed
the percentage would be much higher, but they felt they had to put a
number in the plan that would be, as Don Moses (co-founder, the first
CEO, and current vice chairman) says, "believable" to the investment
community.

You see, they considered the standard thinking of the investment
community—that you start out by gaining a strong foothold in the

domestic market and after a while begin to think global—to be precisely backward.

THE RESPONSE

Yes, Wadia was looking to go global *before* going domestic. From the
very beginning, the co-founders were looking at a global market for
their top-of-the line products. The United States was viewed simply as
one market among many.

Their initial strategy was to talk to as many knowledgeable people
in the industry as possible to secure leads as to who were the best
distributors for products like theirs around the globe. Having done
this for more than a year, they went off to the Consumer Electronics
Show in Chicago in 1988, before founding the company, armed with a
list of twelve targeted distributors to meet with and show their entire
inventory of five prototypes of their first product. They really didn't
know what to expect. As Don Moses says: "There was a strong feeling
that maybe no one would want to buy the product—after all, it was a
black box with a $6,000 price tag." But they were pleasantly surprised.
They came back to River Falls, Wisconsin, with purchase orders from
distributors in six countries, including the top distributor in Germany.

But what they were really after was a top distributor in Japan. They
knew that many Japanese were willing to pay a premium price for a
premium audio product. They had the right idea, but the top distributor, Nakanishi, turned them down. After all, they were an upstart company from River Falls, Wisconsin. Still, they went back to Nakanishi and
asked, "Okay, so who's number two?" The answer was Axiss, so they
talked to them, went with them, and today Axiss is their largest distributor.

So parts one and two of their export strategy are clear: go for the
best distributors and attend the two major Consumer Electronics
Shows held each year in Chicago and Las Vegas. Part three is to do a
lot of face-to-face meetings. They constantly send their people all over
the world, both to nurture current relationships and scout out new
possibilities. In addition, as Moses describes it, "River Falls, Wisconsin,
has become an international center for this industry," as industry people from all over the world travel to their headquarters.

The fourth part could be called the "Field of Dreams" part. In that
movie, the key idea was, "If you build it, they will come." For Wadia, it

was, "If you build the best products, they will be bought." As phrased by Don Moses: "We're considered the benchmarks with what we make. We're what others are compared to."

A final part is to keep churning out new top-of-the-line products. Of their sales in 1992, an incredible 82 percent were from products introduced over the previous twelve months. Seven new products and two upgrades to existing products were produced in 1992.

THE RESULTS

Few companies have had the type of export success that Wadia had so soon in their existence. In each of its first five years, export sales ranged from 70 percent to 80 percent of total sales. By 1994, their products were being shipped to approximately forty countries, with Russia and Vietnam being recent additions.

How? Why? They obviously succeeded in their mission to produce the very finest digital audio and video products in the world. One fact alone speaks volumes: the CD players manufactured by this small company in River Falls, Wisconsin, are the highest-rated CD players sold in Japan. Also, Wadia won the highly prestigious Japanese *Component of the Year (C.O.T.Y.) Award* in three of its first four years. And it has won the Japanese Jazz Lover's Award. Finally, the folks back home recognized they had something special in their midst, as Wadia won the 1992 Wisconsin Manufacturer of the Year Award and the Governor's Special Award for Export Sales.

[
LESSON: From the beginning view the world as your market, go for the best distributors, and build the very finest products so the world will come to you.
]

The Small Can Span the Globe
RUST EVADER

"OUR WHOLE KEY TO SUCCESS IN WORLDWIDE MARKETING HAS BEEN OUR WILLINGNESS TO PHYSICALLY TRAVEL TO THE COUNTRIES WE ARE DOING BUSINESS WITH."
—DAVID McCREADY, PRESIDENT

THE CHALLENGE

Rust Evader faced no particular crisis in the 1980s. The sales of this Altoona, Pennsylvania, company in the U.S. market during its first two years were doing just fine. It simply made a calculation in 1989 that its product, an electronic corrosion control device for motor vehicles, might have better potential abroad than here. Why? Because overseas there is less of the planned obsolescence than in the United States. People keep their cars longer.

THE RESPONSE

Once the decision to go global was made, the company moved rapidly. The first steps were pretty basic. First, they received advice for their export campaign from the Southern Alleghenies Regional Development and Planning Association. Next, it placed a low-cost ad in *Commercial News USA,* the U.S. Department of Commerce's export promotion catalogue-magazine.

The real key to their export success, however, was their commitment to travel to the countries to personally meet with potential distributors and customers. As David McCready, their president, says, "First you go to every country that expresses any interest in your product." After you establish a good network of distributors, you then consolidate. You pull in from your wide range of distributors and concentrate on just a few large ones who in turn have many local people in the field. For instance, in 1994 Rust Evader had just one large distributor in the Far East, who served sixteen different countries, and they had just hired a person to live in Berlin to serve as their representative to the European Community countries.

While Rust Evader operates on a distributor basis in most locations, in several countries it has licensing arrangements with manufacturers to make its product. In India, Rust Evader India was formed as a joint venture to manufacture and sell its products throughout the Middle East.

Though its results are spectacular, the sailing isn't always effortless. Says McCready, "Not all of our overseas relationships are smooth and trouble-free. In fact, most require conferencing and constant communications to avoid conflict. The conflict encompasses different emotional and ethical standards that are peculiar to each market area."

THE RESULTS

It sounds almost unbelievable, but in the first two years of its export campaign, exports accounted for 50 percent of the company's annual sales, and at the end of the two years, the company was exporting 88 percent of its production. Furthermore, in just two and a half years, Rust Evader established distribution channels in nearly half the countries of the world—and on every continent except Antarctica. Its products in 1994 were shipped to thirty-nine countries. These export markets were instrumental in the company maintaining a 100 percent increase in sales in both 1991 and 1992.

The final sentence in the company's corporate profile sums it all up: "International trade has granted Rust Evader continuous growth and at the same time created a recession-resistant growth posture."

[
LESSON: To first establish a global presence, have the CEO travel extensively abroad and establish a broad network of distributors and customers; after a while consolidate your distribution network by focusing on a few major distributors to serve large regions.
]

FOCUSING ON CONTINUOUS IMPROVEMENT

9: PURSUE TOTAL QUALITY

American companies finally began to focus on quality in the early 1980s for one simple reason: they were getting beat by foreign competition. And it was not just lower prices—it was the higher quality of foreign products.

So American companies flocked to Japan, and to their Japanese subsidiaries, to figure out the secrets of high quality. After all, Japan's quality movement had been going on for over thirty years. Under the leadership and guidance of such revolutionary thinkers as Taiichi Ohno and Kaoru Ishikawa, Japanese manufacturers had burst successfully onto the international scene operating under the banner of *kaizen,* or continuous improvement.

America's quality journey has moved quickly and matured significantly since the early 1980s. From an initial focus on product quality—reducing defects—it moved to the American version of *kaizen* called total quality management (TQM). TQM is focused on achieving top quality throughout the organization, not just with products and not just on the manufacturing floor. The goal is to become a quality corporation, highly efficient, with the objective of zero waste anywhere in the system. No companies have yet achieved this goal. The five highlighted in this chapter have come a long way toward achieving it.

There have been other ways that the quality movement has matured in America. It is now more clearly understood that TQM only works when a company finds out what customers really care about. Most companies now focus on the fact that quality improvements can only be justified if they eventually lead to higher profits. This has led to the recent concept of return on quality, which in turn emphasizes customer retention. Finally, there is increased emphasis on maximizing "things gone right" (TGR) rather than minimizing "things gone wrong" (TGW). This is important, for the TGR, not the TGW, emphasis is what will help create great and spirited products.

Actually, despite all the attention directed toward TQM in the 1980s, two harsh facts remain: the majority of American companies have not launched any systematic effort to improve quality, and many companies that did "try TQM" in the 1980s are discouraged or disillusioned because the results just aren't there. This second fact by itself is not disturbing. What is disturbing is that many people, particularly in the media, are leaping to the conclusion that pursuing total quality has been tried and found wanting. Another seemingly good idea to be put back on the shelf.

This type of thinking is dangerous, for it can divert the focus of many companies, which must be on quality in the 1990s, by indicting the quality concept itself. The concept itself is not at fault. The problem was, and still is, the way TQM is practiced at the companies that experience little payback. Just ask anyone who works for one of the five companies highlighted in this chapter. They are all enthusiastic about the results from their quality improvement efforts. They know that high quality "works"—that the payoff can indeed be quite large.

Or ask anyone at the fifteen to twenty other companies that were top contenders for coverage in this chapter. Or one could go to the employees at the twelve companies that have won the Malcolm Baldrige National Quality Award in the manufacturing category since it was established in 1988, including such companies as Xerox Business Products and Systems, Milliken & Company, IBM Rochester, Cadillac Motor Car Division, and Solectron. Certainly one could go to AT&T: after already winning two Baldrige Awards, it scored a double hit in October 1994, winning yet another Baldrige Award and Japan's prestigious Deming Prize for quality control, becoming the first U.S. manufacturer to win this prize. And if any skepticism remains, talk to anyone at each of the companies that have been winners in recent years of the Shingo Award or the numerous state quality award programs or the hundreds of quality awards given by companies to their suppliers. No, all of these companies are testimony to the powerful effectiveness of a well-conceived *and* well-executed quality improvement initiative.

What makes some quality improvement efforts great successes and others flops? It obviously isn't size or industry or education of workforce or type of product. The companies below span the spectrum. The key ingredients of success cited both in the literature and substantiated in the companies we highlight are focus and leadership. Know precisely what you are after, and have top leadership in the company champion it with hands-on involvement.

The quality movement may be suffering a crisis of confidence because of the negative examples cited in the press, but this will prove short-lived because quality has now become a given. It's foundational. It's what's expected of a company that wants to be a world-class competitor.

MOTOROLA SETS THE STANDARD

Motorola is the undisputed quality champ. Since the full case study follows this introduction immediately, we will touch only on the high points.

The first lesson from Motorola is the critical importance of commitment to the quality process by top leadership. When Bob Galvin was CEO at Motorola, he was the quality champion. He set high goals *and* he invested the money to meet the goals. Another important lesson from Motorola is that total quality does not deal just with quality of products but with quality throughout every part of the company: accountants, patent lawyers, software managers, have all been part of its quality crusade.

The primary means Motorola employs to meet its goal of Six Sigma quality (3.4 defects per million) is an almost fanatical dedication to employee empowerment, centered around teamwork and extensive education and training. The company also looks for suppliers and partners that share their quality values: they actually teach many of them their TQM techniques and they expect all of their suppliers to apply for the Baldrige Award.

Motorola does not rest on its laurels. For those parts of the company that have already achieved Six Sigma, they launched a Beyond Six Sigma program with the goal of improving their defect level ten times every two years. And they inserted quality determinators in the line so you can anticipate when a process might be heading for a defect. Now that's a comprehensive quality effort. And it's well worth the effort. They estimate that improved quality has saved them $4.6 billion and most likely double that. They also view quality as a key competitive advantage. And it's instrumental in their drive to become the "perfect company."

TOTAL TRANSFORMATION OFTEN CALLED FOR

We've just seen total transformation at work at Motorola. The quality initiative at two other companies also led to total transformation. United Electric Controls discovered that they almost had to throw everything out since maintaining even one aspect of the old system slows you down. At Hardinge Brothers, the greatest challenge was making all its employees realize that the company's own process and systems were the greatest impediment to achieving its long-range goals. It involved nothing less than turning the culture of the company in a new direction,.

EMPLOYEE INVOLVEMENT AND TRAINING ARE CRITICAL MEANS

At Motorola, employee involvement and training are central to its whole quality initiative. It is far from alone. At United Electric Controls, the total employee involvement program was perhaps the most successful change put into effect. The message to all its employees was straightforward: challenge the way things are done and undo the way things have been done in the past. Hardinge Brothers launched a massive program of total quality awareness education for employees, and it involved three quarters of the workers in employee teams of all kinds in which they manage and continually redesign their own production groups to meet flexible requirements.

AMP came to its focus on employee involvement in an interesting way. In 1988, the company applied for the Baldrige Award and didn't win. It discovered that while it was good in a number of categories, what it needed most was a more participative environment. It became so serious, that "total employee involvement is fundamental to quality improvement" became the foundation of the company's Plan for Excellence introduced in February 1990. The number of product-focused or project-oriented teams shot up to over 500 by 1992.

QUALITY THROUGH BEING THE BEST-COST PRODUCER

Emerson Electric has its own unique quality program. It is the company's Best-Cost Producer strategy. To CEO Chuck Knight, this strategy is a quality program, for the best-cost producer by definition has the highest quality, which in turn means the best product performance. Emerson's goal is to ensure that each product line and business meets or exceeds the highest global quality standards. The real heart and soul of this drive to produce top-quality products is the company's almost fanatical dedication to continuous cost reduction. Every year for the past thirty-five years, the company has set cost-reduction goals at every level and required plant personnel to identify the specific measures necessary to achieve those objectives. Recently, Emerson has shifted the focus of its quality efforts more toward growth. Thus, two vital lessons emerge from the Emerson quality experience. First, quality can be used to drive down costs. Second, the focus of a quality program can shift—in this case, from reducing costs to growth.

Toward the Perfect Company
MOTOROLA

Yes, that's right. Motorola is aiming to be the perfect company. None other than Richard Buetow, senior vice president and director of quality, stated it quite unequivocally as the 1990s unfolded: "We will continue to improve quality till we become the perfect company."

That's a pretty amazing statement. In all our research looking closely at over 200 companies, we never saw another company state this as a goal. Then again, we never saw another company quite like Motorola. If any company may just make it—or at least come very close to being a perfect company—it's Motorola.

A "perfect company" goal makes even its much heralded Six Sigma goal of 3.4 defects per million look tame by comparison. Yet Motorola was the first major company to establish this extremely ambitious quality goal. And they established it in 1987. And they established it, not just for a factory or two, or for a process or two, but for the whole company. And it was to be achieved by 1992.

Well, it's good to see that Motorola is still human. It did not quite meet its Six Sigma-by-1992-goal—the companywide quality level was 5.4 Sigma in 1993.

But what is so impressive is their constant drive: continuous stretch goals, continuous improvement, continuous learning. Combine these three and the almost inevitable result is going to be continuously great performance. Motorola is loaded with great results. How about just these two: it went from $5 billion to $17 billion in sales in less than a decade in large part because of their quality initiative and productivity soared 126 percent from 1986 to 1993.

So what exactly is the quality system at this quality-paragon company? Ask the top quality guy, Richard Buetow, and you hear a direct headquarters perspective: "Our quality system is very simple: take whatever you do and drive it toward perfection in the lowest elapsed time and serve the customer as best you can. That's our simple goal. We just keep doing it and it's done wonders for us."

Go down a bit on the corporate ladder and you hear from Patty Barten, director of manufacturing at the Cellular Infrastructure plant just a few miles north of headquarters, and you hear a bit different emphasis: "People here have a fire in their belly. They want to showcase the health of American manufacturing."

"Now wait a minute," you say. "Fire in their belly. Showcase the health of American manufacturing. You've got to be kidding."

I had a similar reaction when Patty said this in the plant manager's office at the opening interview of the day. But you begin to sense that fire as you walk the production lines, stopping to talk to the operators. Then I unmistakably saw and heard that fire in the seven operators/trainers who related their perspectives on life at Motorola over lunch. This lunch group was truly remarkable. They looked like a small seminar at graduate school. Most were twenty-somethings, dressed casually and eager to tell their stories which were all great. But what really stood out—and was telling in explaining Motorola's quality success—was their educational background and initial predisposition toward manufacturing.

First came Basyl Martynuik, a member of the local education group at this plant with his degree in applied linguistics (emphasis in Russian). Beverly McGhee, veterinary science. Steve Franks in biology. Linda Aleksick, music (emphasis in opera). Linda stressed how she swore while growing up that she'd never come to Motorola. Her mom and stepdad worked for the company for twenty-two years. Needing money, she came to work for a summer, lifting heavy loads on the receiving dock. It's now four years later, she's a trainer, and she has no plans of leaving. Jamie Martinez was an operating room technician, grew weary of it, came here thinking, "It's a factory job. I'll stay a few months and move on." Why is he still here four years later? "I got involved in the business. I took personal ownership. I saw a fellow worker who became a team leader. He ran the show. I saw there was a lot of opportunity here. This place is opportunity. You can reach what Motorola expects of you—to reach your potential."

Quality works at Motorola. Why? Three reasons stand out: (1) the view from headquarters and the view from the factory on quality closely intermesh and reinforce each other; (2) continuous education and training; and (3) teamwork, always focused on total customer satisfaction.

QUALITY: THE HEADQUARTERS AND FACTORY VIEWS

To get the headquarters view, let's start at the end—the final question asked of Richard Buetow and Mauro Walker, senior vice president and director of manufacturing. "What have been the key lessons learned about quality at Motorola?"

Mauro Walker quickly cited four:

1. Quality is free.
2. The need to develop skills in their workers that match what they're seeing in customer requirements and new technologies.
3. Making sure that workers are trained to function as teams.
4. Being best in class in manufacturing and manufacturing technology.

When he was asked why many other companies have failed at their TQM efforts, he pointed out that it's hard to believe you can increase your goals, such as reducing defects two or three orders of magnitude, at no added cost. "They don't believe that."

Three lessons about quality emerged from Richard Buetow:

1. Institutionalize the quality process within the business process.
2. Quality organizations don't fix quality problems—only people with direct responsibility do that.
3. Let go. Once you put the process in place, management must get out of micromanagement. Let the people do it!

Buetow was quick to point out the *key* difference between Motorola's system and most companies who fail at TQM: "TQM in other companies becomes an overlay process and management won't let go." He continually stressed the "let go" theme: "I think the key in Motorola was—and maybe it was good because we didn't know what to do—let things go from a management perspective."

It didn't take more than three minutes of listening to Rick Chandler, plant manager of the cellular infrastructure manufacturing facility, to realize that Buetow practices what he preaches. Here's a manager, talking about his early days of opening up the new facility in 1987, who was obviously not micromanaged from headquarters:

The fundamental thing we decided was rather than work on quality, cycle time, or cost, to devote our energies to building a culture here where people could really go and run the business—to give them a sense of ownership, a sense of pride, of dignity, a sense that they have participated in their future. That's a funny direction for a manufacturing group to go in. And it's based on a belief that if you get people who have that sense about them that they'll go and do all these other things. It's a leap of faith that a lot of companies aren't willing to take.

So it's obvious that Rick, the plant manager, is willing to let go. That this is not just talk was attested to by many of the factory operators. Indeed, a group of them in a wrap-up interview chipped in a host of comments in rapid-fire fashion: "People here care for each other"; "The morale is good"; "We all listen"; "People care about what happens to the business."

After hearing these, Rick felt that the basic message needed to be made clear: This is not a love-in. If we don't produce and ship product at the highest quality level, this isn't going to work. The outcome has to be there—has to be there. We can get there and still have fun.

It became clear that here was an unusual plant manager: one ruthlessly focused on outcome, on quality, on volume, yet getting there by giving the workers ownership and a sense of fun. One operator, in talking about Rick, also gave another clue to Motorola's fantastic quality journey: "Rick could be in a meeting with top executives and if a production worker walks in and says, 'I've got a problem,' Rick gets up, says 'I've got a problem,' and leaves."

A BRIEF HISTORY OF QUALITY AT MOTOROLA

The meeting by now has become legendary. In 1979, then Chairman and CEO Bob Galvin convened the first meeting of his top officers at the Ambassador East Hotel in Chicago. Arthur Sundry, who ran one of the company's most successful divisions—two-way radios—stood up and said, "Our quality levels really stink." Galvin recalls: "It just electrified us. At that one meeting, everything started to change."

It had to change. Motorola had already sold its TV business (in 1974) and it lost stereos (in 1980) to the Japanese. It would soon be threatened with losing cellular phones through a combination of initial quality problems and some "technological theft." It chose to fight rather than surrender.

Jack Germain was named the company's first quality director. He set in motion quality systems reviews and he started measurements of the cost of poor quality. He also set a corporate goal: a tenfold reduction in defects by 1986. He and his staff spent two years scoring the performance of twenty-four Motorola plants. Meanwhile, Galvin and many top executives were benchmarking the best factories around the world. They were stunned to find plants in Japan where quality was 1,000 times better than Motorola's. So when Galvin returned, he was intrigued by a very ambitious proposal contained in a document titled "Six Sigma Mechanical Design Tolerancing," a highly technical treatise. He liked the sound of Six Sigma, so needing something as a dramatic initiative, he established Six Sigma as the goal for the communications business in 1986, which meant they had to achieve near perfection by 1992.

Galvin then took another extensive trip and again had an epiphany. A dozen major customers clearly told him they liked Motorola's products, but they would do 10 percent to 20 percent more business with Motorola if the company served them better. The next step was ordained: take Six Sigma corporatewide—to every level and every location. It was the centerpiece of five initiatives announced to meet the company's new overall objective of total customer satisfaction (the other four are participative management groups, profit improvements, product and manufacturing leadership, and cycle time reduction).

But how? How do you begin getting a multibillion-dollar global company focused on achieving the seemingly impossible goal of near perfection in quality—in five years?

Galvin began by writing a letter in January 1987 to all employees, challenging them with new goals: a tenfold improvement by 1989, one-hundredfold improvement by 1991, and Six Sigma quality by 1992. Every employee was given a wallet-size card stating those goals (they came in thirteen languages). They then, as Buetow has put it, "saturated the company." A companywide education blitz in 1987 involved videotapes, blue-and-white Six Sigma posters hung throughout every building, and a course (Understanding Six Sigma) required for every employee and tailor-made for each division.

That was only the beginning. Throughout 1988, the heat was turned up to embrace Six Sigma quickly, a strategy Buetow refers to as "top-down commitment." Memos on quality were churned out almost weekly from the CEO's office. A Quality Day was held at all fifty-four Motorola locations around the world to celebrate winning the Baldrige Award. New employees had to meet certain quality standards within a ninety-day probation period—or risk losing their jobs. In 1989, Motorola began tying most performance reviews and bonus incentives to Six Sigma requirements. Workers who show steady progress on quality improvements can earn bonuses running as high as 40 percent of their annual salaries. Galvin told all 10,000 Motorola suppliers to join Motorola's quality crusade. He ordered them to apply for the Baldrige Award or lose Motorola as a customer. The number of suppliers dwindled to around 1,000 from a peak of 35,000.

How did all this translate down to actual operations at the plant level? Buetow emphasized in the interview that it began with asking each business to map their process: This is step number one, measure. This is step number two, measure. And so forth. Though they resisted at first, what they found, according to Buetow, was that "it was powerful." It was a good way to run a business. Most important, Motorola found out what the Japanese had discovered: "the highest-quality product is the lowest cost to manufacture."

The biggest initiatives by far in meeting the quality goals were in education and training, and teamwork. It is to these we now turn our attention.

TRAIN, TRAIN, AND TRAIN

Just as Motorola is synonymous with quality, so is it synonymous with training. Indeed, it could easily have been the leadoff case study for the training chapter. For large companies, it has written the book on training since it launched Motorola University in 1981 with just three people. Today, the training facility employs 200 full-time educators and another 400 on contract, with offices in Illinois, Texas, Arizona, Singapore, Scotland, and nine other locations around the world.

Motorola U. was the brainchild of Bob Galvin. His idea was greeted by decided unenthusiasm. "It would be great if it doesn't cost money or take time" was the prevailing attitude. As Buetow relates it, Galvin shot back, "It won't cost you any money and it won't take much time." What he really meant was "you'll learn to love it." And they did. Listen to Buetow: "It is indispensable. Absolutely essential. One of the most important things we've done."

Here's how Motorola looks at training according to Buetow: "It is a necessary ingredient to be successful in your business. Just like buying the best parts, dealing with the best suppliers, hiring the most talented people." What does Buetow think of the cost, which now runs around $120 million to $140 million annually or 4 percent of payroll, putting it at the very high end for major companies? "Training is a nothing expenditure." Just in case the message wasn't getting across, he added: "Without it, you won't survive."

What's truly amazing is that Motorola feels it has just begun on the education and training front. In early 1994, they were beginning a major new campaign centered on lifelong learning. They felt such an initiative was necessary, for in the future high quality will be a given and the real competitive wars will be fought with the weapons of responsiveness, adaptability, and creativity. To this end, Motorola envisions to quadruple by the year 2000 their already high level of forty hours of training per year for each employee.

That's the view from the top. And again, the view from the trenches, at the cellular infrastructure manufacturing facility, was virtually identical. Indeed, if anything, training was more emphasized there as being absolutely essential to their own great success.

Rick Chandler's second statement, after the eloquent one quoted above about giving ownership to the employees, was, "I believe education is the key to our success." His training foundation is twofold: everyone learns and speaks English and has a math equivalency of at least seventh to ninth grade. Beyond that, all employees at the plant must take courses in team building and problem solving.

Much of the education of employees at this facility takes place in-house by the Manufacturing Education Group. But rather than hire ten to fifteen instructors for this group, Chandler chose to pull them off the lines, train them to be a trainer, and let them teach. It's called "The Assignment" and it lasts for about eighteen months. Many people love it because it's widely viewed as a means for advancement when the assignment is over. This way, no instructor gets flat. Another key advantage was pointed out by Linda Alecksick, one of the young trainers at lunch: "We come right off the floor. We know our products, our people, the process."

While classroom training is important at this plant, and throughout Motorola, even more important is what it calls "embedded learning," a process where new employees earn regular wages while learning tasks under a more experienced worker's guidance. Motorola is a national leader in that style of learning.

It comes down to this for Chandler: "The best investment you can make is to invest in people's knowledge. Then you can educate them for whatever comes up. We used to train people for a new machine. We stopped that. Once you educate people, you can just give them a manual on the new machine."

TEAMWORK AND THE TOTAL CUSTOMER SATISFACTION TEAM CONTEST

It may sound repetitive, but again Motorola is state-of-the-art when it comes to teamwork. Interestingly, the word empowerment was not heard much in the interviews. But the basic idea was there. "We found that if you have a process whereby there is some system by which to track, and measure and train, boy are your employees powerful. They can just turn the world around for you," an enthusiastic Buetow exclaims.

And again Rick Chandler breaks the mold in his perspective on teams:

> We don't have classical teams where ten people train and put them back in the plant and say, you're a team. That's dumb. You've created a monster. The process changes, the customers change, the volume changes. Our business changes daily.

So the teams at his plant are more fluid. Any one individual may be on as many as eight teams as the need arises. "I want to educate people so they know how to form a team, operate in a team. So they can go from team to team according to the needs of customers," says Chandler. "It's a passion for me." The result in 1993 was the formation of 168 special teams dedicated to improving quality, cutting costs, and reducing cycle time.

At the wrap-up meeting, Rick highlighted one team in his plant that had set a number of records simultaneously a few weeks back, on both volume and quality. Orlando, one of the team members, then spoke up to indicate how this was accomplished. The team held a brief meeting. They acknowledged that they had been working as five individuals. "We knew what we were capable of. We laughed a bit, griped a bit. It's teamwork, not a fantasy thing. It's reality."

The real excitement of teamwork at Motorola comes in its annual Total Customer Satisfaction (TCS) Worldwide Team Competition. Gene Simpson, former vice president and director of participative management programs, recounts: "When we first devised this competition [in 1990], we saw it as a way to recognize and celebrate teamwork. But it's begun to take on a life of its own. Teams are beginning to deal with problems so that they can enter the contest, and as a result employees are taking it upon themselves to focus on customer satisfaction and product quality." Here's just one example of the tremendous employee motivation the contest provides. Having won a gold medal in 1992, Hassan Tavakoli said he was already gearing up for next year's competition:

> I'm already thinking about another project we can work on to enter the competition. I'm looking around for areas that need improvement, trying to identify problems that are challenging enough to get us entered into the contest. The most rewarding part of this whole thing is that *we* are initiating the process, not top management. We are finding problems and solving them. We have to devise our own ideas for improvement and sell them.

The enthusiasm for the contest spread like wildfire. In January 1994, 4,300 teams entered the contest, involving 43,000 workers. Another

10,000 workers are on 1,000 teams that chose not to enter the contest totaling 53,000 workers—almost exactly half of Motorola's 107,000 person workforce at that time.

After judging at local and regional levels, twenty-four teams travel to Illinois to be judged by Motorola's CEO and other top executives. Each team wins either a gold or silver medal. Top executives, as well as the workers, love it. "Enthusiasm is the key to what the Total Customer Satisfaction competition is all about," according to Tommy George, the president and general manager of Motorola Semiconductor Products Sector:

- Enthusiasm displayed by the Error-Free Team from Seremban in establishing a permanent fix in wafer processing and opportunities for error, saving 7 million die per year.
- Enthusiasm shown by Munich's Entertainers Team in cutting rejects 500 percent, delivery times nearly in half, and improving sales 29 percent on a product for Nokia Corp.
- Enthusiasm exhibited by NML's Shut-up Team in increasing final test capacity 109 percent, reducing test cost 20 percent, and improving visual reject rates by 1,600 percent.

Certainly they are enthusiastic over at Motorola Philippines Inc. (MPI). When the Hi-Tech Team from there bagged a TCS gold medal in the 1994 awards, it made history by winning a third straight gold for MPI.

Other elements that help make the contest a success: teams are encouraged to focus on projects that achieve significant results within six months; several teams include representatives of outside suppliers or customers; the company goes to great pains to make sure all the finalists feel like a winner.

FANTASTIC QUALITY, FANTASTIC SUCCESS

First off, there are the direct quality successes. Though the company as a whole is not quite at Six Sigma, many of its individual operations are and these are already following its Beyond Six Sigma program and goals. Its cellular phones and pagers are recognized worldwide as world-class leaders in quality. This was not always the case. In the mid-1980s, some failed within one to two years. Now on many products the mean time to failure has reached sixty-three-plus years. Adds Buetow,

"Those are the kinds of gains you get when you drive your process toward perfection."

Richard Buetow doesn't hesitate in citing the overall results for the company: "We have the highest-quality products we've ever had. They will compete with anyone in the world. And we can produce them in Northbrook, Illinois, or anywhere in the U.S. as cheap as anywhere in the world." And it is not just Motorola tooting its own horn. The CEOs of the Business Roundtable rank Motorola as America's top practitioner of total quality management.

Then there are the significant financial rewards from increased quality. Buetow cited that the cost of poor quality in manufacturing was reduced by $1.4 billion in 1993 alone through the cumulative reduction in defects over the 1987–1993 period, and the total cumulative savings over the previous six years totaled $4.6 billion. And this figure doesn't include better designs and the plants and equipment Motorola didn't have to provide. The total savings by Buetow's reckoning are probably double that $4.6 billion figure. How much did Motorola spend to get these savings? "Not much at all" was his response. He also hastened to add that over the last seven years, employee productivity had increased 126 percent, or 12 percent annually. All this, and they didn't add any people and there were no increased costs. In fact, prices went down.

In its typical manner of refusing to rest on its laurels, Motorola is now pushing the concept of quality teams into the office. Buetow feels that the company can save an additional $2 billion by encouraging white-collar workers to operate more efficiently.

And for anyone that doubts that high quality translates into healthy sales, just look at these figures for 1993 in its four major product segments: in the Semiconductor Products Sector, sales were up 28 percent; in the General Systems Sector, sales rose 43 percent; in the Communications Segment, up 24 percent; and in the Government and Systems Technology Group, 32 percent.

George Fisher, while he was CEO, said it best: "We view quality as a competitive advantage. Our reputation opens markets."

LESSON: If you want to become the perfect company, you create a total quality, continuous learning culture by emphasizing:

- a vision from the top
- benchmarking against top competition
- setting and clearly communicating "impossible" goals
- empowering people by management letting go
- employing teamwork throughout
- training, training, and training the workers

 ## Total Employee Involvement Is Fundamental to Quality Improvement AMP

"QUALITY IMPROVEMENT GOALS MUST BECOME INTRINSIC TO ALL OUR BUSINESS PROCESSES, AFFECTING LEADERSHIP, PLANNING, INFORMATION DATABASES, HUMAN RESOURCE STRATEGIES, QUALITY MONITORING SYSTEMS, AND CUSTOMER SATISFACTION STRATEGIES."
—WILLIAM J. HUDSON, PRESIDENT AND CEO

THE CHALLENGE

Because AMP has been in global markets since the 1950s, it recognized early on that to be successful in the future, a company absolutely had to be world-class in quality. In the late 1980s, this world-leading producer of electrical and electronic interconnection products and systems recognized that its many successful programs, including its quality program launched in 1983, had to be integrated into a broader program in order to get the synergistic effect it was looking for.

THE RESPONSE

In the period since it launched its formal quality improvement process in 1983, AMP has pursued total quality with a focused commitment and rate of success matched at few other American companies. This is why CEO William Hudson can now say: "Quality is no longer something that's being advertised. Customers assume it's there, and if it isn't then the supplier will be penalized. It's a given."

To understand why AMP has succeeded so well, one should go back to a statement made by the previous chairman and CEO, Harold McInnes: "If you really believe, as we do, that total employee involvement is fundamental to quality improvement, and that quality improvement is essential to total customer satisfaction, then you have to find a way to get everybody involved. The Plan for Excellence offers us a terrific process to do just that."

The company's Plan for Excellence was introduced in February 1990 (and went global in 1992) to encompass a number of programs that had been created in the 1980s to improve quality, productivity, delivery, service, and new product development. Chairman James Marley notes that while AMP had good success with various separate productivity and quality improvement programs during the 1980s, the new Plan for Excellence integrates these programs and places even greater emphasis on total employee involvement and training. The plan is structured around the guidelines for the Baldrige National Quality Award, which AMP first applied for in 1988. The company was pleased when its Integrated Circuit Connector Products division was selected as one of only four large manufacturing companies to receive a site visit by the Baldrige committee in 1993.

The main thing AMP learned from its first Baldrige application was that while they were good in a number of categories, what they most needed was a more participative environment. They began to shape such an environment in a number of ways. Determining that employee product-focused or project-oriented teams had to be a key element of the Plan for Excellence, the number of such teams shot up to over 500 by 1992. The company generates employee interest in quality by sponsoring a yearly Excellence in Quality Improvement competition. In 1993, forty-three organizations entered. One of the winners was a plant in Japan—the company's first global winner. And Hudson believes it's important to empower employees by spending heavily on leading-edge technologies and equipment for both new product development and process improvement. The company has spent over $300 million each year in the 1990s on capital improvements, with two thirds going for new equipment and systems that leverage employees' efforts.

AMP also views training as a vital part of its employee involvement commitment. Its goal in 1994 was 40 hours minimum training per employee per year. It uses a seven-step process, known as the Manufacturing Skills Inventory System, to encourage an individualized skills assessment and training plan for each employee in manufacturing. To make sure all this preparation, time, and effort pays off, two separate evaluations keep track of each plant's training success, or lack of it. This training certainly pays off. The AMP manufacturing employee has between fifty to 300 skills to document. In addition to this, the company also began in 1988 its Engineering Education Program, which has a three-tiered focus aimed at identifying, developing, and instilling the highest quality engineering knowledge and skills. These two training programs, and a host of others, including a 100 percent reimbursement for tuition at accredited schools and universities, allow AMP to say, "This is what you need to know and how and when you can expect to learn it."

A plant manager who is aware that properly implementing the training takes time, has a few words for skeptical and reluctant managers: "Some people say they don't have time to work on their plant job skills matrix and then the individual assessments. But time and your people are all you have. You *must* invest in both of them."

Technology and training for the workers. Here's how Hudson ties it all together:

From the beginning of our improvement process a decade ago, it was clear that real progress would be made only if culture changes were accompanied by a commitment to steadily increasing spending on technology and training to enable our employees to keep pace with greater individual freedom and responsibility.

So quality is closely tied to employee involvement, which itself stresses training.

The other critical leg of the triad is total customer satisfaction—the goal of all its quality efforts. Hudson emphasizes how AMP had to move its quality emphasis from being just the best producer to focusing on the customer and growth and he adds that in facing over 1,000 competitors, AMP's best path to growth is to more closely tie the quality of our products to customer satisfaction. In short, they have carried their quality movement forward to the customer.

AMP works hard at tearing down the barriers between plant workers and sales reps. Two plants that adopted a product-focused team approach with great success are AMP's Williamstown and Tower City, Pennsylvania, manufacturing plants. At these sister plants, four sales engineers cooked an outdoor barbecue lunch for workers on all three shifts as a way of saying thank you to the plant people, who are turning out better products, thus making their job easier. This has now become an annual event. Such direct contact helps boost worker morale. One said: "I sometimes felt that we made millions of these parts and they simply dumped them in the ocean after we shipped them out. Now I know where most of them go."

This same focus on the customer characterizes AMP's activities abroad. It gets 60 percent of its revenues from thirty-five foreign countries. Chairman James Marley says AMP's local overseas ties are so close that foreign customers sometimes say, "Oh, I didn't know AMP had a U.S. subsidiary." Incidentally, AMP went global long before going global became trendy. It started in France in 1952 and began establishing its market-leading operation in Japan as early as 1957.

One key element and contributor to AMP's quality success has been a dedication to measurement. It measures hundreds of variables across every function of the company. Each day, employees and management on a department, division, business unit, and companywide basis receive critical information on such key indicators as quality, delivery, value, and service as these relate to customers, suppliers, internal operations, and (added in 1994) shareholders. This information comes in the form of a quality matrix, with the four variables running along each axis. It emphasizes that one of the most powerful ways to evaluate quality efforts comes in a completely unexpected unit: customer-time saved.

THE RESULTS

AMP's strong results are seen everywhere. At the macro level, though it has well over 1,000 competitors, it is the world leader in electrical/

electronic connector devices commanding about 18 percent of the $17–19 billion-a-year world market. It is four times the size of its nearest competitor and has stayed ahead of its Japanese and German rivals—even in their own countries. On the quality front, its efforts helped it achieve a corporatewide, tenfold improvement in product and service quality from 1986 to 1991.

By the end of 1993, AMP had nearly sixty management systems, covering almost 90 percent of production volume, certified to ISO 9000 standards—and aimed to have everything covered by the end of 1994. They also claimed to be on schedule toward a late 1995 goal on the much more rigorous MRP II Class certification of manufacturing requirement planning systems.

Where the results really show is in customer satisfaction. In independent U.S. customer satisfaction surveys conducted for the past seven years, AMP ranked very high (91 percent in 1991, 92 percent in 1992, and 96 percent in 1993) on specific performance attributes such as defect rate, delivery, service, product knowledge, and technical support—and generally highest on overall customer satisfaction all three years. The company stresses: "Quality is a major ingredient in that satisfaction. In fact, quality now ranks above price, delivery, and service in customer need surveys." General Elecric was so impressed with AMP's customer service techniques that it included AMP among the dozen companies it studies to improve its own management practices. Other customers who named AMP best or outstanding in 1993 were AT&T, Ford, IBM, Northern Telecom, Abbott Labs, Raytheon, Siemens, and UNISYS.

Why are customers so happy? Its on-time performance on ship-to-AMP-promise-date for 150,000 U.S. orders a month had risen to 95 percent in 1993 from 65 percent in 1987. To become even more customer-focused, AMP now carefully tracks ship-to-customer requirement as well. Its success rate is 80 percent, with a goal of at least 90 percent. Customers' phone calls are answered in an average of 3.5 seconds, and if anyone gets put on hold, a strobe light flashes in the phone operator's bullpen. Now that's attention to detail.

[
LESSON: Total quality can only be achieved by linking culture changes centered on a participative environment to steadily increasing spending on technology and training, with its goal being total customer satisfaction.
]

Being Best-Cost in Whatever We Do
EMERSON ELECTRIC

"THE BEST-COST PRODUCER STRATEGY BEGINS WITH A RECOGNITION THAT OUR CUSTOMERS' EXPECTATIONS FOR QUALITY, BROADLY DEFINED, ARE GETTING HIGHER EVERY DAY. TO REMAIN COMPETITIVE, WE HAVE TO MEET OR EXCEED THE HIGHEST STANDARDS IN THE WORLD ON PRODUCT PERFORMANCE, ON-TIME DELIVERY, AND SERVICE AFTER THE SALE. IN THIS CONTEXT, THE IDEAL OF 'ZERO DEFECTS' IS NOT SOME HIGH-TECH DREAM."
—**CHARLES KNIGHT, CHAIRMAN AND CEO**

THE CHALLENGE

It is 1984, and your company has experienced for more than a quarter of a century continually rising earnings and dividends per share. What challenge could there be? Foreign competition—especially in Brazil where they have discovered a product nearly identical to yours but much cheaper.

THE RESPONSE

Chuck Knight, CEO, wasted no time complaining about unfair foreign competition. He understood that in an environment in which it wasn't possible to raise prices because of global competition, the only way to maintain profit margins—which at that time was the company's main goal—was to increase volume and reduce costs. So he formalized and announced Emerson's Best-Cost Producer strategy in the company's annual report. Its underlying objective set a high standard: be best-cost in whatever they do, meaning the lowest cost at a differentiated-quality level. This strategy is Emerson's quality program, for in Knight's eyes the best-cost producer by definition has the highest quality, which in turn means the best product performance.

Of the Best-Cost Producer strategy's six elements, the lead one is "commitment to total quality." Emerson's goal is to ensure that each product line and business meets or exceeds the highest global quality standards. The emphasis is on making products right the first time. To measure progress of the total quality systems of its divisions, Emerson uses criteria for the Malcolm Baldrige National Quality Award and the ISO 9000 series quality standards (international quality standards). And the company is unrelenting in its quest for quality improvement.

Here's the way Knight closes his article in the *Harvard Business Review* highlighting what makes Emerson tick: "One final, basic point: never underestimate the cumulative impact of incremental change and the gathering forces of momentum. When you grind it out a yard at a time, you are in fact moving ahead. I can't say it will work for everybody, but at Emerson we view it as the only way to manage."

The real heart and soul of Emerson's drive to produce top-quality products is its almost fanatical dedication to continuous cost reduction. Knight says that this "has correctly been described as a 'religion' and 'a way of life' at Emerson. Every year for the past three and a half decades (in good times and bad), the company has set cost-reduction goals at every level and required plant personnel to identify the specific measures necessary to achieve those objectives." Currently, its annual cost-reduction goals average about 7 percent of the cost of goods sold. What it all boils down to is that the company sets targets, plans carefully, and follows up closely. As Knight has said, "We do act on our policies, and that may indeed make us unusual."

Another key element of Emerson's strategy is a "commitment to capital expenditures." In the 1988–1992 period, capital expenditures as a percentage of sales increased from 3.3 to 4.5. Since introducing their Best-Cost Producer strategy in 1984, the company has spent over $0.5 billion on restructuring. In the 1980s, Emerson invested $1.6 billion in technology. And the company moved from an export-led to an investment-led international strategy.

Knight acknowledges that these elements of strategy "are not especially new or original." But, he adds, "We think the key to success is closely tracking performance along these dimensions and attacking deviations immediately."

Though it's not part of their quality story per se, it is important to note that in 1993 Chuck Knight decided that it was time to add another important goal: growth. As he put it: "The pressure of the last ten years has been so great that I became tunnel-visioned on [profit margins]. ... We are shifting gears to growth."

Having growth as the new focus means rethinking some cherished concepts like decentralization, changing management's compensation formula, and encouraging risk taking and even tolerating some mistakes. Adding growth means tougher targets than ever under their rigorous planning process. Revenue growth is to be pushed to as high as 10 percent per year, from under 5 percent in recent years. And, of course, profit margins and return on equity should be kept steady.

THE RESULTS

The results that speak the loudest are these: thirty-six and thirty-seven years respectively of record earnings and dividends per share. Yes. That's right—since 1957, the earnings curve for Emerson has sloped steadily upward. Few companies can match that result. But there's another result that competes for dramatic effect: the percentage of Emerson products that are number one or two within domestic markets is a stunning 87 percent.

For a company that does not have a quality department, Emerson's reputation for quality is virtually unsurpassed. The waste disposers it makes for Sears have the lowest failure rate of any appliance item sold by that chain. Its electric clothes dryer motors for the appliance industry are nearing Six Sigma quality (their defect rate is less than one hundred parts per million).

Its major investments in technology and engineering support have made it a new-product-generating machine. New products—those introduced in the past five years—as a percentage of sales has increased from 9 to 24 percent. In fiscal 1993 alone, commercial new product sales reached $2.0 billion, up 11 percent over the prior year.

Emerson's investment-led international strategy has also paid off handsomely. Its international sales have grown annually at 11 percent over the past ten years, to approximately 40 percent of total sales in fiscal 1993. Unconsolidated joint venture sales worldwide more than tripled from $605 million in FY 1988 to approximately $2.0 billion in FY 1995. It has 132 manufacturing locations outside the United States and in 1994 was building plants in India, China, Singapore and Eastern Europe. But recently exports from U.S. factories have emerged as the fastest-growing segment of the company's business. Certainly the manufacturing abroad hasn't held back job growth in the United States. In 1981, its U.S. factories employed 19,000 workers. In 1994, the figure was 43,000.

Investors couldn't be more pleased with the results. The annual total return since 1956 has averaged 17.9 percent. Emerson is one of only eleven U.S. corporations that outearned its cost of capital during each of the past twenty years and one of only twenty-two industrial companies whose ratio of market price to book value ranked in the top 20 percent of U.S. corporations during each of the past ten years.

[
LESSON: Your quality program can be a total commitment to continuous cost reduction. Viewed properly, and in conjunction with capital investment, the best-cost producer by definition has the highest quality and the best product performance.
]

 Total Transformation from a Little Book
UNITED ELECTRIC CONTROLS

"YOU ALMOST HAVE TO THROW EVERYTHING OUT. YOU CAN'T JUST ADOPT A KANBAN-DRIVEN [JUST-IN-TIME] PRODUCTION SCHEDULE. YOU HAVE TO USE JUST-IN-TIME SCHEDULES, REDUCE SETUP TIME, AND ELIMINATE DEFECTS—ALL AT THE SAME TIME. MAINTAINING EVEN ONE ASPECT OF THE PREVIOUS SYSTEM SLOWS YOU DOWN."

—BRUCE HAMILTON, VICE PRESIDENT, MANUFACTURING

THE CHALLENGE

In late 1986, United Electric of Watertown, Massachusetts, realized it was in the midst of a downward trend—deliveries were poor, lead times were up, inventory was high, and employee participation was at an all-time low. In 1987, the company posted its worst loss ever. Bruce Hamilton, vice president of manufacturing, knew change was necessary. He never particularly had liked the status quo or seeing himself as a caretaker: "Somebody who becomes a change agent is not in the same business as the type of person who is a career job protector." But he wasn't sure exactly what needed to be done.

Until a little book was literally dropped on his desk one day about a month after he assumed his new VP for manufacturing position in late 1986. This book, he found, had just what his company needed.

THE RESPONSE

Of all things, the book that set the company on its way toward a thorough transformation and turnaround was a novel—*The Goal* by Eliyahu Goldratt and Jeff Cox. It's the simple story of a plant manager who discovers how to turn around the quality, production, and delivery problems within his own company. The book's message was simple: challenge the way things are done and undo the way things have been done in the past. One particular problem that the book addressed and that was a real one at United Electric was overproduction—building parts or components far faster than the next department could use them.

All of the managers found it compelling reading, so much so that the company purchased copies for *every* employee, about 450 at the time. Not everyone read it, but it transformed the thinking of those who did. "Until *The Goal,* I don't think I had ever read anything about manufacturing, and it flat out contradicted everything we believed," notes manufacturing supervisor Charlie Thompson, a forty-one-year UE veteran.

The book led to a *Goals* workshop and then two other workshops that focused on how the message of the book applied to UE. More than a hundred employees voluntarily attended these workshops and began to challenge their own work areas as "education is action" became bywords at UE.

At this point, Bruce Hamilton knew that all the answers to what needed to be done—and the solution to the long puzzling and frustrating dilemma of how to improve productivity—could be found in the minds of the employees. Let them take the lead: "Maybe you should call me an antihero, because I think leadership should be more like a flock of geese, with different people leading every day." But he also knew that creating the dissatisfaction with the status quo for his employees and the tremendous change that was required was not going to be easy: "Change is the management of pain. It involves a lot of people, a lot of emotion. And you have to have that structure—that support system—not only for the change agent, but also for the people who are going through the change."

The employees emphasized that UE needed change—change in processes, techniques, and employee roles. Drawing on various production systems, the company began to alter its philosophy and methods. Lot sizes, inventory, systems, jobs, and education were all scrutinized with an eye toward reducing waste, improving the process, and tapping the creative resources of the organization's employees.

Perhaps the most successful change put into effect was the Total Employee Involvement (TEI) Program. Under this, the company has three main tools for harvesting ideas. One is the Valued Ideas Program, under which a flat $100 in cash is handed out for every usable idea. Then there are Action Centers, which resemble the quality circles of old. Employees can form these at any time (with management's approval) to solve a specific problem. In the first month of the program (February 1987), employees set up more than forty such groups. Then there is CEDAC, which stands for Cause-and-Effect Diagram with the Addition of Cards, a method used when the cause of a problem needs to be defined. This group usually meets for at least three months.

Hamilton shares an important insight about tapping into people's ideas. He emphasizes that companies do themselves a disservice by evaluating ideas purely on the basis of how much money they save. "It's the process of arriving at those ideas—even thinking about them —that we want to reward, not just the result. A person may come up with nine ideas that save a dollar apiece, then the tenth saves $50,000. People hate rejection. If you reject the first few, you don't get that last one."

THE RESULTS

United Electric is well on its way to solving the productivity dilemma and that was vividly attested to in 1990 when it became the sole recipient of the North American Shingo Prize for Manufacturing Excellence.

Certainly their TEI program has worked wonders. Between roughly 1968 and 1988, a twenty-year period, employees had slipped around twenty ideas into the company's suggestion box. Within a few years of the start of TEI, over 1,000 ideas were pouring in—a virtual invasion of imagination. Everywhere, workers are using devices that they themselves invented. This is employee involvement made very concrete in the form of improved inventory controls, more efficient machines, better quality-testing tools. Some were big changes, others quite small. But added together, they brought on dramatic positive results.

Within just four years of *The Goal*'s arrival on Hamilton's desk, lead times (the time from raw stage of a product to when it is finished) were slashed from sixteen weeks to one or two weeks, with 60 percent of its orders built and shipped within three days. Lot sizes went from about 200 to ten, which in turn helped to cut finished-goods inventory by 75 percent and work-in-process by 80 percent. Setup times dropped from ninety minutes to less than three.

Best of all, these changes didn't cost too much. Says Hamilton: "This is not a problem you need to throw money at. There is more than enough information out there in the public domain" that will let a company "improve productivity on a shoestring."

[
LESSON: Don't underestimate the power of new ideas (which may be found in a book) to change the way things were done in the past, unlock people's minds, encourage creativity, and create a quality-conscious culture.
]

TQM Is Something You Are
HARDINGE BROTHERS

"THE BIGGEST OBSTACLE WAS BRINGING ALL EMPLOYEES TO THE REALIZATION THAT THE COMPANY'S OWN PROCESS AND SYSTEMS WERE THE GREATEST IMPEDIMENT TO ACHIEVING ITS LONG-RANGE GOALS. ACCORDINGLY, IN JULY OF 1987, HARDINGE COMMITTED ITSELF IRREVOCABLY TO TOTAL QUALITY MANAGEMENT AS THE NEW COMPANY LIFE-STYLE."

—ROBERT AGAN, PRESIDENT AND CEO

THE CHALLENGE

Along with most other American machine tool companies, Hardinge Brothers of Elmira, New York, experienced the 1980s as a time of threat and uncertainty, primarily because of international competition. Japanese producers in particular began to offer CNC (computer numerically controlled) machine tools in all sizes and across all functions, thus becoming capable of supporting the requirements of even the largest manufacturers.

Hardinge made several (limited) attempts to penetrate these new, larger markets but by the mid-1980s found itself in a precarious position. The demand for manual machine tools was clearly giving way to new technologies. The need for change was obvious.

To chart a new business course, Hardinge first had to improve its manufacturing and control procedures. In 1985 and 1986, it implemented a new MRP II (manufacturing resource planning) program, both for controlling manufacturing and for planning sales and operations. But even the success resulting from MRP II was not enough, though the success did provide the confidence that the company could manage major change. The greatest obstacle was making all its employees realize that the company's own processes and systems were the greatest impediment to achieving its long-range goals since they were not customer-oriented and were too slow to respond to customers' changing needs.

THE RESPONSE

Accordingly, in July of 1987, Hardinge committed itself irrevocably to total quality management (TQM) as the new company life-style. This was not a spur-of-the-moment decision. They had been looking for some time for a vehicle to improve product quality. Around this time, a close corporate neighbor, Corning, had adopted a TQM process. They decided to play off Corning's lead.

Hardinge's TQM process has three focal points: the primacy of satisfying the customer, eliminating rework through continuous improvement (as gauged by statistical analysis), and a management philosophy that stresses planning to prevent mistakes (to make correcting them unnecessary).

TQM was installed at Hardinge first by obtaining a total commitment from top management. This was followed by a massive program of "total quality awareness" education for employees, in which more than 26,000 classroom hours were logged. Education was enhanced by an improved employee communication system and an employee recognition program that operated immediately and on the spot. And it resulted in three quarters of the workers participating in all kinds of employee teams in which the workers manage and continually redesign their own production groups to meet flexible requirements.

One gets the impression that TQM has worked at Hardinge because of Bob Agan and his perspective on it. Few people have such a thorough understanding of the importance of TQM:

> I believe TQM is the most significant thing to happen to American business life since the invention of the assembly line. There are still people who believe that TQM is just another exotic "management flavor of the month." But TQM is here to stay because, by every yardstick, whether it's profits, productivity, market share, or customer satisfaction, TQM companies are more successful.

THE RESULTS

As a Hardinge report says, TQM has brought it "a host of benefits." Today it produces machine tools capable of achieving accuracies of 15 millionths of an inch. Indeed, the reliability of its products has been so greatly enhanced that the company now offers the first two-year warranty in the machine tool industry.

Speed, in many different ways, has greatly increased. By 1993, the company's goal of shipping any one of its more than 30,000 standard collets within two hours of receiving a customer order was achieved on 94 percent of all orders. Further, the use of simultaneous engineering concepts has reduced product development time by over 60 percent, and has helped Hardinge introduce twelve new CNC machine models to the marketplace during the past five years.

But to Hardinge, the bottom line of its TQM efforts is this:

Perhaps the most important result of Hardinge's efforts is that all have been generated by workers trained and motivated here in the United States. All thoughts of divestment, or of seeking foreign ownership or capital, were discarded by Hardinge in favor of using the company's home-grown talents and capabilities. By restructuring to focus on continuous improvement in production, and by removing an entire layer of management, Hardinge has been able to build an environment that takes full advantage of the creativity and industry of all its people.

[
LESSON: TQM is not an event, it is a process that drives every activity in a company. It may mean turning the culture of a company in a new direction, which in turn may mean re-forming work groups, finding ways to create stakeholders instead of employees, and learning how to create a process of shared decision making.
]

10: ACHIEVE ENVIRONMENTAL EXCELLENCE

The theme of this chapter, which is the way that companies must look at environmental issues in the future, is stated clearly, succinctly, and forcefully by Frank Popoff, chairman and CEO of Dow Chemical.

Environmental protection makes good business sense—from both ethical and economic viewpoints. How well we perform in this arena will impact our ability to build new facilities, renew permits, manufacture new products, attract new employees, and ultimately, compete in a global marketplace. I don't believe it's an exaggeration to say that companies that fail to adequately address environmental issues will face extinction as we move into the next century.

ENVIRONMENTAL PROTECTION MAKES GOOD BUSINESS SENSE

That's a pretty radical statement. For many companies, it may seem like an oxymoron. Cleaning up and complying with pesky, even nasty, government regulations is a pain and an expense, pure and simple.

That certainly was the prevailing perspective and ideology for most of corporate history in America. But over the past two decades, a small but growing number of companies are discovering an exciting win-win type of situation: that environmental benefits and corporate financial benefits often go hand in hand.

Virtually all the companies in this chapter demonstrate the truth of this principle. The godfather of them all is the 3P program (Pollution Prevention Pays) of 3M. Started by 3M in 1975, the program had spawned 4,100 projects by 1993 that have made substantial reductions in a broad range of corporate pollutants, all the while saving the company over $710 million (in first-year savings alone). In the mid-1980s, 3P evolved into the 3P+ program—a more business-oriented view that integrates environmental goals into the overall business strategy. It continues to stay ahead of the game with state-of-the-art corporate environmental thinking such as this statement by Robert Bringer, staff vice president for environmental engineering and pollution control:

> We don't see pollution as something to be cleaned up at the end of a production process. It's an environmental goal. But it's also a productivity goal, and it's a quality goal. They all work together. 3P+ is a holistic approach to pollution prevention. This is a process that will help us meet our environmental and business goals simultaneously, and it can be a part of our overall quality improvement process.

It took other companies a while longer to recognize that pollution prevention really does pay, but in the 1980s a number did and have benefited greatly. Dow Chemical features the fact in its WRAP program —Waste Reduction Always Pays—initiated in 1986. Chevron got SMART (Save Money and Reduce Toxics) in 1984.

Most companies don't have a clever program name, but they definitely see that environmental protection can make good business sense. Searle's Augusta, Georgia, plant took on the specific challenge of inventing a nonpolluting cleaning process. After a two-year effort, the new process was implemented and led to an 87 percent reduction in toxic air emissions, a 71 percent reduction in liquid hazardous wastes generated, *and* a 40 percent increase in productivity. Eastman Chemical now views environmental management as one of its core competencies that give it a competitive advantage.

MAKE EMPLOYEES "ENVIRONMENTAL MANAGERS"

The companies featured in this chapter engaged in many types of responses to environmental challenges. The two approaches that most clearly emerged were making your employees frontline "environmental managers" and being willing to invest heavily in environmental R&D.

Again, 3M led the way with encouraging its employees—all its employees—to be responsible for creative environmental initiatives that would help prevent pollution. Indeed, a good deal of 3M's effectiveness as an environmental leader for nearly two decades is captured in this cleverly phrased corporate truth: "We have 85,000 employees looking for waste minimization ideas." Management encourages employee involvement, an important part of the 3P program, in three principal ways. First, they hammer away at the message. Second, literally thousands of their employees have by now received company awards for their contributions to the 3P program through the company's overall recognition and reward system. Then there is the Environmental Leadership Award, started in 1991, which recognizes employees not only for the work they do at 3M but for improving the environment outside 3M as well.

Other companies pursue different ways to involve their employees. Dow Chemical has a number of very direct means. For plant managers, salaries and bonuses are partially pegged to how well they meet environmental goals. For all employees, it added in 1992 an environmental category to their job appraisal form. And senior managers meet four times a year with eight environmental leaders from around the world for a full one and a half days. Cooper Tire & Rubber, when it wanted to reinvigorate its environmental thrust, formed its employee task force on waste minimization.

INVEST IN R&D

A company should also be willing to invest in R&D that may lead to breakthrough products and processes. Eastman Chemical, as a result of extensive research into plastics recycling, is on the verge of putting into operation an automated sorting system that could revolutionize—and boost dramatically—plastics recycling. 3M has demonstrated a huge commitment to environmental research. More than 15 percent of its yearly $1 billion in R&D spending—$150 million in 1993—is devoted to environmentally related projects.

INSTITUTIONALIZE ENVIRONMENTAL EXCELLENCE

Dow Chemical, 3M, and a number of other companies have gone so far as to institutionalize environmental excellence into the company culture. They keep strengthening their environmental efforts to such a degree that achieving environmental excellence becomes a natural part of the company's operations and a key part of its overall business strategy.

SIGNIFICANT RESULTS CAN APPEAR QUICKLY AND THEY CAN BE CONTINUOUS

One myth that has generally prevailed is that environmental results of any significance will take a long time to achieve. Cooper Tire & Rubber certainly belies that myth. In their first year of operation, the employee task force on waste minimization had a broad array of dramatic reductions in pollution, including increasing the amount of waste recycled by 38 percent and reducing the amount of waste taken to the county landfill by another 38 percent.

There's also the myth that a company will take on all the relatively easy challenges with big results up front, but after that the law of diminishing returns sets in. Jim Lindsly, Dow's issue manager for waste reduction, takes this one on directly: "With every year, we see more and more impact. Once you get the 'easy pickings' out of the way, the power of your quality program comes into play."

Further, what's really encouraging is that the twin economic and environmental benefits can continue to be realized year after year. The 3P and 3P+ program of 3M is nineteen years old and dozens of employees still receive the company's Environmental Leadership Award each year for new efforts that are helping the company meet its very challenging environmental goals, which are continuously being set: ultimately to "become a sustainable growth company and move toward zero emissions."

▶ Pollution Prevention Really Pays
3M

The year was 1975, and few corporations were "thinking environ-ment." If they were thinking about it at all, it was in the sense of "how can we avoid, or keep our costs to a minimum in responding to these annoying new regulations beginning to spring forth from this new regulatory kid on the federal block—the Environmental Protection Agency."

But one company over 1,000 miles from Washington was thinking differently. It knew that waiting to eliminate pollution at the end of the pipe would be expensive and counterproductive to business goals. Plant managers saw this as money spent unwisely with absolutely no return. So 3M established the 3P (Pollution Prevention Pays) program to eliminate pollution at its source. The board of directors in February of that year adopted a proactive (a key word at 3M) corporate environ-mental policy with one of its six main principles being to "prevent pollution at the source wherever and whenever possible." The com-pany then had the genius to ask its people to look for projects that not only prevented pollution but saved money. This program was strictly voluntary for the employees, yet after nineteen years over 4,100 proj-ects have been accepted for 3P recognition, over 1.3 billion pounds per year of pollution have been prevented, and over $710 million has been saved (in first-year savings alone).

But the impact of 3P went far beyond Minnesota. It proved that pollution prevention can pay in many instances and 3P became a model for other industries. It helped lead to the adoption of pollution prevention as the preferred approach to environmental protection by the U.S. government, by most states, by the United Nations and most foreign governments, and by the environmental community.

That's quite a set of accomplishments. But 3P was only the start for 3M. As Robert Bringer, the company's senior environmental official, said in 1991, "our greatest opportunities for pollution prevention in 3M still lie ahead."

In 1985, 3M began to build on its 3P legacy and since then has launched a number of environmental initatives that continue to put it at the forefront of creativity and effectiveness in meeting corporate environmental challenges. Specifically, 3P evolved into the 3P+ program, a more business-oriented view that integrates environmental goals into the overall business strategy.

Are they still excited about this approach, which has now been underway for nearly two decades? It's clear they are more excited and committed than ever.

MAJOR MILESTONES IN ENVIRONMENTALLY CREATIVE THINKING

Meeting environmental and business goals simultaneously. Sounds like an idea of the 1990s that a company like 3M would finally come to based·on long experience. But 3M has had it in its blood for some time:

> It's only in recent years that conservation of natural resources has become of interest to people generally. Even now there are too few who consider conservation a major part of business operations.
>
> In industry, almost any saving of materials is at least an indirect saving of natural resources—and manufacturers who realize this are probably operating at a much higher level of efficiency than those who do not.
>
> That efficiency, through more thorough use of materials, means more economical production. That in turn means more total production for each dollar invested . . . more jobs, more prosperity.

These words were written by former 3M CEO William McKnight back in the 1940s.

This company culture, or attitude, was the first thing Robert Bringer brought up in his interview. He stressed that it was a combination of this attitude and things happening in the world that have led to where 3M is today. He pointed to three outside forces:

1. Command-and-control regulation is the biggest market incentive right now. It puts many restrictions on 3M that the company wants to get out from under.
2. Global competition is the second force. Decreasing waste is important to being a low-cost producer.
3. The quality push is the third force. Processes with low environmental impact often lead to high quality.

But then he hastened to add that "the setting of corporate goals really raised the importance of the environmental issue in the company." This goal-setting milestone—a change in 3M's approach to the environmental issue and its movement toward sustainable development—began in late 1985, ten years after the start of the 3P program. Then CEO Allen Jacobson asked if anything was bothering Bringer and his staff about the company's environmental status. They replied that they were concerned about the sheer volume of solvent air emissions. At that time, these emissions accounted for 80 percent of 3M's total emissions to air and water and were a direct result of its major manufacturing processes, which coated value-added materials suspended or dissolved in hydrocarbon solvents onto thin backings.

In 1987, the Operations Committee approved an air emmissions reduction program for all of 3M's major uncontrolled sources worldwide. The goal was to reduce global air emissions by 70 percent by 1993. When Bringer was asked how the 70 percent goal was chosen, he stated it was a simple matter of going through all their plants and calculating the reduction that could be achieved when all the controls were put on. Two thirds of its plants installed thermal oxidizers, mammoth contraptions that remind one of a machine from *Star Wars*. They're expensive too. The company had to spend over $175 million for what was mainly pollution control equipment. But it was wise enough to recognize that pollution prevention alone—particularly voluntary efforts—could not do the whole job.

Even this pollution control approach was very proactive. It anticipated legislation that now requires them to reveal all their emissions to the public; it anticipated 1990's Clean Air Act Amendments, which will require future controls; it reduced some potential liabilities; and it has given them incentive to eliminate the use of solvents rather than replace that equipment.

Here we should introduce Jim Clapper, the plant manager of the tape plant in St. Paul. This plant, one of 3M's oldest, has been at the forefront of 3M's initiatives in reducing air emissions. Here, loosely paraphrased, is the fascinating story Clapper told.

As a manufacturer, one of their goals was to take out a layer from one of their tape products. Specifically, they had to look at ways to take the layer out without decreasing quality. Many experiments were run in the factory. (They run one hundred experiments a month in his plant alone.) Short-run production lots were run so they could use normal equipment. They also utilized product and process engineers, who are located right in the plant. Together they came up with a method that did not require coating both sides of the tape. Best of all, the new method met three key criteria: quality was better, costs were saved, and the environmental impact was reduced. All in all, the new process resulted in forty-three fewer tons of solvent discharged into the atmosphere. For this, the cross-functional team that worked on it was given a 3P Award.

Jim Clapper and his people are not ones to rest on their laurels. Indeed, the week before the interview, they were the focus of a landmark environmental agreement between the state of Minnesota and 3M when both sides signed an innovative air quality permit for the St. Paul tape plant.

Basically, the permit allows the plant the flexibility to change operations in response to market demands without obtaining numerous permit amendments. Clapper spoke glowingly of how the new permit works: "Our new permit, which took almost two years to develop, places a cap on total emissions from this facility. That allows us to decide how to keep our overall emissions within specified limits, making permit amendments for existing sources unnecessary." That cap is substantially below 3M's past emissions levels and regulatory limitations. Here's the way Robert Bringer described the value to the company of the new flexible approach:

> This kind of flexibility is important to us because this plant has several dozen different manufacturing processes with emissions which might require numerous different state permits. As we try to be more competitive globally, we move things around from production line to production line. There are a lot of things that require changes, and what we don't want are delays and stop-and-start manufacturing every time we need to modify operations.

The enthusiasm for the innovative new permit goes right to the top. Chairman of the Board and CEO L. D. DeSimone said: "This is the kind of arrangement which benefits the state, the environment, and the economy. It encourages us to operate with increasingly lower emissions."

As for the goal of reducing air emissions by 70 percent by 1993 from the 1987 base, the company met the goal. But as Bringer said, "This is not a long-term solution." It was necessary and they did it. This pollution control phase constituted Phase 1 of 3P +

Phase 2 of 3P+ began in 1989 with two goals to be accomplished by the year 2000—a 90 percent reduction of emissions to air, water, and land, and a 50 percent reduction in waste generated. This is on top of the 50 percent reduction as a result of nineteen years of 3P.

These Year 2000 goals were approved by the Operations Committee. In 1990, the Challenge '95 program began. It set goals of a 35 percent reduction in waste and a 20 percent reduction in energy use by 1995. It was an important milestone, for it is the first time a productivity improvement program in 3M has environmental goals.

Challenge '95 serves as a formal measurement tool. It is one of the most comprehensive control systems for continuous performance improvement of any corporation in the country. For example, all waste-stream products and by-products must be measured by weight and reported on a quarterly basis—allowing management to measure progress by each product division in reducing its waste 7 percent a year, or 35 percent over five years. With such objective data, management can adjust R&D and other expenditures to maximize pollution prevention efforts to attain its long-term objectives.

The third phase of 3P+ involves a major new emphasis on the environmental impact of products. They use the phrase product life cycle analysis to look at all aspects of a product's life from inception to final disposal. "Each of the stages in a product's life offers many opportunities for environmental improvement which are often accompanied by commercially valuable benefits—both tangible and intangible." The life cycle model is truly an iterative process. All elements of the life cycle need to be considered in the concept and design phases, as well as anytime a change is made to the product design or process during the development program.

The life cycle model is a tool to assist business units in developing products with an optimum balance of performance, cost, environmental, health, and safety characteristics. Importantly to an innovative company like 3M (indeed it could well have been the lead company for the chapter on new product innovation), the model is not intended to impair creativity and innovation. Rather, it is intended to encourage business units to make prudent choices in developing products (and packaging) that can be manufactured, distributed, used, and disposed of safely.

Bringer sums up the environmental policies and programs at 3M since 1985 in this manner: "3M recognized several years ago that our business and environmental interests were merging. And while the voluntary 3P approach of the past is still viable, we needed to add structure and goals to our environmental programs to ensure the protection of our business interests."

COMMITTED, CREATIVE EMPLOYEES

Employee involvement is an important part of the 3P program. How do they do it? Three ways, according to Rick Renner, the corporate host for our interviews. First, they hammer away at the message. Jim Clapper, the plant manager, had a vivid way of describing the process: "It just gets burned into your brain that we're doing this. I can't even describe all the ways you get indoctrinated about 3P+."

A second method is the Environmental Leadership Award, which was started in 1991. Employees are recognized not only for the work they do for 3M, but for improving the environment outside 3M. CEO DeSimone calls it "one of the most important awards" given at 3M because it recognizes "individual contributions to society at large as well as to 3M's environmental goals." The number of awards each year varies. In 1993, six awards involving more than one hundred people were given.

One of these awards was given in 1991 to a team of process engineers at the Aberdeen, South Dakota, plant. What they did was a perfect example of "thinking globally, acting locally." The task at this plant was particularly intriguing because it makes round respirator masks out of square fabric. When they began looking at the process, 33 percent of the fabric that went into the process came out as waste. The team's goal was zero waste for the mask product. They began by seeing the waste as a supply of raw materials. By reformulating the product, fibers in the waste could be used in a new line of products for hazardous waste clean-up. "Our goal," said team member Tim Stump, "is that everything that comes into the plant goes out as a useful item." With the success of the respirator mask project, that is beginning to look like a reasonable goal at the Aberdeen plant. Another team member, Roger Stumo, said, "We need to look at products from cradle to grave and then eliminate the grave."

This same type of employee initiative and creativity is occurring throughout 3M's worldwide operations. Of the many fascinating plant stories, one in particular stands out for individual employee initiative.

Andrew Shell was a team leader in three innovative projects. When he and three colleagues were visiting a plant in Illinois they saw Coag, an unwanted by-product of the manufacturing process. A nearby landfill could no longer accept the Coag, so it was being transported 350 miles away. "The idea hit all of us at the same time," Shell said. "We could incorporate the Coag back into the parent product." So the team went to work and modified the product. The project resulted in lower disposal and raw material costs—an annual savings of $660,000 and waste reduction of more than 300,000 pounds per year.

In another project, Shell led a team that substituted solventless materials in a product that had used the usual hydrocarbon-based solvents. The result was a reduction of 3 million pounds of solvent emissions a year since 1988, and a cost savings of more than $2 million. In a third program, Shell's team substituted a solventless treatment in another abrasives product, resulting in 1,350,000 pounds less of solvent emissions per year and savings of $800,000 per year.

The third factor in promoting employee involvement is the overall recognition and reward system. There are a number of levels of awards, most for employees but three for operating units as well. Many award winners receive recognition from management, in 3M publications, and award ceremonies and recognition. No financial rewards are involved because the company tries hard to get these to be shared efforts.

A HUGE COMMITMENT TO ENVIRONMENTAL RESEARCH

3M is definitely a company that puts its money where its mouth is. More than 15 percent of its yearly $1 billion in R&D spending—$150 million in 1993—is devoted to environmentally related projects. What is going on in its laboratories? The use of recycled or recyclable materials is being investigated. More environmentally compatible materials are being developed. The use of materials that trigger regulation is being reduced. New solventless coating processes are being developed.

Environmental research goes on everywhere. Fifty operating units have their own labs, and major pieces of analytical equipment can now be easily deployed to the various production sites.

At Central Research—the corporate research lab—one of its directors, Ted Bolles, stressed that they work hard at getting the newest technologies out to the divisions. The lab's major thrust is to work on creating solventless processes, which they've already accomplished in a number of cases. When he was asked how research priorities are established, he said they aim for a mix. About half should come from heads of business units saying, "Hey, I think we can use that." The other half should be the long-range stuff like their work in phototonics, which spanned ten years; it wasn't until the eighth year that the business unit people began to like it.

A SUSTAINABLE GROWTH CORPORATION

In looking to the future, 3M continues to think big. When asked about new goals, Bringer replied, "Become a sustainable growth company and move toward zero emissions."

What is a sustainable growth company? Bringer defines it as one whose products, facilities, and operations have minimal environmental impact so that its business can continue to grow without adverse effect on the earth. It will also be a corporation that has maximized the business opportunities the environmental issue has presented.

How does 3M plan to become a sustainable growth company? They plan to use both a process and an all-inclusive umbrella organization because the environmental issue involves so many aspects of 3M operations.

The process they are using is holistic pollution prevention—a process that is an integral part of its total quality management process and an opportunity to demonstrate progress toward TQM goals. Holistic pollution prevention will continuously minimize the harmful environmental impact of 3M products, facilities, operations, employees, customers, and suppliers.

The umbrella under which the process operates is called Pollution Prevention Plus or 3P+. It builds on the base established by the 3P program and includes all existing and future programs that have a pollution prevention component. Most importantly, it directly incorporates environmental goals into the overall business strategy. There are three advantages to the umbrella approach:

1. It will identify all related programs as seeking the same goal.
2. It will allow management commitment to the process rather than individual programs.

3. It will minimize the time for 3M to become a sustainable growth company.

The number of 3P+ type programs that already exist within the company and that will fall under the umbrella of 3P+ already exceeds fifty. The ones that are manufacturing-plant-related are 3P, Air Emissions Reduction, Year 2000 Goals, and Challenge '95. Others include Underground Storage Tank Upgrades, Asbestos Survey and Management, PCB Elimination, Ozone Depleting Chemicals Elimination, HF Storage and Handling Upgrade, and Resource Recovery. Some are related to facilities other than manufacturing such as paper recycling, some are transportation-related like van pooling, others are more employee-related like paper use conservation, and still others are oriented toward the public like the Responsible Care Program.

So what does it take to move a corporation to that new level of performance called sustainable growth? Bringer cites four factors:

1. Recognition—that such a move is not only in the world's best interests but in the corporation's best interests.
2. Commitment—to becoming a "sustainable growth" company. This includes commitment of adequate resources.
3. Goals—publicly stated with time deadlines.
4. Process—preferably part of an ongoing, never-ending improvement process such as total quality management.

LESSON: The best way to protect the environment is to focus on pollution *prevention* because it not only protects the environment, it makes it possible to cut costs and it improves quality. To take advantage of all these benefits, pollution prevention should be embedded into the culture and business strategy by:

- setting ambitious goals, especially eliminating all waste
- involving all employees as "environmental managers"
- investing in environmental R&D
- giving rewards and recognition to employees for achieving environmental progress
- having good measurement systems

Quick Results
COOPER TIRE & RUBBER

"OUR WASTE MINIMIZATION PROGRAM HAS BECOME PART OF OUR DAILY WORKING LIVES. RECYCLING IS NOT ONLY SOCIALLY RESPONSIBLE BUT ALSO MAKES GOOD BUSINESS SENSE. AS WE PUT LESS WASTE MATERIAL INTO THE LANDFILL, WE SAVE MONEY."
—PAT ROONEY, PRESIDENT

THE CHALLENGE

Cooper Tire & Rubber of Findlay, Ohio, had always been conscious of controlling waste, reducing scrap, and protecting the environment generally. In the late 1980s, it wanted to put more teeth into its efforts, focusing both on minimizing waste and recycling its company-generated scrap tires.

THE RESPONSE

Its first step was to form an employee task force on waste minimization. Its mission was to initiate new programs to further reduce waste and to recycle, reuse, and recover additional by-products and the energy content from materials that, in the past, had been disposed in landfills.

In July 1991, the company formalized a long-term commitment to waste minimization with the issuance of a written policy, which lists nine specific ways in which Cooper is committed to finding practical ways to minimize waste. In August 1991, an office waste recycling program and a home recycling education program were introduced and enthusiastically accepted by employees.

Cooper had already launched a program in April 1990 to recycle 100 percent of its company-generated scrap tires into other products such as asphalt rubber, floor coverings, and playground cover. In 1991, they solicited the assistance of their raw material suppliers in eliminating unnecessary packaging and in identifying outlets for other manufacturing waste.

THE RESULTS

For those who feel that significant results take a long time to generate, they need look no further than the accomplishments of the employee task force on waste minimization in just its third year of operation (1993):

- reduced the total waste landfilled at the Findlay facility by 48.3 percent in three years
- converted 76 percent of all raw materials shipments to tire plants to systems using returnable containers, reusable packaging, or bulk loads
- recycled 323 tons of paper and cardboard, and 738 tons of plastic
- recycled 390 tons of trimmed tire vents by donating it to area parks and playgrounds as ground-cushioning material
- recycled over 58 percent of wastes generated in the Findlay plant and corporate offices, diverting over 8,000 tons of material from the local landfill into productive uses

Gerry McCullough, Findlay's materials conservation foreman, said he is "overwhelmed" by the success of the program so far: "We have just scratched the surface. There is no reason, in my mind, why we can't get to recycling 75 to 80 percent of the materials we were throwing away just two years ago."

[
LESSON: By getting everyone involved from the beginning in employee task forces on waste minimization (and other environmental goals) you can achieve significant results quicker than you think.
]

Innovate to Meet Impossible Standards
SEARLE

> "WE ARE HERE TO COMMEMORATE SOME VERY SKILLED AND DEDICATED ACTIVITY WHICH PRODUCED SOME VERY POSITIVE RESULTS FOR THE ADDED PURITY OF THE AIR, THE SAFETY OF THE EMPLOYEES, AND THE REDUCTION OF TOXIC WASTES, NOT TO MENTION THE EFFICIENCY OF OPERATIONS."
> **—RICHARD U. DE SCHUTTER, PRESIDENT**

THE CHALLENGE

It goes without saying that pharmaceutical manufacturers must attain high purity of product. This in turn requires an extraordinarily high degree of equipment cleaniness. Searle, a subsidiary of Monsanto, estimates that more than 700 separate equipment-cleaning sessions will take place each year. This results in two problems: substantial amounts of downtime and heretofore the use of chemical solvents that are toxic, flammable, and generate significant quantities of both hazardous wastes and toxic air emissions.

The challenge for Searle was to develop a cleaning method that would reduce downtime and related expense, eliminate toxic air emissions and hazardous waste, and provide a safer work environment for employees. Specifically, they were seeking a high-pressure water-cleaning method. Considered in the past, such methods had not been developed to meet strict FDA standards. The goal of Searle Augusta was to develop a water-cleaning system that would satisfy all desired conditions.

THE RESPONSE

Over a two-year period, the project team assigned to meet this challenge tested and evaluated a number of possible approaches. They adapted existing technology to create a water-pressure cleaning method that purifies production equipment with 6,000 pounds of water pressure. The system is called Aqueous Clean-In-Place, the first and, for now, only high-pressure water-cleaning system in the pharmaceutical industry that is successful and in compliance with stringent FDA requirements.

THE RESULTS

The results of ACIP, as Searle puts it in correspondence with the authors, "proves that efficiency and profit improvement need not be sacrificed for environmental protection." First on the environmental front: the new process reduced toxic air emissions from cleaning by 87 percent and it reduced liquid hazardous wastes generated during cleaning by 71 percent.

Two major results contributed positively to the company's bottom line: it increased productivity by as much as 40 percent by significantly reducing the downtime required for cleaning during changeover, and it saved $500,000 in 1992 alone by increasing production capacity, lowering raw material costs, and eliminating waste disposal costs.

[
LESSON: It is possible to reduce waste, improve the environment, increase productivity, and save dollars with just one new operation.
]

Tying Environmental and Quality Improvements Together

DOW CHEMICAL

AT DOW WE ARE COMMITTED TO THE CONCEPT OF SUSTAINABLE DEVELOPMENT
—BALANCING ECONOMIC GROWTH WITH ENVIRONMENTAL CONCERNS. CLEARLY,
THE TWO MUST BE MUTUALLY SUPPORTIVE."

—FRANK POPOFF, CHAIRMAN AND CEO

THE CHALLENGE

The challenge that Dow saw before it was to totally revamp its culture regarding environmental protection and regulations. The company once was fiercely opposed to what some executives called "nitpicking, riduculous regulations." It wanted to begin demonstrating the truth of what its new chairman and CEO, Frank Popoff, believed: that "environmental protection makes good business sense."

THE RESPONSE

Dow's first formal environmental waste reduction initiative was its WRAP (Waste Reduction Always Pays) program initiated in 1986 in the United States. The basic concept behind the initiative is to reduce waste as far upstream in the manufacturing process as possible, recognize employee efforts, track progress, and seek out cost-effective reduction projects.

Not all environmental waste reduction projects are cost-effective and most emission reduction projects aren't. But that's all right, according to Joe Lindsly, Dow USA issue manager for waste reduction: "We have a basic responsibility to prevent adverse environmental and health impacts on the communities in which we operate and to reduce waste and emissions. The primary objective is to focus our limited resources on reduction projects that have the greatest environmental benefit."

Annually a small amount of seed money has been made available to help promote the concept of seeking out environmental waste reduction projects. Winning projects are selected first on the basis of the amount of waste reduced (primarily at its source), and then on such criteria as environmental impact, cost-effectiveness and, currently, whether or not the waste material is covered under the Superfund Amendments and Reauthorization Act. Dow has provided $11 million over the last three years to fund projects that will reduce an estimated 56 million pounds of hazardous and nonhazardous materials. These projects have the potential to save Dow over $12 million.

Many people feel that a program such as WRAP works well in its initial stage because the easy projects with major impacts can be picked, but once these are gone, the law of diminishing returns sets in. Lindsly doesn't see that happening at Dow:

> Wherever you have a waste stream you have at the very least an "opportunity" to save. With a corporate culture of continuous improvement and a strong quality performance program, the identification and prioritization of new reduction projects is almost a sure thing.

Dow's other major environmental initiative has been its pioneering work in opening up serious dialogue with the environmental community. Four times a year, it brings to its Midland, Michigan, headquarters eight environmental leaders from around the world. They spend a full one and a half days in meetings with senior managers and board members. This same type of consultation takes place at the local level between Dow plant managers and its community advisory panels.

Dow continues to deepen its environmental focus. In 1992, it added an environmental category to every employee's job appraisal form. It then put its senior environmental officer, David Buzzelli, on its board of directors. These actions, and the consultation with environmental leaders, are all firsts and remain unique actions by a major American company.

Dow is involved in a host of other environmental initiatives. It is taking cradle-to-grave responsibility for the chlorinated solvents used to clean industrial equipment. It established an Advanced Cleaning Systems business to assist customers in finding the best cleaning option —aqueous, semi-aqueous, or ultra-tight solvent systems. Dow phased out the practice of injecting hazardous waste underground, which means that its TRI (toxic release inventory) releases per dollar of sale are now among the lowest in the U.S. chemical industry. And its overseas environmental goals are also ambitious. Dow not only voluntarily subscribed to the EPA's 1991 campaign to get companies to reduce their use of seventeen chemicals by 33 percent by 1992 and 50 percent by 1995, but its foreign businesses took on the same goals. Dow Europe went even further, targeting sixty more chemicals in addition to the seventeen on the EPA list.

Finally, Dow does not run shy of the concept of sustainable development, which some business leaders see as controversial. As David Buzzelli puts it, "The question isn't 'Have you achieved sustainable development?' The answer is always no. The question is, 'Are you moving toward it continuously?'" Frank Popoff does not equivocate about the importance of the concept:

> Our company recently announced ten "Global Principles for Sustainable Development," which, among other things, include commitments to "integrate environmental decisions into all business decisions" and "design or modify our products to minimize their environmental impact." Plain and simple, sustainable development is the right way to manage.

THE RESULTS

The WRAP program has certainly demonstrated that waste reduction can pay—and quite handsomely. In 1991, Dow reviewed the efforts of waste reduction teams in all its plants and selected five projects to recognize for outstanding achievement in 1990. These five projects had eliminated nearly 13.5 million pounds of waste annually and generated net savings of $10.5 million. There were ninety-five other projects reviewed for the award.

Here's one factory example of how environmental protection makes good business sense. At its latex plant in Midland, teams of workers and supervisors made a few simple changes in production equipment and pipes, process control improvements, and implemented some "good housekeeping" practices. These simple, straightforward efforts eliminated 60 percent of the waste previously headed for landfills, saving $310,000 in annual fees. Further, by making latex production more efficient, the plant saved an additional $420,000 a year.

Dow has also discovered that another benefit of its WRAP programs is that they often lead to improvements in quality. One example is Dow's Licking River Films Center in Hebron, Ohio, a project to upgrade film-winding equipment and improve gauging equipment. It produced a 400,000 pounds per year reduction in the amount of film scrap going to landfills. As Lindsly has stated, "If you have a strong quality program, it will embrace many forms of quality, including the quality of your environmental performance. The two are very much interrelated."

[
LESSON: Environmental excellence requires leadership from the top and a culture that ties environmental and quality improvement together. This can be further encouraged by regular consulting with environmental experts, tying job appraisals and salaries to meeting environmental goals and establishing a corporatewide waste reduction program.
]

Investing in Environmental R&D
EASTMAN CHEMICAL

"ENVIRONMENTAL MANAGEMENT IS ONE OF THE COMPANY'S 'CORE COMPETENCIES' THAT GIVE IT A COMPETITIVE ADVANTAGE."
—**EARNIE DEAVENPORT, PRESIDENT**

THE CHALLENGE

As the world's largest producer of polyester plastic (known as PET) used to make beverage bottles and other packaging, Eastman Chemical has long realized the value and the necessity of recycling as an important part of its business activities. Its main challenge in this arena is to continually look for ways to increase the recyclability of plastics.

THE RESPONSE

Its first initiative was to build a huge recycling facility right on its property in Kingsport, Tennessee. This came about from a proposal by its Tennessee Eastman Division to WMX (then Waste Management Inc.) to form a novel partnership. Recycle America, operated by WMX, handles paper, plastic, glass, and aluminum. In addition to handling all the materials generated in the huge Eastman Chemical complex, it also reprocesses recyclables collected by nearby communities. To increase the public's awareness and participation in recycling, Eastman developed and implemented a partnership with the University of Tennessee and WMX to recycle stadium cups (90,000 cups per football game) in special containers at sports events.

Eastman Chemical is also actively engaged on the recycling R&D front. As incentives to recycle PET grew, Eastman responded by helping start the Plastic Recycling Research Center at Rutgers University in 1985. The center has become the industry's principal source of research into recycling and its components.

Eastman launched two other major R&D initiatives in recent years. It improved parent Eastman Kodak's existing methanolysis process (used for years to recycle X-ray film) and applied it to recycling plastic bottle polymer in order to reclaim the original raw materials for production of new plastic. The other initiative has President Deavenport excited. It involves their applying for patents on a breakthrough technology that has the potential to "revolutionize" the plastics recycling business. Rather than sorting plastics by hand, it would allow total automation through "molecular markers" built into plastic resins that could be detected electronically. The potential impact is sizable. According to Deavenport, it "could pull from the waste stream over 600 million pounds of plastic soda bottles, more than double the amount currently being processed for recycling." Not only does the new sorting system have the potential to increase plastics recycling to the same rate as aluminum, but the system is also fast, low-cost, and virtually error-free, ideal for large and small operations alike.

THE RESULTS

During 1992, Recycle America processed over 5 million pounds of materials from the huge Eastman complex, saving 19,200 cubic yards of landfill space. Recycle America serves as a solid waste recycling center for over half a million businesses and residences in nearby communities. The facility now receives all of the plastics collected in the Great Smoky Mountains National Park and it spurred the city of

Kingsport to adopt a curbside recycling pickup program. Eastman was awarded the first-place 1991 Keep America Beautiful Recycling Award, which recognized it as the first corporation to initiate a comprehensive recycling program for a municipality.

The Eastman/University of Tennessee recycling program is the nation's largest stadium recycling effort. Another beneficial result of the program is that it has spurred a number of public schools across Tennessee to initiate their own recycling programs.

In 1992, Eastman received a patent for improving the methanolysis process and spent over $2 million on a pilot plant for further testing. Eastman is now prepared to meet the increasing demands in the marketplace for food-grade containers with recycled content.

Eastman's environmental efforts extend far beyond recycling plastics. In recent years, its overall expenditures on environmental protection and improvements have shot up. From less than $100 million in 1989, they were nearly $200 million in 1991 and well over $200 million in 1992. At that level, they were around 5 percent of sales—the largest percentage of any major chemical company.

Eastman Chemical was a winner of the 1993 Malcolm Baldrige National Quality Award. The very first entry under "quality improvement characteristics" in the government's written announcement of the award winners (in *Business America*) was: "Eastman is well accepted by its surrounding communities and has a strong environmental record."

[LESSON: Major recycling results can be achieved through development of state-of-the-art facilities, providing opportunities for public participation in recycling, and a major commitment to investing in environmental research and development.]

11: INCREASE SPEED AND AGILITY

Successful companies today have to constantly increase speed and agility and they can do so through the vast array of new and powerful information technologies currently available. But the solution is not just technology per se. To enjoy the full productivity-enhancing power of these technologies, companies must also restructure themselves and how they work. The "formula" is simple but powerful: technology + organizational change = higher productivity.

Increasing speed and agility is one of the more recent additions to total quality management. As the attention moved from quality of product to quality of the whole organization as a result of the TQM emphasis, companies began to focus more on efficiency of production. This in turn involved a closer look at production processes and supplier relationships. Companies also recognized that they had to get products to their customers quicker and they had to offer more variety. To attain this increased speed and agility, companies have turned to a vast array of advanced and sophisticated manufacturing technologies that have become extremely powerful instruments in the past decade.

While many technologies are available, two stand out for their widespread application and powerful impact: CAD (computer-aided design) and JIT (just-in-time) production. In a 1994 survey of manufacturing companies, CAD was found to be the most widely used technology, with 85 percent of those surveyed using it. JIT is aimed at efficiency of production, particularly reducing cycle times, a primary goal for most manufacturers. It should be noted that this same survey showed that CIM (computer-integrated manufacturing), the most advanced and sophisticated technology that "puts it all together," was used by only 40 percent and just 3 percent of respondents reported that they were extremely skilled in its use. Still, while CIM remains only an ideal for many companies, the Allen-Bradley and Peavey Electronics stories show its tremendous power today.

The unfortunate fact is that many U.S. manufacturers still have not implemented these technologies in an effective manner. Some aren't aware of the benefits they can bring. Others feel they're too expensive. Still others have tried them, but didn't do the necessary training of their workers to obtain the full benefits. Some are simply frightened of a "computer-integrated" world. The fortunate fact is that more and more companies are seeing great benefits—for in the first four years of the 1990s, U.S. industry was spending more on computers and communication equipment than on all other capital equipment combined. The computer is becoming the common technological bond drawing every industry and every trade and profession closer together through digitizing work products and processes into the ones and zeros of computer language.

Certainly all companies can learn from those that have successfully implemented advanced manufacturing technologies. And they will want to learn once they realize what these companies are capable of doing and the results they are achieving.

At Ross Controls, just one person is needed to design a valve and program all of the tool paths for machining and manufacturing the valve. No manufacturing engineers, machinists, or inspectors are required. At Badger Meter, the production manager programs every morning which of the over one hundred components are necessary for the day's orders. And who wouldn't want the phenomenal revenues per employee of Kingston Technology: an astounding $2 million per employee.

While advanced manufacturing technologies are important, the key point to remember is this: they are usually not enough on their own. Many companies will be required to change their entire manufacturing process, as Badger Meter discovered. This company began its transformation with flexible manufacturing but soon found that it had to move beyond that to continuous flow manufacturing in order to get the greater efficiency and quality it desired. And all companies will have to closely combine training of its employees with its new equipment while many will find that employee empowerment is the real key to maximizing the effectiveness of the technologies. Finally, a few companies will want to begin exploring the route that Kingston Technology took: creating a wholly new form of corporate organization to achieve just-in-time manufacturing.

So in looking at the issue of how to attain speed and agility, we're not just talking about computers, hardware, or even technology. In each instance, we're talking about a new, exciting process capability the company has achieved that helps it to respond better, and more quickly, to its customers' ever-changing needs and desires.

IT'S ALWAYS TECHNOLOGY AND PEOPLE

When you want to learn how increasing speed and agility should be done, you go to the top, which in this case is Allen-Bradley's EMS1 facility in Milwaukee. It's the best in speed and agility, and it's the best in integrating highly advanced technology with comprehensive training and employee empowerment to get the very most out of its new capability. In this factory of the future, computer-integrated technology may be the driving force, but one also sees the full power of people and organization, which enable the technology to be so powerful.

Training at this facility is extensive. "Boot camps" come first; then there are "summer camps," which occur anytime they make a major change; and finally the really serious stuff is a college-level program in surface mount technology put on by the Milwaukee School of Engineering.

Peavey Electronics invested heavily in computer-integrated manufacturing in order to integrate the electronic and mechanical sides of the business. It realized that all of its sophisticated hardware and software requires highly skilled workers. Hence, training is a very important part of life at Peavey. Close to 1,600 of its employees have learned to handle various aspects of CIM at the local college where Peavey donated and installed a Peavey CIM system.

Because of its emphasis on "virtual products," Ross Controls likes to highlight the uniqueness of its training and the individual that emerges from it: "We've spent seven years training graduate engineers, who've never worked anywhere else, how to do this. We couldn't hire an engineer already in the marketplace, because he'd say, 'You're trying to get me to do three jobs.' They are a whole new breed."

VIRTUAL PRODUCTS AND A VIRTUAL COMPANY

Two of our companies are at the leading edge of what could well be two major revolutions in manufacturing. Ross Controls produces "virtual products" and Kingston Technology is the closest thing today to a "virtual company." What's fascinating is how the two companies achieved their visions in dramatically different ways: one emphasized heavy investment in sophisticated CAD technology while the other chose to create a wholly new type of corporate organization structured around close partnerships with vendors.

The vision that Ross Controls had in the mid-1980s was to sell "virtual products"—unique products that do not exist until the customer needs them and which are "owned" by the customer, who can make continuous changes to the product at very little cost. It was an innovative idea, and the company was willing to put a lot of money behind it: $30 million in sophisticated CAD systems and automated production equipment. The two most significant innovations in its process are the direct involvement of the customer in designing the product and the multidisciplinary functions of its employees.

Kingston Technology has what every company wants: speed, and lots of it, throughout the company. But they didn't get it through investing in advanced technologies or even through restructuring their manufacturing processes. Rather, they achieved it by creating a wholly new type of corporate organization structured around a closely knit network of partners—a virtual company. These are not simply subcontractors, but vendors that lead overlapping corporate lives with Kingston, sharing know-how, capital, and markets. What they have done is taken the new focus on suppliers by American manufacturers beyond quality and into the area of increased speed and agility. But as important as its vendor partners are, they come second at Kingston; the employees are seen as the most valuable asset. Family-style management, no supervisors or secretaries, and very few contracts—just handshakes. Sounds like a crazy way to run a business.

But who can argue with $2 million per employee in revenues?

The Factory of the Future Today
ALLEN-BRADLEY

The "factory of the future" has been talked about for fifteen or twenty years. Trouble is, few people have seen one. That's primarily because not too many exist.

But one does. And it isn't where you would expect to find it—in one of the oldest buildings of an old-line manufacturing company on South Second Street in Milwaukee, Wisconsin, in the middle of the region once called the Rust Belt.

In this very unlikely place sits a facility that *Industry Week* (June 15, 1992) describes as "a factory within a factory, a crucible of the best manufacturing processes to date." *The Wall Street Journal* says simply, "Allen-Bradley has become the Lourdes of advanced manufacturing." But perhaps Nick Everett, a senior project engineer with thirty-two years at the company, says it best: "This is about as state-of-the-art as it comes."

All of this excitement is over A-B's EMS1 (electronic manufacturing strategy) facility, which manufactures printed circuit boards for the company's solid-state products. It is unique in that it has a production line with total seamless flow (defined later in story) from one end to the other. It is here that one must come to really see the future in manufacturing—to see the full power of technology. But while computer-integrated technology is the driving force, one also sees the full power of people and organization, which enable the technology to be so powerful. Throughout the interviews, employees kept mentioning training, teams, customers, quality, vision, and shaking things up. In short, this facility has put into practice most of the ten paths for business success highlighted in this book.

Just how big—how important—is EMS1 for Allen-Bradley and for American manufacturers? The company says, "EMS1 was first and foremost a cultural change for all functions originally in the Industrial Control Group at Allen-Bradley." It also claims that "it sets the pace for computer-integrated manufacturing (CIM) for the twenty-first century." But that's not all. According to Glenn Eggert, vice president of operations, "This is not just another computer-integrated manufacturing facility. EMS1 is a solution to a complete business approach."

All of this sounds pretty heady. It did to us also until we had a chance to visit the old building on South Second Street. As the old saying goes, seeing is believing.

A NEW MANUFACTURING STRATEGY IS BORN AND DEVELOPS

By 1985, A-B's Industrial Control Group knew that the growth opportunities for solid-state electronics products were going to far outpace those for the group's traditional electromechanical ones. However, designing and assembling enough of these complex products to meet customer requirements would be impossible without first putting together a new manufacturing strategy. Why? Because essentially they were looking at the necessity of making a major transition from "low mix, high volume" to "low volume, high mix."

Listen to John Field, the production manager at EMS1, describe the high volume, low mix situation back in 1985.

> We had minimal manufacturing criteria for design. Consequently, you would be doing things over and over again to get it right. We had minimal pilot production and process capabilities. And, so far as surface mount is concerned, it was almost nonexistent. We did have a couple of pick and place machines. High inventory investment. Because of this batch approach, we had to have a lot of product around all the time. There were long production cycles based on this minimal manufacturing criteria. It wasn't unheard of to take weeks to get something through. And then there were extended new product introduction cycles because of these iterations. Okay? In other words, we really didn't have any expertise back then.

Their first step in putting together a new manufacturing strategy was to bring together a core team that drew on employee representatives from all over the company—a dozen departments in all from test engineering to receiving, and from finance to facilities and maintenance. Nick Everett says this process was "really instrumental," as "everybody got involved and coordinated those efforts and spent a lot of hours here."

The team came up with an overall electronics manufacturing strategy in 1987. Top-level objectives of the strategy were:

- Provide enough capacity for 800 percent growth by 1992.
- Reduce time to market on new products.
- Achieve unsurpassed quality.
- Achieve lowest total lifecycle cost in factory floor operations.
- Significantly improve internal and external customer satisfaction.

Before anything else was done, the EMS1 project team went out to measure themselves against the best in the world in circuit board assembly. In North America, they visited AT&T, Hewlett-Packard, DELCO, Digital Equipment, Northern Telecom, Motorola, and A-B's Twinsburg, Ohio facility and its parent company, Rockwell International. In Japan, they saw Sony and Nippondenso. Just how well this team learned and later implemented what they learned is vividly attested to by the fact that most of the companies A-B visited have come to benchmark EMS1.

Allen-Bradley emphasizes that EMS1 is called that because it is only the first step in the total electronic manufacturing strategy. Other parts of that strategy were being developed concurrently, and many more are planned for the future.

Before any equipment was ordered or a site for the new center selected, the implementation team developed the vision for a world-class assembly operation based on strategic objectives. EMS1 had sixteen objectives in all, many of which were extremely demanding: assemble boards in lot sizes as small as one, provide one-day throughput of boards, strive for near zero setup time, and implement total computer-integrated manufacturing.

EMS1 was planned to unfold in three stages. In Stage I, what the company calls the survival stage, Allen-Bradley met existing demands for capacity. It is known as the "islands of automation" stage and took place in 1989–1990. Stage II, mechanical integration (1990–1991), was where Allen-Bradley put itself on a par with the competition by increasing throughput and quality and decreasing inventory. Stage III was the key one, for it is here that total computer integration is taking place. It began in 1991 and is still being refined and perfected. Since EMS1 is America's state-of-the-art CIM facility, it is important to understand exactly how Allen-Bradley defines CIM in its company document of that name.

Computer-integrated manufacturing integrates the "factors of production" to organize every event that occurs in a manufacturing business from receipt of a customer's order to delivery of the product. The ultimate goal is to integrate the production processes, the material, sales, marketing, purchasing, administration, and engineering information flows into a single, closed-loop controlled system.

To get this degree of integration of course requires the simultaneous operation of many CIM systems throughout the process.

Here's the beauty and power of total computer-integrated manufacturing at work:

Standardized panels containing as few as one or as many as eighty-four printed circuit boards are *automatically* routed to all appropriate assembly operations (as many as five distinct methods). This flow-through capability means that the boards flow from the first laser scribing to the last circuit test operation without leaving the automated line. Overhead conveyors are in place for the purpose of bypassing a process technology if the product being manufactured does not require that process. At any time, as many as six different types of panels may be flowing through the center.

That's the broad overview. The fascinating parts are in the details of how this facility was put together.

CHOOSING THE TWELVE PIONEERS

You can have all the greatest technology in the world, but if you don't have the right people, it just isn't going to work. Allen-Bradley knew it was putting together one of the most highly automated factories in the world. How to choose the right people?

John Field described the process:

We posted the jobs. And we brought people in and we interviewed them. Because they didn't have any experience in solid state, our interview process consisted of their past history. Are you reliable? Are you a good communicator? Are you willing to make a change? What kind of attitude do you have? Do you have a wide-open attitude to learn? That's how we picked them. Not necessarily on ability.

Some of the more fortunate workers were asked to join the start-up team. One element they all seemed to have in common was ambition. Diana Grandaw definitely worked her way up—way up—in the company in a fairly short period of time. As she put it, "I started right at the bottom. When I started out, I had a tweezers in my hand, and I was placing some of these components manually, and I repaired them and did the screen printing—all the things that we're doing here automatically today." She went from assembler to group leader and then to technician.

Things weren't so easy for Larry Hanson. But here's where ambition and determination and perseverance come into play. After twenty-five years with the company, he decided he wanted to be part of the World Contactor Facility, another highly automated facility at Allen-Bradley and an immediate predecessor to EMS1:

> I was interested in that when it first started out, and I didn't make it. So I set out with a plan to make sure that when the next one came along, I would be available, with all the credentials for it. And I was very successful at it. So I set about taking a lot of classes on my own, a lot of computer classes, robotics classes, everything that I thought would help my objective of getting into this department. That's what the main objective was—to better myself—and to find something new and interesting.

That was what a man then in his mid-forties, who had "never touched a computer prior to that," chose to do to get in on the best facility there was.

BOOT CAMP AND OTHER EARLY FORMS OF GETTING EMS1 OPERATING

Right from the start, the plan was for employees to provide the motivation and for A-B to provide the education. This it has done through "boot camps," "summer camps," and a rigorous three-year technology program with specialized college courses at a neighboring university.

Boot Camps came first. Six two-day boot camps were attended by more than one hundred A-B personnel from more than twelve different departments. Why they were developed and what they did depends on who you listen to. An official company document states: "The guidelines for design and data transfer were not mandated by EMS1 to the rest of the division but were fine-tuned during a half-dozen, two-day 'boot camp' sessions." John Field presents a more personal picture of their early development and purpose:

We were going along well in implementation but we were not communicating to the outside world [the rest of A-B] exactly what we were doing. All they could see was "there are an awful lot of restrictions in your new facility. You mean I have to panelize. What do you mean I have to have these types of spacings, etc., etc?" So, we came to a conclusion that we need to sit down and discuss with every individual that works in solid state what we're trying to do here. What are our objectives? How do we try to go about it? Why are we putting these types of restrictions on? So we developed a two-day seminar called boot camp. The whole idea was to communicate what we were trying to do and break down this barrier.

Field went on to say that they have also had summer camps, which occur anytime they make a drastic change. They get the same people back in for a "one-day deal going through the design guidelines."

Finally, there's the real serious stuff—a college-level program in surface mount technology put on by the Milwaukee School of Engineering. Just how serious? It is 150 hours of training a year (one Malcolm Baldrige winner believes that ninety hours of training should be considered world-class). Employees attend voluntarily, on their off hours two days a week from 3:30 to 5:30. And it lasts for three years (future programs will be two years in length). The curriculum starts with basic math (for individuals that need it) and proceeds through geometry and trigonometry right into electronic systems, electronic design, and working with surface mount components. Remember, most of the people taking these three years of college courses are twenty-, twenty-five-, and thirty-year employees who hadn't been to school in as many years.

The program started shortly after the start-up of the EMS1 facility. It was developed jointly between A-B personnel and professors at the Milwaukee School of Engineering. The courses were tailor-made to the requirements of the sophisticated CIM facility that EMS1 is. Most of the first-shift people were graduating the week after our interviews in May 1993. All together, about three fourths of the twenty-eight Allen-Bradley people employed on the two shifts volunteered for this program and made it through.

Guess who was the first employee to enter training in this program? Thirty-one-year veteran Larry Hanson, who says that one of his personal goals is to continue learning and perhaps one day earn a technician's rating, even though he's just a few years from retirement.

All of this training feeds directly into empowered employees and self-directed work teams. Here's how John Field describes the interaction:

> The objective is not to make engineers out of the individuals. Basically the objective is to enhance their communications skills, problem-solving skills, and try to get to this empowerment that everybody talks about. It's the team approach, being able to look at a product and understand basically what it is you are trying to do. And if there's a problem, you stop and you fix it.
>
> And they have authority to do that. If you walk out on the floor, you won't see any supervisors. The people running the floor are the ones that have been going to school, and they're self-directed work teams.

And employees aren't likely to forget that teamwork is the critical factor. A sign quoting Allen-Bradley President Don Davis welcomes each worker to EMS1: "The key to competitiveness is not necessarily working faster, or even working cheaper. It's working together."

Davis feels deeply about this, not only for the highly trained professionals at EMS1 but for everyone at Allen-Bradley:

> I've said it before, and you're going to hear me say it often. Teamwork can really make a difference in our efforts to outperform our competitors. Teamwork among people on the plant floor or in an office or on a business trip. Teamwork among people in different departments, in different plants, in different divisions, in different states, in different countries. That's the key to achieving our vision of being the world leader in our business by the year 2000.

An important part of this emphasis is that the team extends far beyond the four walls of the EMS1 facility. It includes the Milwaukee School of Engineering; Automation Technologies, a chief supplier; Digital Equipment for its VAX systems; Hewlett-Packard for in-circuit testing. And finally, Universal Instruments, an important supplier of most of the equipment on their highly innovative conveyor line. The company says that this system in particular illustrates the power of forming outside partnerships. The teamwork resulted in cleaner integration of the new machinery into EMS1. So important was this partnership that Allen-Bradley presented Universal with an unprecendented Partners in CIM Award in October 1991. The company formed similar partnerships with dozens of other suppliers—all with the purpose of making existing systems even better.

EMPLOYEES' ENTHUSIASM FOR THE TECHNOLOGY

In a totally computer-integrated environment, one question that immediately comes to the fore is what the workers think of this. They are
surrounded by highly sophisticated machines that automatically take
care of so much of the production process. Does this cause a sense of
alienation? Of not really being needed? A feeling that the machines are
really in charge and thus there's not much of a challenge in the job?
These are serious questions as information technologies spread, and
what better place to address them than at EMS1.

The responses from Sandi Hammel and Larry Hanson are particularly revealing, for they have lengthy experience with the company
(twenty-eight and thirty-one years respectively), are operators, not
management, and both had virtually no experience with computers
before joining EMS1.

Hammel, when asked if she was concerned about the computers
taking over and controlling things, said, "I don't know. Maybe at some
point they will (laughs). But right now, they need a lot of help (laughs
again)." She then provided an interesting operator perspective:

> But I don't think, in the section that I'm working in back there, that it will ever
> become boring because you've always got the challenge. Sure, that screen
> says, "This is what failed on that board." But that's not always true. There could
> be something else making that failure. So you've always got the research to do
> —to get the schematics out once in a while and dig into it a little further and
> find out, "Why is this resistor reading low? I've changed it and it's still reading
> low. So it's not a bad part. What's making it do that?"

She was later asked whether she tells her friends that she works in
a factory:

> This really isn't a factory. It's like a factory within a factory is what it really is.
> It's like a little company within a company because Allen-Bradley's departments
> are our customers. This isn't anything like a factory—not only the way it looks,
> but the way it operates. It's much cleaner up here than it is in a factory. Up
> here, people listen if you have an idea. You're not treated like a dummy just
> because you didn't graduate from college or you don't have an engineering
> degree. In a factory you have maybe one engineer that's trying to service three
> or four departments. Here you almost have an engineer for every person, which
> is great. And I consider the team atmosphere is so different. Elsewhere it's just
> nothing at all.

If the word enthusiastic best describes Sandi, the word for Larry Hanson would have to be excited. This is a man who absolutely disproves the popular opinion that older workers cannot learn, and certainly cannot enjoy, computers, particularly in very sophisticated applications. When asked what he liked best about EMS1 and its CIM capability, he replied, "That's exactly what I like—the computers and the technology—and that just really gets me excited about doing my job."

"But Larry, some people view computers as either a threat or—"

They're afraid of them—I have run into that all the time. People don't want to touch the computer. They're just absolutely petrified of it. At one time, I probably was in the same situation, but I'm not anymore, and I can only see everything expanding for me.

"In this state-of-the-art, computer-integrated facility, are there still some interesting challenges?"

Oh most definitely. Yes. Yes, most definitely. The computer doesn't do everything. Each day, there are decisions that have to be made, however large or small they may be. As operators, everything is not done for us. We have to make decisions on repairing the circuit boards or inspections or operating one of the pieces of equipment. The computer may put most of it together, but it still has to have the human contact.

Is Larry an isolated example—a case of a hidden computer junkie that just needed the opportunity to release these hidden urges? He emphasized that this type of highly sophisticated computer environment appeals to a broad range of workers:

When other people down in the shop see us here, they want to know about this. This gives them the same thing that I had, years ago, with World Contactor. It gives them something to strive for, something to work for. They see this fancy facility up here, with all this computer stuff, and they really seem to be excited. I talk with a lot of them. They want to know "How can I get up there? What do I have to do? And how did you get up there?" These are the questions I've been asked for the last four years, in a constant barrage.

The last question asked of Larry was, "So you really do look forward to coming to work each day?"

Let's put it this way. I have never hated it. I didn't even hate it when I worked in the assembly department. I have a different perspective, a different outlook. This has all been because of having like a new life—a new life that I wish I could have had twenty years ago. It would have been really fantastic, a real good shot in the arm.

RESULTS SECOND TO NONE

The results that have flowed from the total computer-integrated manufacturing environment at EMS1 are far too numerous to enumerate in any detail. The following list provides most of the key quantifiable improvements:

- one-day throughput (often four hours) for complete printed circuit board assembly and test (compared to two days when EMS1 started and two weeks before that)
- one-day new product implementation
- twenty-six inventory turns per year for work in process, which lowers inventory costs and makes products more competitive
- reduced total product introduction time to as little as five months from as long as three years, an 85 percent decrease
- lot sizes as small as one
- scrap down to 0.09 percent and rework to 0.26 percent (in 1992)
- customer reject rate plummeted from 39,337 parts per million in May 1991 to 7,982 ppm in October 1992
- reduction of environmental impact of solid state manufacturing by 100 percent through chlorofluorocarbon elimination (utilizing a total no-clean flux and solder paste process)

A single example shows what all this means for the company's customers and business. One of the leading automotive companies came to Allen-Bradley in September 1990 requesting a remote-I/O unit for their engine manufacturing operations. By January 1991, the new unit was delivered to the customer. This could not have been accomplished without EMS1 integration of design and manufacturing. For this particular product, EMS1 did both prototype and pilot manufacturing simultaneously.

John Field, production manager, provides the big picture when he was asked what he felt were the most significant benefits of EMS1:

First of all, we've got the strategic advantage now. That gives us the leading-edge technology. I can work toward any schedule that industrialization or engineering comes up with. Second, if you take a look at our total business, this has been very instrumental in the total team approach here at Allen-Bradley. It's allowed us to grow at the rate that we've been able to grow, without having something catastrophic happen.

It also allows John Field to say with a gleam in his eye: "I'm not in full agreement that the Japanese are way ahead of us. In our facility, I've had a lot of Japanese in, and we are ahead of them." (Laughs.)

LESSON: Computer-integrated manufacturing that is state-of-the-art:

- can unfold in stages
- ultimately becomes a cultural change for all functions
- requires choosing the right people (aggressive and willing to learn) and training them properly
- utilizes sophisticated technology that improves all performance features of the production process
- is a new capability offering a solution to a complete business approach
- can bring new enthusiasm and excitement to the workers

Selling "Virtual Products" to Customers
ROSS CONTROLS

"WE ARE SELLING 'VIRTUAL PRODUCTS' TO OUR CUSTOMERS. THE CUSTOMER
CAN MAKE A CONTINUOUS STREAM OF CHANGES TO THE PRODUCT—AT [VERY
LITTLE] COST. WE CAN NOW DO IN TWENTY-FOUR HOURS THINGS THAT USED TO
TAKE A YEAR. AND THE BEAUTY OF IT IS, THE CUSTOMER IS TAKING OWNERSHIP.
IT'S NOT OUR PRODUCT ANYMORE. IT'S HIS. WE'RE NO LONGER JUST A SUPPLIER
—WE'RE A PARTNER."

—HENRY DUIGNAN, FORMER CHIEF OPERATING OFFICER

THE CHALLENGE

The term "virtual products" may not have existed back in the mid-
1980s, but that was the vision that this company in Troy, Michigan, had.
Their idea was to be able to produce unique products that don't actually exist until a customer needs them. Quite different from the traditional approach of selling standard products, from a catalogue—their
primary focus since 1921. But the new products would have to meet
each customer's specific needs and still allow for prompt delivery, at a
reasonable price. After all, Ross manufactures industrial controls, not
luxury trinkets. In short, it saw its challenge as finding out what its
customers really wanted and needed—and then finding a way to make
it happen.

THE RESPONSE

It was an idea with a lot of potential, but it would require time and
money; no one really knew how much. Under the leadership of Chairman Russell Cameron, the company invested $30 million in sophisti-
cated CAD systems, state-of-the-art production equipment, and a major
retraining and reorganization of people. Traditionally trained workers
organized under separate disciplines like engineering, manufacturing,
and marketing couldn't accommodate the necessary acceleration in
product development. Old structures and thinking also didn't allow
for the most critical innovation of all: bringing one or more people

from the customer's organization directly into the product design pro-cess.

Here's how the company describes its new process: "One or more individuals must be able to sit down in front of a terminal and design a valve. They must also have the capability to program the tool paths for automated machining on advanced CNC (computer numerically controlled) production systems and send an electronic stream of data to waiting machines on the shop floor." After the component parts are manufactured, they are assembled by special teams who receive their instructions via video, from the designer. That's it. No manufacturing engineers, no machinists, no inspectors. As Henry Duignan, now a consultant and former chief operating officer points out, "What the customer is really buying is our ability to design and manufacture a product unique to his particular needs—and to do it almost instantane-ously."

Beyond the investment in computers and other sophisticated equip-ment, they also had to invest in training. Duignan emphasizes the uniqueness of this training and the individual that emerges: "We've spent seven years training graduate engineers, who've never worked anywhere else, how to do this. We couldn't hire a lot of experienced people in the marketplace, because they'd say: 'You're trying to get me to do multiple jobs. How do I know who's in charge? Where's all the paperwork?' Our ROSS/FLEX people are a whole new breed—they have to be." Indeed, the company's perspective is "the hardware and the software are easy to acquire—the *humanware* is the hard part."

THE RESULTS

The ROSS/FLEX program has eliminated the most time-consuming as-pects of manufacturing, and found a way to fully integrate the cus-tomer's needs and desires right into the manufacturing process. Thus, Ross can put working prototypes of customized valves into a cus-tomer's hands in as little as seventy-two hours. And as we saw in Duignan's opening statement, the customer can make a continuous stream of changes to the product, making sure it keeps pace with his future needs. He never has to "go shopping" again.

Little wonder that Henry Duignan calls this "a whole new business for the twenty-first century."

[
LESSON: Aim for selling virtual products to your customers—unique products that don't actually exist
until the customer needs them and that the customer
can make a continuous stream of changes to. This
will require the right investment in equipment and
training.
]

The Power of Continuous Flow Manufacturing
BADGER METER

"EACH MORNING THE PRODUCTION MANAGER SIMPLY KEYS INTO THE PROGRAM
WHICH AND HOW MANY OF THE 110 DIFFERENT HOUSINGS OF BRASS, BRONZE,
STEEL, OR ALUMINUM HE WANTS FOR THE DAY BASED ON ORDERS RECEIVED THE
DAY BEFORE."

—JOHN JANIK, VICE PRESIDENT OF OPERATIONS

THE CHALLENGE

Like most American manufacturers, Badger's operations were organized in traditional departmental fashion. Finished goods were produced to a forecast, customer orders were filled from stock, and
manufacturing replenishment orders were batch-processed sequen-
tially from operation to operation.

Manufacturing lead times ranged up to twelve weeks, and lot sizes
varied from one month's usage for high-volume parts up to six months'
supply for low-volume parts. Final test yields were in the 70 percent
range, necessitating substantial rework. Overall inventory turnover
ranged from two to three times per year.

In the mid-1980s, this Milwaukee-based company recognized the
need to make changes in its manufacturing system. Competitive pres-
sures had grown intense and customers were demanding higher levels

of quality along with quicker response to their needs. The company had to make dramatic improvements if it was to survive and prosper.

THE RESPONSE

Flexible manufacturing was seen as the way to meet the challenge. Beginning with its longest lead-time processes—machining of meter housings—the company installed two flexible machining systems, one for large, low-volume, high-variety meter housings used in utility distribution systems and large industrial applications, and a second system for small, high-volume residential water meter housings. These changes eliminated ten stand-alone machines, some of which had setup times as long as twenty-eight hours.

As significant as the machining improvements were, however, management recognized they were not the whole answer and the company began to examine its entire approach to running its manufacturing operations. First, the manufacturing operations were separated into smaller focused factories, each specializing in the production of large or small water meters, industrial lubrication meters, and automatic meter reading technology. Then in 1989, a formal continuous improvement program was launched incorporating a team-based total quality philosophy.

Teams were formed in each plant. They were charged with examining all facets of manufacturing and developing plans for improving quality, throughput, and productivity in all operations. The guiding philosophy of the program was implementing continuous flow manufacturing, in which all manufacturing processes are linked together to provide a continuous flow of value-added operations from raw material to finished tested product.

Here's how continuous flow manufacturing works. With the new flexible machining systems as their centerpiece, all operations from receipt of raw material to completion of a finished meter are linked. First, the new machining systems are integrated with the plastic molding operations. Next, meter assembly is moved to the machining and molding area, creating a flow of product from raw castings and plastic resin directly to assembly. Finally, meter testing is automated and linked to the assembly processes.

While more subtle, the change in the job-place culture has been equally important. Employees are empowered to make improvements in their activities and now feel they contribute directly to the success of the company. Union members were highly involved in the teams from the start, and in a move that would have been considered unthinkable five years ago, a member of the bargaining committee and former president of the union was made team leader for one of the plants, sharing vital information on all details of the company's manufacturing operations.

THE RESULTS

The up-front improvements from flexible manufacturing alone were dramatic. In the large-meter machining system, any one of the hundreds of varieties of housings could now be machined with zero setup time. The result is that housings can literally be machined upon demand. In the small-meter machining system, quality was improved dramatically, all material handling steps were eliminated, and a finished housing can now be produced in minutes compared with weeks for the previous method.

The final results from the implementation of continous flow manufacturing are stunning. Yields increased to the 98 percent plus range, productivity increased substantially, work-in-process inventories were slashed, and throughput time to produce a complete tested, packed meter was cut to less than one day. A finished product could now truly be made to customer order.

The company found the initial results from continuous flow manufacturing so good that they expanded it to their lubrication meter plant. Further, they hope to adopt the concepts to their automatic meter reading technologies once the unit volume justifies the investment.

And then there are the enthusiastic workers. According to team member Larry Ahrens, "It's a great time to be a Badger Meter employee. Never before has a union employee been given the opportunity and ability to not only create and structure their own position within Badger Meter, but also to contribute to the decision-making process that ultimately shapes the manufacturing concepts that guide and control the future of the corporation." Adds team member Ray Shilter, "I really appreciate the opportunity to contribute my knowledge to improving the company's operations. There is a great deal of experience on the factory floor and now we are able to put it to use so that everyone can benefit."

LESSON: Flexible manufacturing centered around flexible machinery systems can help meet customers' demands for higher quality and quick response. If you want even more dramatic results, including the ability to make finished products according to customer order, transform manufacturing operations by linking all operations (including the flexible machinery systems) together to achieve continuous flow manufacturing.

The Closest Thing to a Virtual Corporation
KINGSTON TECHNOLOGY

"YOU'VE HEARD OF JUST-IN-TIME INVENTORY? THIS IS JUST-IN-TIME MANUFACTURING. YOU ALWAYS HAVE TO THINK OF YOUR PARTNERS. THEY ARE THERE WHEN WE NEED THEM, AND WE ARE THERE WHEN THEY NEED US."

—DAVID SUN, VICE PRESIDENT

THE CHALLENGE

It was 1987 when John Tu and David Sun (both immigrants from Taiwan) saw a market niche. There was a shortage of a certain type of chip used in memory-upgrade modules that could be easily filled by altering another chip in ample supply to produce a similar product. *Voilà!* Cash started to pour in from memory-starved distributors.

But, thought Tu, this was so easy that soon competitors would catch on and simply copy what they had done. He went so far as to bet Sun a Jaguar that Kingston would be out of business within six months.

Needless to say, Sun soon had a great new car and this Silicon Valley company has been going like gangbusters ever since. How?

THE RESPONSE

Kingston's success has a lot to do with speed and putting employees first. But there's something more fundamental at work. It sounds a bit soft, even philosophical—but it works. Here's how Sun sums up their secret for success:

> What we do today is better than what we did yesterday. Revenue is nothing. Let's make sure the base is right. So in a certain way we are very relaxed. We're patient. We say, "Let's just do it the right way, build ethical, honest products."

An article in *Inc.* (October 1992) featuring Kingston was entitled "Built on Speed" and it emphasized how the company had "institutionalized speed at every level." This is true, but Kingston hasn't done it through major investments in technology or even through restructuring its own manufacturing processes.

Rather, Tu and Sun have done it by creating a unique brand of corporate organization that comes as close to being a "virtual company" as any in America. At the core of this new organizational model is a closely knit network of partners—vendors to whom Kingston farms out much of its work. What makes the organization unique is that far beyond a mere subcontracting relationship, Kingston and its vendors lead overlapping corporate lives, sharing know-how, capital, and markets.

From the very start, Tu and Sun had long-term relationships with vendors as a fundamental corporate goal. They felt this was the best way to give stability to a company in a volatile industry. This focus on vendors means that Kingston never cancels purchase orders, always works with the vendors to schedule the manufacture and delivery of chips, and does not pressure suppliers on price, preferring instead to receive a consistent supply at good quality.

How does the just-in-time manufacturing partnership with its vendors work? Here's one example. Bank of America called a ComputerLand store with an order for one hundred IBM PCs. They wanted them quick and they also wanted lots of extra memory and other upgrades. ComputerLand called Kingston, which accepted the order despite the products being out of stock. Kingston immediately contacted Express Manufacturing, a partner company in the Kingston virtual organization. Express cleared its lines and produced the needed parts within a few hours. After testing all the products, Kingston Fed Ex'd them to ComputerLand to arrive the next morning. How could the vendor respond so quickly? In 1988, it had one assembly line. It now has eighteen, each built to meet the growing demand from Kingston. This is where David Sun's philosophy bears fruit: "You always have to think of your partners. They are there when we need them and we are there when they need us."

In effect, what Kingston and its vendors do is hold the customers' inventory. As Sun puts it, "We are sitting here as a broker of services from our employees and vendors to our customers." He adds, "If we ship the same day, then there are no back orders. They create extra work. We say instead, 'We'll support you. We'll ship to you every day.' The distributor is not forced to take a lot of product all at one time."

Just-in-time manufacturing automatically creates just-in-time inventory. For a company with sales approaching $500 million, Kingston's inventory takes up four rows of shelves, each running about twenty feet deep—about four days' worth of parts.

But this is only half the story, and not even the most important half. For as much as Kingston values its relationships with its vendors, they come second. The customer must come first? No. Here's Sun's view of the priority of relationships: "Your employee is your most valuable asset, and your vendor is your second most valuable asset. Take care of the first two, and the customer is taken care of."

It's all part of family-style management. And Kingston is quite a family to manage, as it is a highly multiracial company, where whites, blacks, Chinese, Vietnamese, and Hispanics work without divisions or barriers between them.

The informal, fluid environment of the company tends to keep any barriers from being established. There are no doors, no titles, no secretaries, no ties, no supervisors. There are no commissions for the salespeople, for Tu and Sun believe that their success would not be possible without the group's efforts. And few contracts—"we do almost all our business on a handshake," says Tu. The company's books are open to everyone. Much of this springs from John Tu's number one priority: a sense of obligation to his employees. He thinks: "Suppose the company stops growing tomorrow. We want to make sure our employees will not be hurt."

A small plaque inside the front door in the lobby states the company's four core values very simply: "Courtesy . . . Compassion . . . Modesty . . . Honesty."

THE RESULTS

As we begin to look at Kingston's results, remember when David Sun said, "Revenue is nothing." Tu and Sun really believe that. So with "doing what is right" as the goal rather than growth, here is what Kingston has achieved. In 1992, it stood at the top of *Inc.*'s 500 list, the 500 fastest-growing private companies in America. Started in 1987, its sales by 1991 were $141 million, in 1992, $253 million, and they approached the $500 million mark in 1993. Moreover, they achieved this spectacular growth with no debt, no venture capital, and no plans to go public.

It has 45 percent of the memory-upgrade market. It sells its upgrades in over thirty countries and derives 32 percent of its revenue from international sales.

But here's the truly remarkable result. Its revenues per employee come out right around $2 million. The 270 full-time employees benefit greatly from this high productivity, receiving not only salaries that average 20 percent to 30 percent above industry norms but also a bonus each quarter that comes as the company distributes 5 percent of its pretax profits.

With all their speed, one would think they had a lot of misses when it comes to new product introductions. Far from it. Indeed, the ratio of successful products to product introductions is a phenomenal 90 percent. And they constantly push into new niches, keeping the entrepreneurial spirit alive despite their rapid growth.

[
LESSON: Become a virtual corporation through just-in-time manufacturing. This can be achieved by putting employees first in family-style management and establishing long-run, closely interlocking, rock-solid relationships with partners—vendors to whom you farm out most production.
]

CIM Provides the Competitive Edge
PEAVEY ELECTRONICS

"CIM [COMPUTER-INTEGRATED MANUFACTURING] HAS BEEN AN AWFUL LOT OF WORK BUT DEFINITELY WORTH THE EFFORT. WE HAD TO DO IT TO ATTAIN AND MAINTAIN OUR COMPETITIVE EDGE. THIS IS ESPECIALLY IMPORTANT WITH THE NUMBER OF PRODUCERS OF THE DIGITAL EQUIPMENT SUCH AS KEYBOARDS THAT WE OFFER TODAY."

—RODGER WHOBREY, DIRECTOR OF ENGINEERING SERVICES

THE CHALLENGE

In the mid-1980s, Peavey Electronics (Meridian, Mississippi) was doing quite well but it wanted a competitive edge that would help secure its leadership position in the United States in the production of guitars, other musical instruments, and portable sound equipment. It also wanted to continue its burgeoning export thrust.

It first tried computer-aided design and manufacturing with some MRP (manufacturing resource planning) applications and a variety of personal computers and terminals scattered around the company. The results were disappointing. It considered robots but discovered on an observation field trip that robots were not appropriate to its applications.

THE RESPONSE

It called in IBM, which conducted an application transfer study. This study uncovered a lot of problems, particularly in communications and data accuracy, that were causing mistakes, worker frustration, and poor product quality. What Peavey needed was a centralized database and integration of the electronic and mechanical sides of the business.

Peavey went to work learning computer-integrated manufacturing "on the job" according to Rodger Whobrey, director of engineering services and the leader of Peavey's CIM implementation efforts. By 1989, it had over 400 terminals, fifteen CAD workstations, and T-1 communications to link its manufacturing sites, its sales force, and to provide electronic data interchange for direct customer order entry anywhere in North America.

By 1992, Peavey's CIM operation was about as good as they come. In addition to its 550 terminals and twenty CAD workstations, all fifty CIM applications were integrated. Here's a partial listing of the alphabet soup that a full-scale CIM environment entails: IBM's CATIA (Computer-Assisted Three-Dimensional Interactive Applications) for product design and development CBDS (Circuit Board Design Systems), and PROFS for communications; Cincom Systems' Control: Manufacturing for manufacturing resource planning; IBM's DB2, an SQL-compliant relational database; and other packages for project management, statistical analysis, and business graphics.

So what does all this fancy technology do for the company? Whobrey provides a simple, straightforward answer:

> CIM means never having to make the same mistake twice. With CIM, we can find errors on screen that would otherwise take three to four weeks to find and fix during a prototype run. This allows us to get a product to market sooner than might otherwise be the case. In a volatile market such as ours [with some product life cycles of a year or less], speed is very important.

All of this sophisticated hardware and software requires highly skilled workers. So training is an important part of life at Peavey. The company donated and installed a Peavey CIM system at the local college, where close to 1,600 of its employees have learned to handle various aspects of CIM. Indeed, at any given time 12 percent to 15 percent of its employees are in continuing education, ranging from high-school-level vocational training through postgraduate work at the local campus of Mississippi State University. Says President Melia Peavey, "Obviously, implementing a true CIM environment has been a big factor in the success of Peavey, but the people who work here are the real reason why Peavey is where it is and why it continues to grow."

THE RESULTS

And grow it does. It now exports its products to an incredible 103 countries. Its CIM system has enabled it to introduce 150 to 200 new products annually. Indeed, CIM, which seemed to most employees in 1989 to resemble a foreign language, is now the "business-as-usual" standard.

And oh yes, the chairman and CEO, Hartley Peavey, may have been thwarted in his dream of becoming a great blues guitarist like Bo Diddley, but how many CEOs can claim to be a member of Hollywood's rock 'n' roll Walk of Fame?

> LESSON: To get the full range of benefits from a CIM environment and all advanced manufacturing technologies requires extensive training to develop a highly skilled workforce.

12: SHAKE UP THE ORGANIZATION

All of the companies featured in this chapter are great comeback stories. Every one was in serious trouble in the 1980s. As market share eroded and profits slid, a few saw their very survival at stake.

How did things get so serious for formerly very successful companies? Therein lies a major reason: great success had gone to their heads. They relaxed. They lost their focus. They had it too easy. Chairman Benjamin Rosen of Compaq sums up how many of the top officials now feel at all these companies: "There will never be a time when we can relax. We relaxed once, and don't ever want to go through that again. Prosperity is very dangerous."

When you relax, you allow giant, stifling bureaucracies to develop. Layers of management pile up. Numerous committees review every decision to death. Your reaction time slows. New products don't get to the market quickly enough. Complacency—even a simple conservatism—is the great enemy of success.

The cure is obvious. Stop relaxing. Act. Shake things up!

Each of the five success stories involves a thorough shaking up of the organization. Massive change—not incremental change—was deemed necessary for survival and growth. Why? Jack Welch, chairman and CEO of General Electric, provides the clearest answer: "If your change isn't big enough, revolutionary enough, the bureaucracy can beat you. When you get leaders who confuse popularity with leadership, who just nibble away at things, nothing changes."

Leadership—that's what it all comes down to. A great many corporate leaders today embrace the new concepts of empowering employees, training continuously, delighting customers—but they don't do anything. It's been said that 95 percent say the right thing—5 percent to it!

This chapter is about the doers.

Harry Quadracci, CEO of Quad/Graphics, lays it right out: "People think the president of an outfit has to be the main organizer. No, the president is the main disorganizer."

When you shake up an organization, you launch attacks on many of the fronts described in this book. Five, seven, or even all nine of the previous paths to success have been put into play at these companies. In every case, their bold shaking up was amply rewarded. Indeed, Compaq's 75.4 percent increase in sales from 1992 to 1993 and Intel's 50.3 percent increase ranked number 1 and 2 in biggest increases in sales among Fortune 500 companies.

GET FOCUSED, SET TOUGH GOALS, *ACT*

Before any shaking up can go forth, you have to know what the problems are and what the company really should focus on. When Eckhard Pfeiffer took the reins of Compaq in 1991, he spent the entire first weekend going over and over the same few words on a piece of paper that he felt best identified what had gone wrong and the problems that must be rectified. When Tracy O'Rourke became CEO at Varian Associates in 1990, he quickly recognized the company's fundamental problem: loss of strategic focus. At Intel, having a clear focus has been, and still is, a distinct advantage. At no time was this more evident than in 1985 when it made the tough, and emotional, decision to get out of the DRAM (dynamic random access memory) business, a product Intel had introduced. And Andy Grove still has the big picture sharply in focus in the mid-1990s as he sees Intel shifting the focus of its attention to the field of communications and interactivity.

Setting tough goals is not mandatory, but it sure can help. Pfeiffer soon announced that Compaq would cut production costs, and hence prices, by 50 percent. And, Compaq was to compete in every segment of the PC market—both on price and performance. Pfeiffer set such "ridiculous" targets because he believes that only by asking for dramatic, transformative change can people see their way out of old habits. O'Rourke also believes in the shock value of tough goals. So he stunned his managers early on by announcing that the company would apply for the Malcolm Baldrige National Quality Award within one year —not the three years everyone thought would be needed to get the improvements. And here's the shock value: "When you're not doing well, you want to improve fast, but it was hard for us to get people to understand that they could attain quantum leap improvements."

Finally, you act. And the quicker the better. Perhaps no CEO acted quicker or asked for faster action than Pfeiffer. He identified the company's numerous problems in the first weekend. All of these were attacked during his first year on the job. Nine hours after he was appointed, he convened a group to start planning the company's new low-cost PCs.

Get focused, set tough goals, act. Each of the five companies did all three and did them well. But for sheer drama and boldness, Tenneco's story of the early 1990s stands out, for when Mike Walsh in essence locked in all of its top officers after a casual dinner meeting at a hotel until they got things straightened out, he wasn't even on board yet as the new CEO. But he recognized the serious situation they were in and felt he had to act: "The action plan challenged every part of this company. It was gut-check time for everyone in this room and hundreds— probably thousands—of other people. It took real-life courage to take these difficult steps—to commit to actions that seemed impossible, especially in a hundred days."

THE BIG FIVE—COSTS, EMPLOYEES, CUSTOMERS, PRODUCTS, AND PROCESSES

These companies acted on a lot of fronts, but five paths to success stand out: cut costs, empower employees, exceed customer expectations, create new products, and attain agility and speed (through major process changes).

Cutting costs in a bold and immediate fashion was a prime response at Chrysler, Tenneco, and Compaq, achieved through major corporate restructuring.

When it comes to employee empowerment, Chrysler is the place to begin. For it is a story first and foremost of the power of American teamwork. In late 1988, senior management began dismantling its traditional, hierarchical organization and began to install four cross-functional "platform teams"—one each for small cars, large cars, minivans, and Jeep vehicles and trucks. In the new platform team organization, people at all levels in the company are empowered with the authority —as well as the responsibility—to participate, to innovate, and to make decisions. The result is a new spirit, a new enthusiasm, and an invaluable sense of commitment and "ownership." An important feature of teamwork at Chrysler is its comprehensive scope, covering Chrysler's "extended enterprise"—white-collar employees, suppliers, and dealers, as well as blue-collar employees.

Varian Associates also used employee empowerment as a key action in its transformation. The reason, according to O'Rourke, was that the company's production problems were actually rooted in personnel issues.

Customers were a top priority to a number of the firms. Pfeiffer leaves no doubt as to their important focus in Compaq's transformation: "Most importantly, we had to go from being a business-centered company to being a customer-centered company. Our new strategy began with its primary focus on the customer and on customer support." Varian's efforts to exceed customer expectations involved hands-on involvement by the CEO. O'Rourke and Richard Levy, then chair of the company's Baldrige Award steering committee, personally visited each of the company's thirty-one operating units. At every place, they started with the section on customer requirements and asked how these were translated into strategies. Chrysler has its commitment to Customer One, a $30 million training program for its dealers. Intel transformed itself from a technology company alone to one that involves customers right from the beginning of its design process.

New products were at the heart of the transformation at Intel, Chrysler, and Compaq. The Intel decision to drop DRAMs allowed it to focus its resources on microprocessor development and production, leading to its eventual successes with the 386, 486, and Pentium chips. Chrysler chose not to cut back on spending for new products and went on to introduce three highly successful new vehicles in a short space of time. Compaq decided that it had to enter the low-price, entry-level end of the PC market and it set out to do so with a vengeance. Within nine months, it was successfully introducing forty-five new personal computer products.

Finally, many of the companies saw the need for major changes in its processes to become more agile and increase speed. Intel had a rude awakening about its manufacturing processes in the mid-1980s. As COO Craig Barrett describes it, "Basically, all our results—yields, throughput time, capital utilization—were pretty abysmal." Three blockbuster changes were instituted. First, they changed the relationship between process technology development and manufacturing. This change had historic significance for Intel, as it had always taken pride in the fact that it developed its manufacturing processes in the factory. Another historic change was their decision to move to sole-sourcing, which came with the introduction of the 386 chip. Finally, CEO Grove ordered that they "double up" on design, so he launched work on the P6 generation chip two years before the planned introduction of the Pentium chip.

QUICK RESULTS

It is encouraging to see that major transformation does not mean that results won't show up for years. Indeed, at *all* of these five companies the results were amazingly swift. In addition to the forty-five new PC models for a total of seventy-six, price cuts ran as high as 32 percent. In one year, Compaq tripled its manufacturing volume, cut costs and prices across its whole product line, and doubled the number of its distribution outlets.

Chrysler went from flirting with insolvency in 1990 and 1991 to recording 1993 operating profits of around 2.5 billion, with its stock soaring some 500 percent. Varian's loss in 1990 was turned into $58 million in earnings in 1991, and throughout the early 1990s, sales and orders remained at or near record levels, gross margins grew, net debt declined, and cash flow increased.

IT ALL COMES DOWN TO LEADERSHIP

You have undoubtedly seen that the CEOs and the presidents of these companies have been frequently cited and quoted. That is because real shaking up of an organization requires first and foremost a person at the helm that understands true leadership. Dana Mead, the CEO of Tenneco, is one such leader. His words, directed right at Tenneco's top leaders, who were seated before him, are words that can benefit each corporate leader who hears them:

> This is a personal challenge to you: Remove the roadblocks. Don't let the old ways of thinking block your path.
>
>   It's easy to say what can't be done. The challenge for leaders is to overcome inertia and to apply your resources where results can be achieved. We must, you must, exercise initiative to do it.

 ## The Paranoid Survive, and Thrive
INTEL

"Only the paranoid survive." After reading thousands of words about Intel's great comeback and accomplishments in recent years and conducting a full day of interviews there and touring one of their "fabs" (fabrication facilities where semiconductors are produced), those four words of Andrew Grove, current president and CEO, stand out as best "explaining" Intel—at getting to the heart of what has made Intel such a great success.

Being paranoid not only enabled Intel to survive its tough midlife crisis in the mid-1980s, but has caused it to absolutely thrive in the years since 1986. But what does being paranoid really mean? A paranoid company culture helps Intel continually recognize that if it doesn't bring out products that make its older ones obsolete, someone else will. As Chief Operating Officer Craig Barrett puts it, "Our goal is to be the best possible cannibal in the world and to eat our children as fast as we can." And being paranoid is a reality to Intel employees. Vinod Dham, the "godfather" of first the famous 486 chip and then the Pentium chip, had a sign hanging on the bulletin board right above his desk. In big, bold letters, it said "D2000," and then listed some very ambitious goals for the year 2000. When asked to explain it, he said that it shows the kind of things we should have in place. "Do it or die. This is the paranoic and chaotic aspect of living here." Adds Craig Barrett, "We're competitive paranoids."

"Only the paranoid survive." Grove also deliberately used the word survive, for that is what was on the minds of top management at Intel in the mid-1980s. They had to make some very tough decisions. They had to break some sacred rules—set off in new directions. The tough times, and the key elements of their transformation, are examined below.

The important point is that what they did worked wonders. Even after becoming quite large, Intel was still doubling in size roughly every two years in the early 1990s. Intel is now America's, and the world's, largest chip maker (it was tenth in 1986). It is also the most profitable chip maker, and the most profitable company of its size in the world—in 1993, it had quarterly net margins that rose above 25 percent and its profits soared to $2.3 billion, more than double the $1.1 billion in 1992, and nearly six times the 1989 level on sales of $8.8 billion. Both of the first two quarters of 1994 set new quarterly records for net income and revenues. Total 1994 profits were estimated to reach $2.65 billion. It commands a position of almost unparalleled dominance—in 1993, nine out of ten of the world's 150 million PCs, contained "Intel Inside"—the microprocessor brains of a computer.

Dataquest, a respected market research firm, says it all when it calls Intel "the most powerful semiconductor firm in existence."

The big question is how? How did it accomplish this, particularly when it faced such tough times in the mid-1980s, totally losing out to the Japanese in its major market, one that it helped develop and previously thrived on? The transformation involved first an emotional decision to drop out of this market and then to rebuild around five major initiatives: a manufacturing overhaul, doubling up design, continued emphasis on old-fashioned capital investment and R&D spending, getting close to customers, and empowering and training employees.

THE TOUGH TIMES

Intel was on a roll. Revenues were rising smartly each year: $789 million in 1981, $900 million in 1982, $1.12 billion in 1983, $1.63 billion in 1984—and then $1.36 billion in 1985. What happened?

It was a combination of external and internal problems. Externally, Japanese semiconductor manufacturers had invested so heavily there was substantial overcapacity. This precipitated the industry crash of

1985–1986. EPROM (erasable, programmable read-only memory) prices were in free fall. Japanese manufacturers were slashing prices to less than half of their actual manufacturing costs. Intel, which had invented EPROM back in 1971, along with other U.S. producers, was rapidly losing market share. U.S. companies fought back by filing a Section 301 case against Japanese manufacturers for dumping.

But Intel didn't only gripe and point the finger at the Japanese. It had enough sense and courage to point the finger at itself as well. The mid-1980s industry downturn gave the company a rude shock about its manufacturing processes. As Craig Barrett puts it, "We suddenly realized we weren't so hot." Intel then benchmarked itself against the world's best, many of them competitors. Barrett declared that all its key performance results—yields, throughput time, capital utilization —were "pretty abysmal."

It was a tough combination. Getting killed by foreign competitors. Seeing your own manufacturing processes not measuring up at all. Clearly, dramatic, swift action was called for.

THE EMOTIONAL DECISION TO DROP DRAMS— "THE BEST BUSINESS DECISION WE'VE EVER MADE"

Overhauling the manufacturing process was going to take time. The first decision was what to do about their rapidly declining share in the DRAM (dynamic random access memory) market. Remember, Intel had been the first to introduce the product and build the business in the 1970s. It had been clinging to the idea that its DRAM market would come back. Indeed, in 1985, it was still spending 33 percent of its development dollars on these products—an amazing percentage considering DRAMs at the time only accounted for 5 percent of its revenue.

Andy Grove muses, "In retrospect, it's fascinating to see how long we held on, basically deluding ourselves." Finally, he asked Gordon Moore, co-founder and CEO at the time, " 'What would someone do with this business if they came into Intel from the outside?' The answer was clear: 'Get out immediately.' "

Grove acknowledges this was an emotional decision. But he proudly points to the decision as being absolutely key to Intel's future success:

In retrospect, getting out of DRAMs when we did was the best business decision we've ever made, both for us and for the industry. We'd have been of no value to the industry as one of many limping memory suppliers. As it was, we were freed to put those resources into microprocessor development and production, which enabled us to become the technology powerhouse for the PC industry. We didn't act a moment too early.

Thus freed, Intel could focus its efforts on the far more sophisticated microprocessors—the brains of computers. Having a clear focus was, and still is, a distinct advantage of Intel. In 1994, microprocessors provided about 55 percent of Intel's sales and most of its profits, which Grove vows to "fight with everything we've got to protect."

OVERHAULING THE MANUFACTURING PROCESS

Ask any Intel employee who was most responsible for turning Intel's manufacturing processes around and bringing them up to world-class standards and they'll all point to one man: Craig Barrett. Vinod Dahm called Barrett "the real hero in turning that side of the world around." He later added, after bemoaning the fact that no one seemed to have the vision to say, "How do we take a quantum leap here and how do we create best-known methods of doing things and proliferate those best-known methods?":

Barrett was the man instrumental in having the vision and more importantly in driving the vision through the organization and implementing it to where it starts showing results. Today, manufacturing is an order of magnitude better. He created the environment, the expectations, the infrastructure.

Because of his prowess in this capacity, Barrett was made executive vice president in 1991 and the third member of the executive office (joining Chairman Gordon Moore and president and CEO Andrew Grove). He became the COO in January 1993.

So it was that we looked to the interview with Barrett with high anticipation. Thus, it was quite a surprise when he was led down a long row of cubicles, most running between eighty to 120 square feet, to the final cubicle that served as Barrett's office—maybe 30 percent larger than the average analyst's cubicle. Hard to believe that this humble space was the operations center for the chief operating officer of the world's largest and most profitable chip maker.

And with characteristic modesty, Barrett said relatively little about his own role in Intel's transformation. Rather, he directed us to Intel's main operating document, which reads, "Our Mission," "Our Values," and "Our Objectives" from left to right. This, he stressed, was the real secret of Intel's success—the fact that every Intel employee knew and lived by these values and objectives. And sure enough: the document was ubiquitous throughout the company, hanging in people's offices and often on the long outside walls of the cubicles.

The six values are: customer orientation, results orientation, discipline, great place to work, quality, and risk taking. Important to Intel's transformation is that three of the six were added since 1985: customer orientation, great place to work, and quality.

The objectives, he noted, point to the drive and energy of the company—and we may add, a bit of the paranoia. Under the first objective, "Strengthen our number one position in the microprocessor segment," were such specific goals as:

- make the Pentium processor ramp the fastest in history
- double system performance at every price point
- ensure 90 percent of major new PC introductions are Intel verified

Under objective number two, "Make the PC *the* ubiquitous interactive information device," were goals such as:

- make the PC accepted as the interactive information device in the home
- be number one in PC connectivity devices (desktop and mobile)

"Do the right things right" was the simply stated third goal, but it included:

- build 2X upside capability into our planning, scheduling and delivery systems
- double the size of our standard semiconductor business by 1995

These are the points that Craig Barrett—"Mr. Manufacturing"—emphasized. But from other people and company sources, here's the revolution in manufacturing that Barrett oversaw in the 1980s.

First, the company in the mid-1980s went back to basics. Barrett recalls: "We set our expectations higher. We trained our engineering staff in statistical process control. We gave more attention to equipment selection and management. We pushed our technology development."

The points that Vinod Dham raised in his interview show how much of this was fleshed out, first focusing on "more attention to equipment selection":

> When I came in 1979, we were a bunch of young hotshots who created these wonderful EPROMs and DRAM products and processes. We did it all individually. There was no synergy—no sharing of the knowledge or the processes. There was no shared learning.
>
> The change that first took place is you couldn't just go out and order whatever you wanted. Instead of four individuals doing their own thing, ordering their own materials, they coordinated as a team. We were too autonomous. Shared learning creates its own rewards you don't see when there are just little fiefdoms creating their own little things.

Vinod then talked about Barrett's "setting higher expectations":

> We presented to him [Barrett] our improvements on yield. He said, "What will the yield be a year from now?"
>
> We'd say, "10X." "My God, what a great number" we thought.
>
> He'd say, "Have you looked at the Japanese. Their model?"
>
> "No."
>
> "Look at the Japanese. We want 20X."
>
> He was damn bloody right. He really was. I don't know whether he just faked it or whether he really knew it. He set that expectation for us and within the year, we were at 20X.

The last item mentioned in Barrett's list was "pushed our technology development." This involved changing the relationship between process technology development and manufacturing, which had historic significance for Intel. The company took pride in the fact that it developed its manufacturing processes in the factory. Finally, it became clear that interrupting production to tweak its processes was too disruptive. The big switch was to turn Fab 5 (a large fabrication plant) over to technology development. Then when it got yields up on a new process, the manufacturing teams replicated the process exactly.

Barrett proudly cites the astounding results:

> We've made several quantum leaps. For example, in the mid-1980s, fewer than 50 percent of our chips were functional at the end of the line. Today, we regularly have yields of more than 80 percent. Equipment utilization has risen from below 20 percent to as high as 60 percent today.
>
> People who were in manufacturing ten years ago think the yields we have

today should be impossible. It's a great example of how you can always do better.

The next big transformation for manufacturing was a move to sole-sourcing. Until the mid-1980s, the pattern of the industry was to sec-ond-source most products. That pattern was no longer attractive as Intel's microprocessor line increased in value and candidates for ex-change did not keep pace. The turning point came with the introduc-tion of the Intel 386 chip. As Andy Grove recalls, "We just didn't want to put the chip on a silver platter and ship it off to other companies. We wanted to be sure we would get something of value in return." To ensure this, Intel decided to remain the only manufacturer of the 386.

It may not sound like much, but this decision pushed Intel to new heights in manufacturing according to Grove:

> We had to commit to supplying the entire needs of the industry. That motivated us to get our manufacturing performance up to snuff. We developed multiple internal sources, so several factories and several processes were making the chips simultaneously. We made major commitments to production ramps, and we didn't hedge.

The manufacturing changes were visible in the tour we took of D2 (their process technology and manufacturing fabrication facility) in Santa Clara, California. First came the "behind the scenes" part, the "basement" floor below the clean room. It was huge, filled everywhere with pipes, valves, meters—all spotless, all expensive, and all necessary to the clean room manufacturing going on above. John Carpenter, the production manager of this facility, proudly pointed out the waffle ceiling, which gave them flexibility in allowing them to bring in new pieces of equipment fast. Since this was their technology development facility, such flexibility was very important.

Carpenter pointed out the changes that he had witnessed there in recent years. Before, all manufacturing employees were operators. Today, they are technicians. As technicians, they are often asked to do engineering-type work, as well as sleuthing work to see what is wrong. Before, everything was manual. Now there is a great deal of robotics. All technicians must become computer literate. Before, it was unheard of for manufacturing people to get together to exchange best practices. Today, it's common practice.

DOUBLING UP DESIGN

It's quite strange. Intel's special silver anniversary book, which high-lights each of the company's first twenty-five years, doesn't even men-tion what was one of the biggest shake-ups at the company in the last decade. Up to mid-1990, Intel's standard practice was to wait until one generation was ready for production before starting work on the next. Because of paranoia (there it is again) over looming competition, Grove doubled up on design. He launched work on the sixth-genera-tion chip, code-named P6, two years before the planned introduction of the fifth-generation chip—the Pentium processor. The Pentium processor was introduced in the spring of 1993. Before that time, the core design team from the Pentium process was directed to work on the P7—the seventh-generation chip. In essence, what all this does is halve the time between chip generations. By 1994, Intel was at work designing five generations of new chips.

Now is the time to meet Vinod Dham more closely. For just as Craig Barrett is Mr. Manufacturing at Intel, so Vinod could be considered "Mr. Processor." It is Dham who helped design and head the team that introduced the 486 chip, which put Intel on the map, and it was he who helped design and then head the team that introduced the Pen-tium chip. He now heads the Pentium business program, with the task to, in his own words, "make it mega-successful." Dham points out that this doubling up on design "creates its own challenges, but the reward is you are out there much more frequently with higher performance and you provide higher value to your customers."

He was asked, "What is the interaction between the P6 and the P7 team?"

When we started P6, the guy who managed the 486 project headed it. We sent dozens of people working on P7 up to Oregon, to the P6 team, to not just learn but to contribute to P6 because the best way to learn is to contribute.

"Isn't it possible for the P7 team to leapfrog the P6 team?"

In computer architecture, there is no magic that happens overnight to make a project go away. We know where we'll be with architecture improvements through the end of the decade. There is a logical progression. The next team picks up the next chunk, the next team the next chunk, etc.

One thing is clear: the process of design and manufacturing is not usually smooth. A mix of high-powered designers and technologists always makes for some degree of "creative tension" on the job. This was certainly the case for the Pentium processor, Intel's successor to its highly successful 486 chip series. It was nearly four years from the summer of 1989 when initial brainstorming took place to the Pentium's unveiling in the spring of 1993—a stormy four years. The chip's design was a radical departure from previous Intel microprocessors. It computes two instructions at a time instead of one. Soon, "real estate" squabbles began as engineers fought with getting their share of the 3.1 million transistors that were crammed onto the 0.7-inch-square chip. As different circuits were patched together, more strains erupted, as one design crew often blamed another's work. To ease the friction, design milestones were celebrated with pizza parties, beer bashes, and dinners out. The project leader, Vinod Dham, once piled everybody into a bus for a party at the Academy of Sciences in San Francisco. The final product was a true breakthrough. It handled 100 million instructions per second, five times more than the heralded 486 chip and 100 times more than the 286 chip introduced just eleven years earlier. And the Pentium didn't hesitate in becoming a smashing success, as it was expected to gross up to $4 billion in 1994—almost 30 times more than the 486 in its second year.

PLENTY OF OLD-FASHIONED CAPITAL INVESTMENT AND R&D

Now we get back to some real basics at Intel. To put this into perspective, let's go back to the tough times. From 1985 to 1986, the company closed seven factories, abandoned several businesses, and cut head count by one third. What did *not* get cut were investments in the future. Intel stuck to its long-term orientation, with combined R&D and capital expenditures totaling 30 percent of revenues in 1986. And the investments just kept coming.

By year-end 1993, their twenty-fifth year as a company, Intel had spent more on capital programs in the three previous years than it did in the first twenty-two. As recently as 1991, Intel's capital spending was running at "only" around $1 billion. By 1994, its budget called for capital spending of $2.4 billion, more than twice what any other company in the industry spent in 1993.

It's not too difficult to see why capital spending must be so high.

Each new fab (fabrication facility) that it now builds will cost around $1.5 billion, which means that in 1994 it was spending $3 billion just to develop two new fabs in New Mexico and Arizona. Incidentally, this expansion in New Mexico and its new plant in Arizona means that 85 percent of Intel's processors will be made in the U.S. Meanwhile, R&D expenditures in 1993 inched close to the $1 billion a year mark, nearly three times that of 1988.

BECOMING CUSTOMER-FRIENDLY

When Vinod Dham was asked if close interaction with the customer is fairly new, he replied, "You bet. Ten years ago, we were a technology company alone, where we created tremendous innovations and passed them on to the user and the user had to figure out how to use those innovations." Remember, "customer orientation" was a fairly recent addition to Intel's list of values.

So Intel committed to putting on a new face with customers, involving them right from the start. In designing the Pentium chip, the designers first visited every major customer plus major software houses to ask those companies what they wanted. The list of features grew to 147, many of which were different from what Intel expected. The company also surprised many of its customers by furnishing software simulations of the Pentium so the customers could start engineering their new computers. As Vinod said, "We learned along the way, particularly with our microprocessors, that we need to listen to our customers, understand what they need, and design things to their requirements."

One of the most important things Intel does to ensure customer satisfaction is to test each chip thoroughly before it leaves the factory. Because chips may end up in applications ranging from automobile engines to airplane control panels and factories, they must be able to withstand a wide range of environmental stresses.

Perhaps the best way to delight customers is to deliver high value to them. Grove has set this goal for the company: to enable PC producers to double the performance of their machines at every price point this year.

EMPOWERING AND TRAINING EMPLOYEES

Grove has his own unique way to empower Intel employees. His desire is to create a corporate environment that fosters creativity and innovation. Believing that pulling no punches is the most efficient way to proceed, he told the employees that anyone can demand an "AR"—action required—of any executive on any issue. He encourages his employees to speak their minds in order to iron out disputes. He personally attends an ongoing series of forums where he asks workers to download what they're thinking. He's also been known to barge into a cubicle (there are no offices) and demand an on-the-spot defense of a decision.

Other Intel managers can also be creative in stimulating innovation. In June 1993, the microprocessor products group held its first "innovators day," with $100,000 in development cash to be given to the three or four employees coming up with the freshest new ideas. As Albert Yu, head of the groups, says, "It's management's job to encourage innovation every day. Our worst enemy is complacency."

Empowerment takes many forms. All employees receive equal access to all information. Before, Intel could exercise control by denying information to lower-level workers. Employees receive a bonus twice a year. They also receive an eleven-week paid sabbatical every seven years to combat burnout. And the employees receive a lot of training, both technically and to encourage creativity and promote greater awareness of new product and manufacturing technology.

A CONSTANT SCANNING OF THE HORIZON

Perhaps the greatest strength of Intel is that it is definitely not a company resting on its laurels. It is restless—always scanning the horizon for new business opportunities. Andy Grove has the big picture sharply in focus: "Many of you have followed Intel through its transition from the 70s to the 80s, as it moved from a semiconductor memory to a microcomputer focus. In a similar fashion, we now are shifting the focus of our attention to the field of communications and interactivity."

It's already come a long way in this direction. In recent years, it has moved resources into areas such as networking products, mobile computing, and its recent ProShare personal conferencing products.

This does *not* mean that it is leaving the PC world behind. Quite to the contrary, as Grove makes dramatically clear: "The PC is it. That sums up Intel's business plan and rallying cry."

Specifically, Grove wants to move into the home market big-time. His goal is to transform the Intel-chip-powered PC into an all-purpose consumer device that will ultimately subsume your telephone, answering machine, TV, VCR, set-top cable TV box, and video game console. In short, Intel brains will make your PC the family vehicle for cruising down the Information Highway.

Meanwhile, Grove is not exactly abandoning the business market: "We see incredible opportunities in the area of business communications—making the PC a truly full-functional, real-time communications tool. The PC has the ability to obliterate time and space barriers in dealing with information."

There are always the naysayers when it comes to moving into new markets. Grove remembers back in 1971 when Intel introduced the 4004, "One of our board members asked me, 'You're a semiconductor memory company. What business is it of yours to do CPU development for other people?' "

Groves's comments on this indicate why it is likely that Intel will be a pacesetting company for some time to come:

Today, some people have asked me essentially the same question: "Where do you get off making end-user-ready telecommunications products?" It has the same flavor to me as our venture into microprocessors—it's a risk, but it's enormously exciting.

We have no guarantees that it will work, but it seems like something people will want. It just feels right.

Once again, we're leading with our chin into a brand-new arena. Historically, it's our best mode.

LESSON: To get ahead of the pack with new products, and stay ahead, a company must:

- get focused on the right thing, which may mean killing projects that aren't flying
- make sure everyone knows, and lives by, the company's mission, values, and objectives
- invest heavily in modern plants and R&D
- increase speed significantly by doubling up on design
- be willing to completely restructure the manufacturing process
- involve customers right from the start in new product development
- always scan the horizon for new business opportunities

 ## Shake Out the Complacency
COMPAQ

TODAY, THE CUSTOMER IS THE CENTER OF OUR ATTENTION. EVERY DECISION WE MAKE IS GUIDED BY CUSTOMER REQUIREMENTS. IN SHORT, WE HAD TO TOTALLY CHANGE THE WAY WE DID BUSINESS—THE WAY WE DEFINE OUR PRODUCTS, THE WAY WE SELL THEM, WHERE WE SELL THEM, THE WAY WE SUPPORT THEM, AND THE WAY WE COMMUNICATE AND ADVERTISE THEM."

—ECKHARD PFEIFFER, PRESIDENT AND CEO

THE CHALLENGE

No one has articulated more clearly the challenge that Compaq, based in Houston, faced in late 1991 better than its chairman, Benjamin Rosen:

> From our start-up of operations in 1983, we enjoyed an unbroken eight-year run of rising sales, earnings and stock price. We went from start-up to $3 billion sales in record time, achieved Fortune 500 status in three years, an all-time record, and were flying high. We were recognized for producing PCs with the highest performance and quality, but also with the highest prices. No matter though, for the market clearly was willing to pay up for the best.
>
> And then, in the second quarter of 1991, a funny thing happened on the way to prosperity. Our sales flattened, our earnings dropped and our stock price plummeted. In the third quarter, we faced our first-ever quarterly loss. What had happened was that competition was intensifying and product price was becoming much more important to customers. Yet we were locked in to a product line characterized by high costs and high prices.
>
> Compaq Computer, after a period of meteoric and profitable growth, ran into serious difficulties engendered by fundamental shifts in the marketplace. Our historical recipe for success was out of tune with the new needs of customers. For the first time, the board and management differed on the fundamental direction of the company.

It is interesting to note, and most instructive, that before the fall of 1991, the survivors of Compaq's glory days felt its strategy of "premium products, premium prices" was good for another five to ten years. It took the sudden rebellion of a large number of Compaq's customers switching to less-expensive brands to wake the company up. But even then, many at Compaq just didn't get it. This included Rod Canion, the company's co-founder and chief executive. He and his management team in September 1991 presented a recovery plan to the board that called for a major reorganization and the company's first layoffs. *But,* their plan placed no urgency on countering the low-priced clones— Compaq's own low-end product launch wouldn't come until the first quarter of 1993, and meanwhile, customers would come back to the company's superior products.

The board understood that the computer industry was witnessing a sea change while top management saw no such change and therefore no need for fundamental transformation. The board quickly elevated then Chief Operating Officer Eckhard Pfeiffer to president and CEO and challenged him to turn things around.

THE RESPONSE

Just as Ben Rosen provided the best summary of the challenge, so Eckhard Pfeiffer provides the best summary of the key thinking and first steps in the turnaround:

> I met with the Compaq management team and spent endless hours struggling to develop new corporate objectives, strategies, and plans. Together, we came to the fundamental conclusion that we had to aggressively defend and expand our position as one of the top three PC suppliers in the world. But to be a worldwide leader in the current PC market, we could no longer follow our strategy of being only a high-end player.
>
> We needed to know what went wrong after Compaq's ten years of success —and face those issues head-on. We had to recognize our key strengths and define the new market requirements in order to build our new strategy.
>
> We knew that we had to bring our costs and prices down 35 to 50 percent. We knew today's customers required a high level of customer support and broader distribution. And we knew we had to reposition the company in this new market. But we also knew that people liked many of the values traditionally associated with Compaq—quality, reliability, compatibility, high technology, and performance.
>
> All this meant extraordinary changes were necessary to accomplish significant improvements and—hopefully—a complete corporate turnaround. We needed to direct our organization to address new market opportunities—in fact, the total market opportunity. We needed to define and develop new products that would enable us to capture new market segments and compete with low-priced clone products. At the same time, we had to lower the cost and pricing requirements of our traditional high-end products to satisfy the needs of our existing customer base.
>
> We needed to expand our skills in all the product areas we had already pioneered—and add the cost capability and marketing requirements.

That's quite a sweeping agenda. How does one begin to implement it?

Compaq first identified six priorities: products, cost, pricing, distribution, corporate positioning, and customer support. Products and cost led the way. In order to redefine its role in the PC industry, Compaq recognized that it had to defend its market share and meet total market needs—including the entry level. So it needed a host of new products, particularly low-end models, and it needed them quickly. To do this, it had to cut costs dramatically, which meant spurring the company to new ways of thinking.

The key step was creating an Independent Business Unit, which was charged with developing an early low-end clone launch. Housed in a warehouse removed from Compaq's main offices, this IBU began work on an entry-level product line code-named "Ruby." It purchased low-end computers from competitors and found they weren't so bad, making it tough for Compaq to break into that end of the market. The only hope was to break some of Compaq's sacred rules—including those related to long-term relationships with a few select suppliers. Team Ruby sought bids directly from a variety of parts suppliers and pressured them to lower prices. Those that didn't take them seriously were soon dropped. New suppliers were looked at and Compaq discovered that offshore manufacturers could save the company tens of millions of dollars.

This alarmed other Compaq employees, seeing the massive loss of jobs that loomed. They offered to compete with the other manufacturers for the business. Working together with members of the IBU, they discovered they could match most of the outsiders on price. As one example, board manufacturing was greatly simplified, enabling the new line to crank out a computer every minute compared to the old way of one every eight minutes.

The Ruby team had scrambled hard, and presented its proposed models to Pfeiffer shortly before Christmas. One problem: they didn't look at all like Compaqs. He sent them back to the drawing board to redesign the product.

Just three months into their work, team Ruby was reincorporated into the rest of the company. At once, they began to spread the gospel about cutting costs and development time. People listened. On June 15, Compaq publicly launched its New Era and forty-five new personal computer products. It had proved to a skeptical world that it could implement its strategies to successfully address the total market opportunity. As Pfeiffer puts it: "I'd like to think that Compaq had two turning points—October 25 was our corporate turning point in terms of our new strategic direction, June 15 was the day on which we were finally able to communicate the total message and see the company's fortunes beginning to turn around."

His point about being able to communicate the total message is a critical one, for he has said that "communication was our greatest need and our toughest challenge throughout the first 200 days. From the moment of the change in our corporate leadership, we were under constant pressure from everyone—inside and outside—asking us, 'What's going to happen, what are you going to do now?'"

Compaq began its manufacturing revolution in 1992 when it began for the first time to give some subassembly work to contractors. This in itself was a wrenching change for a company that had built a reputation on the MADE BY COMPAQ label. But the company still maintains rigorous testing standards for its suppliers and its own products, ensuring that Compaq's reputation for quality, reliability, and integrity is upheld.

It also began its customer-focus revolution in 1992. We say "revolution" because as Gus Kolias, its vice president for customer service and training, acknowledges, "We had acquired the reputation for being standoffish." With its new focus on serving customers well, it immediately enlarged its customer support staff in 1992 by 40 percent, by redeploying workers from all parts of the company. In December of that year, it extended the normal business hours for its 800 telephone number to twenty-four-hour, seven-day-a-week service. Calls increased 81 percent in less than a year.

It also launched a major effort to get its products closer to potential customers. It quintupled the number of North American outlets from 2,000 to 10,500 in just two years. Worldwide, it now has 21,000 marketing partners. Retailers in early 1994 accounted for more than 20 percent of Compaq's shipments compared to only 5 percent in 1992.

In its drive to develop new products and enter new markets, Compaq increasingly works through its strategic alliances. It already has had a very successful alliance with Microsoft, along with Novell, that has enabled it to become the biggest maker of servers, high-powered PCs that anchor office networks (37 percent of the market in 1993).

Meanwhile, Compaq relentlessly creates new products, enters new markets, and continues to cut prices. In June 1994, it made its boldest play yet, introducing the Armada, which is a six-foot-high server designed to replace mainframes in computers. It plans to launch an assault in 1995 on new consumer markets, including set-top-TV boxes, game players, and stand-alone home PCs. The overall goal is to make the PC the center of a range of consumer appliances in the home. Also in June 1994, it cut the prices of its computers yet again, by up to 29 percent.

Pfeiffer, after his first tumultuous but highly successful year, said that the experience had taught Compaq some valuable lessons about adapting to change. The four key messages are:

- keep your vision of the future constantly in mind
- find the right technology for the right time
- form the alliances necessary to meet the challenges head-on
- anticipate and leverage change

THE RESULTS

First came the accolade from *Industry Week* in early 1993: "It has been hailed as the quickest and best-implemented corporate change ever." In early 1994, *Fortune* said: "In the two years since Eckhard Pfeiffer became CEO of Compaq Computer, he has engineered such a stunningly complete turnaround that it's surprising the company still has the same name."

One of the major set of results has already been noted above: the introduction of forty-five new products in June 1992—only nine months after the new direction was set. In one year, Compaq tripled its manufacturing volume, cut costs and prices across its whole product line, and doubled the number of its distribution outlets.

Looking out two years from Pfeiffer's arrival, Compaq more than doubled its share of the PC and workstation market, from 3.8 percent to 10.5 percent. The Presario, its new consumer product introduced in August 1993, quickly became the top-selling computer for under $1,500. In 1993, it boosted sales from $4.1 billion to $7.2 billion, which was good enough to have it ranked number 6 on the Fortune 500 list of "Biggest Increase in Sales" with a 75 percent increase over 1992. It made more money that year than its two top rivals—IBM and Apple—combined.

Meanwhile, its net profit continued to soar. In the first quarter of 1994, Compaq made $213 million—more than double its net profit for the first quarter of 1993—on sales of $2.3 billion, up 41 percent. Second quarter profits also more than doubled to $210 million. Many were estimating that 1994 sales could hit $10 billion. And sales per employee isn't too bad either: a whopping $716,000, tops in the computer industry and more than double that of IBM and Dell Computer, and well over double their own figure in 1991.

Remarkably, as its volume doubled and it introduced 35 new products in 1993, total manufacturing costs came down almost $10 million. Cost cutting across the board has been remarkable: in 1992–1993, combined labor and overhead costs per computer fell by an amazing 75 percent. Its general goal is to cut costs and prices by 15 percent to 20 percent a year.

For all these reasons, it is not surprising that when Pfeiffer announced, in September 1993, that Compaq intended to become number one in PC and workstation market share by 1996, few people laughed. Even fewer were laughing just a short time later when in each of the first three quarters of 1994 Compaq edged aside both IBM and Apple to become the world's largest PC maker.

> LESSON: Total company transformation—change completely the firm's culture, cut costs by 35 percent to 50 percent, create a host of new products, undertake a manufacturing revolution, become customer-focused, and rely more on strategic alliances—may be called for and it can succeed quicker than you think.

Reinventing Auto Making
CHRYSLER

"THE ONLY WAY WE CAN BEAT THE COMPETITION IS WITH PEOPLE. THAT'S THE ONLY THING ANYBODY HAS. YOUR CULTURE AND HOW YOU MOTIVATE AND EMPOWER AND EDUCATE YOUR PEOPLE IS WHAT MAKES THE DIFFERENCE."
—ROBERT EATON, CEO

THE CHALLENGE

Lee Iacocca didn't pull any punches in describing the tough times Chrysler faced in the late 1980s. Here are just a few of the phrases he threw out in the interview with him: "the volume was dropping like a rock"; "we lost our commercial paper rating and we got downgraded to junk"; "we couldn't finance any cars." And on top of it all: "We weren't talking to one another."

And this was all after the great Chrysler Comeback of the late 1970s and early 1980s. That was the dramatic one involving the federal loan guarantees and the catch phrase of "equality of sacrifice" to save the company. In looking back at it, Bob Lutz, the current president, calls it "good old-fashioned top-down management at its finest." And, he adds, "It worked."

So what went wrong? The economy for one. The go-go 1980s were coming to a screeching halt. Seeing a recession coming on, Lee Iacocca thought, "Oh my God. We're going to tank again." The Japanese automakers were growing increasingly tougher. Profits were sliding and market share was eroding. Bob Lutz adds that "it was equally clear that some of the organizational and human resources strategies that had worked pretty well in the 1980s would not work so well in the 'leaner' 1990s."

Chrysler faced a tough choice: follow the usual Detroit path of cutting new product development programs to save costs or keep spending on new models?

THE RESPONSE

They decided to keep spending on new models. But they also decided to cut costs substantially. And far beyond that, they also decided to overhaul Chrysler's top-down autocratic management structure. And at the same time, why not totally transform the organizational infrastructure—the very way that cars are made? From that point on, Chrysler was to be a much more nimble, agile manufacturer, quick to introduce a host of new products, primarily through extensive use of platform teams.

And the leader of what is now called Chrysler's Second Comeback was none other than Lee Iacocca. According to Robert Eaton, current CEO, "Lee Iacocca laid the groundwork. He created an environment in which radical change could occur. He was the godfather of that, and it is irreversible."

So what does the godfather have to say when asked what it mainly was that drove the success of Chrysler's recent transformation. "Fear. Fear of going broke."

Iacocca has much more too say about other key driving elements of Chyrsler's transformation, but before turning to them, it is fascinating to note one element that is *not* included: market share. Bob Lutz is clear about this:

> We don't have a market share goal. We might put something down on our business plan, but if you set a goal, you focus on the wrong thing. You end up mishandling customers, shaving margins, planning capacity you don't need, making foolish acquisitions. Bob Eaton agrees. Neither of us sees our role as killing competition or carving up more share. These are outdated concepts. Our goal is to design and produce exceptional vehicles, vehicles that stand for something, that don't pander to the middle-of-the-road.
>
> Set a goal, and what is the easiest way to get there? Oversupply and rebates, which trashes the equity of our customers. We want to be marginally undersupplied.

So, besides fear, what has driven Chrysler's Second Comeback? It's a fascinating blend of the old and the new: good old-fashioned cost cutting and virtually all the paths to success cited in this book, with empowerment and teamwork at the center.

How important was cost cutting? Just listen to Iacocca:

> We said what we should do is take $4 billion out of the company. And they said, "You have to be nuts; you can't do that and keep the product going." I said, "Well let's start with $1 billion," and we started. In fact, we said that instead of cutting your pay, or me taking a buck a year again, what you could do is bet your check. If you as a group can make the $1 billion cost reduction, you can bet 10 percent of your pay and we'll give you double your money back if you make it.
>
> After the first billion, a funny thing happened. We didn't have to put incentives on the second, third, and fourth billion.
>
> They found it. It had to be at the grass roots. That really was the guts of saving the company. If we hadn't done that four billion, we wouldn't even be talking today; we'd be bankrupt again.

Iacocca went on as to what this cost cutting entailed: "What you had to cut out was all the 'frills.' In a big company, it's everything from flying first-class to getting tough on telephone calls."

Bob Lutz acknowledges the importance of the cost cutting but what he likes to emphasize is the other half of the scissors—all the new initiatives and new structure. Here's his capsule summary:

> I submit that the key watchwords of this turnaround have been, all things considered, "teamwork" and yes, "empowerment." It applies, not just to blue-collar workers, but to what we call our total "extended enterprise" at Chrysler —white-collar employees, suppliers, and dealers, as well as blue-collar employees.

Empowerment began at Chrysler by giving employees an opportunity to vent what was on their minds. Scores of town hall meetings were held. Iacocca pointed to his active participation: "I held fifty of them, with 200 people apiece. I talked to 10,000 people direct and let them take me apart for two hours as to why we weren't getting the work done and why we had to have a culture transformation."

The initial culture transformation was hard but occurred relatively quickly for a big company. It came in the area of new product development and integrating design, engineering, and manufacturing. In the 1980s, Chrysler was a textbook case of how *not* to develop new products. Organized around separate standing "chimney's"—vertically oriented, functional departments—what they all too often ended up with, in Lutz's words, were "huge costs, uncompetitive product development times, and last, but not least, uninspired cars and trucks."

The big breakthrough was the introduction of platform teams in 1989. Most people have by now heard of these teams at Chrysler. But what few people know is the real-life drama and struggle that lay behind their introduction. It's a fascinating case study of how major change at a company often hinges on personality and perseverance. In Chrysler's case, a key person in François Castaing. His important and fascinating story was related to the authors by Bob Lutz.

The story begins with great resistance, bordering on outright rebellion in some instances, when Castaing was made chief engineer. First, many managers and employees didn't like the wholesale changes he wanted to make in dismantling rigid departments and replacing them with product development teams, pulling together experts in design, manufacturing, marketing, purchasing, finance, and outside suppliers. They especially didn't like such radical change coming from an "import"—he was brought in from American Motors—and from a guy with a heavy French accent and a first name like François (this just wasn't the Detroit image). Nasty, sometimes hostile, letters were sent (often anonymously) to Lee Iacocca demanding that he get rid of Castaing and his plan for major overhaul. But both Bob Lutz, who placed him in his position, and Iacocca stuck by him.

Furthermore, both Iacocca and Eaton insisted that all the top managers undergo extensive training on how to work better as a team, with one another and the line workers. They believe that teamwork and empowerment can only succeed if the people at the top believe in it. An entire chapter could easily be devoted to teamwork at Chrysler. Here are just a few highlights:

- The forerunner of platform teams was "Team Viper," an all-volunteer team of eighty-five people that brought the Dodge Viper to life in only three years for a cost of just $80 million.
- Chrysler quickly moved to put four platform teams into place: one each for small cars, large cars, Jeep vehicles and pickup trucks, and minivans.
- The key to these teams' success is empowerment: in virtually every way possible, senior management defines only the "what" of a given vehicle, leaving the "how" totally up to the teams.
- Many major Chrysler plants have experienced their own turnarounds because of employee empowerment:
  - at New Castle, Indiana, a worker says, "The pride has come back";
  - at the Dayton, Ohio, thermal products plant, they chose to virtually eliminate a half-century-old style of union-management relations, the centerpiece being a gainsharing system;
  - at the Kenosha, Wisconsin, engine plant, worker participation programs "have been instrumental in improving every category of quality measured."

Remember that Chrysler sees its teams as extending well beyond Chrysler's own employees. Iacocca emphasized that the company was able to "develop the best relationships with our suppliers. In four years they said Chrysler's got the best procurement and supply group in the world today." And empowerment involves training the workers. In Detroit, the old assembly plant was torn down and replaced by one of the most modern "lean production" facilities in the world. The workers there, even though they had an average of twenty-six years of production experience, were given an additional 900,000 hours of training to build the new 1993 Jeep Grand Cherokee.

There are many other facets to Chrysler's Second Comeback. The major one is that it became a world-class design leader. Long known for a single car product—the dowdy, boxy K-cars—it is now known as the company with the bold curves, introduced first in the Dodge Stealth and Viper, then in the revolutionary cab-forward LH cars (such as the Dodge Intrepid), and finally in the Neon. These were the result of a risky decision the company made in the late 1980s to develop designs that would make its cars striking standouts. Says Tom Gale, its vice president for design: "Design can add value faster than it adds cost."

Other facets can only be briefly noted. One is Chrysler's investment and commitment to Customer One, a $30 million training program for their dealers. Another is their new focus on exports. By the end of the decade, the company aims to ship 200,000 assembled vehicles a year overseas—double the 1993 level. And because the quality of its products has not caught up with their popularity, Robert Eaton has made himself the company's number one quality advocate. The responsibility for quality is now at the plant level and Eaton has even been willing at times to sacrifice profits for quality.

Eaton sums up the depth of the Chrysler commitment to hold on to their gains and to constantly strive to get better. He wants Chrysler to be the premier car company in America by 1996 and the best in the world by the year 2000. Such goals would have generated peals of laughter just a few years ago. Now, competitors aren't even smiling.

THE RESULTS

On the financial front, Chrysler went from flirting with insolvency in 1990 and 1991 to recording 1993 operating profits of $2.5 billion. During this period, its stock soared some 500 percent. It achieved a rare double: high volumes *and* high margins. In the first quarter of 1994, it set a record quarterly net profit of $938 million, a 77 percent increase from the first quarter of 1993. And it set another record in the second quarter with profits of $956 million. It is also the American auto industry's low-cost manufacturer.

But perhaps what it is most proud of is that it is now the acknowledged world leader in new car development. In 1994, it introduced the Neon, which it brought to market in just thirty-one months at a cost of $1.3 billion. The low cost means they could make a profit on the car right from the start. Prior to the Neon, Chrysler had turned out three tremendously successful vehicles in a row—the Jeep Grand Cheorkee, the LH sedans, and the Dodge Ram pickup truck. Overall, it introduced five new chassis designs in 1992 and 1993, compared with three in the previous twenty years.

Specific gains in competitiveness and performance include:

- compressed vehicle development time from a domestic industry norm of four to five years to a world-class thirty-one months
- reduced vehicle development costs by as much as 50 percent
- improved quality, reducing the "quality gap" with major Japanese manufacturers to just one-half defect per car
- increased exports from a virtual standing start in 1987 to more than 112,000 vehicles in 1992 shipped to more than seventy countries
- captured 14.8 percent of the North American car market, its best showing in twenty-three years

> LESSON: The second turnaround of Chrysler is a story first of cutting costs across the board and then of building a transformed organization centered on the power of American teamwork, the bold design of innovative new products, and dedication to continuous quality improvement.

Perpetual Revolution
VARIAN ASSOCIATES

"THE COMPANY'S PRODUCTION PROBLEMS COULDN'T BE SOLVED BY COMPUTER-INTEGRATED MANUFACTURING, AS MOST WERE PEOPLE PROBLEMS."

—TRACY O'ROURKE, CEO

THE CHALLENGE

When Tracy O'Rourke arrived as the new CEO at Varian Associates in February 1990, he was already viewed as a turnaround genius, having helped three other companies in their transformations. Thus, it didn't take him long to see the company's fundamental challenge: "Varian had trouble with strategic focus. Like a hummingbird, we were going from opportunity to opportunity, only to abandon them when the competition got too hot. We were simply spreading ourselves too thin."

There was another major problem as well that lay behind Varian's lackluster performance: high manufacturing costs. O'Rourke found that these resulted from poor cycle time, an inadequate quality delivery system, and poorly managed inventory.

To understand just how tough the situation was when O'Rourke arrived, here are the challenges he highlighted during a short interview:

- quality: "we were not world-class"; "we were probably twenty years behind the times"; "had businesses that had 40 percent cost of quality to percentage of sales"
- factories: "not responsive and intractable"; "average life in the factory in some cases of more than 300 days"; "we were late on everything—had some factories which shipped nothing on time"; "in many cases, we announced products and we didn't have them commercially available for another two years"
- employees: "we had a demoralized and demotivated group"
- research: "could show you dozens of successes but ultimately they didn't lead to any business"; "they succeeded at the wrong thing"
- finances: "we were going broke"

All of this meant that while Varian, based in Palo Alto, California, had established an excellent reputation as a technological innovator, it was not world-class in its manufacturing systems. As one market analyst said, "It used to be a terrific technology company that couldn't make a buck."

THE RESPONSE

Believing that he had a short window of opportunity, O'Rourke launched a rapid-fire, one-hundred-day turnaround. The master plan called for Varian to eliminate underperforming products, launch Operational Excellence, and accelerate profitable growth.

Step number one was to achieve focus. This meant divesting itself of noncore activities. In May of 1990, just three months after arriving,

O'Rourke announced the decision to sell five businesses and nine product lines. This allowed Varian to concentrate on its core businesses: electron devices, instruments, semiconductor production equipment, and health care systems. This was the relatively easy step.

The big step was a companywide drive directed toward what O'Rourke called Operational Excellence. Operational Excellence was centered around five principles: commitment to quality, customer focus, top-notch time to market, flexible factories, and organizational excellence.

It's ironic that employee empowerment or employee involvement is not mentioned explicitly in the five principles, for that is the key action step to Tracy O'Rourke. You begin there, according to him, because "people had not been properly trained, led, motivated, or integrated into the manufacturing process." The drive to operational excellence can thus be seen as a means of identifying bad habits and empowering people to effectively change them. With this perspective, O'Rourke led the effort to transform Varian's "engineering-pushed" culture toward a "customer-pulled" ethos, primarily through employee empowerment.

To O'Rourke, empowerment is a slow and multiphase process, but the steps are really quite basic. First, you talk with your people. This means a lot of listening. In his first year O'Rourke visited every company location at least three times. He repeats a similar tour about annually. Step two is to make sure you actually take action to solve some of the problems the employees are raising. Step three is to train. Training budgets at Varian nearly tripled in a two-year period in the early 1990s. All employees, including top management, receive at least sixty to seventy hours a year. Some high-tech service people spend 20 percent of their time in training.

Trust, as we saw in Chapter 3, is the critical underlying ingredient in creating employee empowerment. O'Rourke is quite clear on this:

The journey toward empowerment of both the leader and the team is really a psychological kind of program. It involves getting comfortable with each other and developing levels of trust between the leader—not "manager"—and the team. Both leaders and team members have to understand the boundaries in which they operate. As a leader, I've got to give the team the tools they need— be they educational tools or machines—so that they can succeed on their own. It's going to take enormous fine-tuning for companies that do not believe in empowerment or trust to convert themselves into firms that really do believe in trust.

Varian's oncology systems unit in Palo Alto is a prime example of how the company has successfully implemented employee empowerment in recent years. Already an established world leader in medical linear accelerators, its manufacturing manager, Jim Younkin, wanted to make this winner even better. The basic means was to transform a reactive workforce to one that was extremely proactive. "I am now watching my people emerge as leaders as they take over ownership of the manufacturing process." This thinking reflects the company's implementing employee empowerment via its concept of leadership. The underlying premise, according to O'Rourke, is that "the sheer speed of change in our business makes it impractical for one person to make all the decisions needed for us to be competitive. Individuals must step forward in situations that call for their specific mix of skills and judgments."

After the employee comes a sharp focus on the customer. Customer satisfaction is the last of seven sections in the Baldrige application, but it is a principal driver behind Operational Excellence. O'Rourke and Executive Vice President Richard Levy, who initially chaired the company's Baldrige steering committee, personally visited each of the company's thirty-one operating units to discuss their draft applications for the award. "We started with the section on customer requirements and asked them to tell how these were translated into strategies," relates Levy. "How have you measured and improved your performance against those customer-driven strategies?" Some very telling discoveries emerged from this process. One unit had shown significant improvement in key quality indices under the previous quality improvement process but sales actually fell. The problem was that customers found the firm difficult to deal with in terms of getting information. Levy nails it on the head: "We were substituting our definition of quality for the customer's."

From this, they saw that proper measurement is critical. Levy found that measurements used to track improvement often excluded the customer. Customers wanted ease of use or reliability, but measurements would focus exclusively on inventory turns or the number of employees trained in SPC (statistical process control).

Here's a good example. A number of customers weren't happy with the long time it took to set up its radiology equipment at hospitals. After identifying several hundred possible solutions, Varian changed many of its standard practices. The results were good for both the hospitals, which saved ninety-five hours in setup time (worth up to $50,000 per order), and Varian, which saved $1.8 million a year.

To meet the goal of flexible factories, all of Varian's processes implemented what O'Rourke calls "demand-flow technology," which is basically JIT manufacturing. Three Varian units in its instruments business pioneered this process in the mid-1980s because they were under intense competitive pressure. At the time, experience with JIT concepts in small-lot, made-to-order facilities was rare in the United States. The company's other units began the process in 1990.

Demand flow technology is perhaps best seen at the firm's nuclear magnetic resonance instruments (NMRI) plant, which produces only 200 instruments a year. The plant is divided into three minifactories, each of which has teams of fifteen to twenty-five employees that build the three major subassemblies constituting each NMR machine. It is these self-driven JIT teams that are spearheading the plant's efforts to smooth the production process through continuous improvement. According to Russ Perry, the production manager for the NMRI operation, "The challenge for our JIT teams is to eliminate non-value-added elements of our cost while making product and process improvements." As in the oncology systems plant, supplier integration has been a key element as well. In recent years, the number of suppliers has been reduced from 1,000 to 240.

THE RESULTS

The good results at Varian came quickly. Its 1990 loss was turned into $58 million in earnings in 1991. Throughout the early 1990s, sales and orders remained at or near record levels; gross margins grew; net debt declined; and cash flow increased. In 1994, net earnings for the first nine months shot up 88 percent, to a record $52 million, new orders rose 29 percent to $1.3 billion, and the company was headed for a record year.

Speed and agility have increased significantly. According to O'Rourke, Varian has become "without exception very flexible and the fastest in our various businesses." The average life for its products in the factory has been cut by more than half. Other major goals of Operational Excellence have been met, such as a sizable increase in on-time delivery and a reduction in the cost of quality.

These good results are there because employees understand and buy in to the Operational Excellence program. The company took a survey of its employees and found, according to O'Rourke, that over 80 percent of the people understand the Operational Excellence program and over 93 percent understand their personal contribution to the quality effort. "I mean, it was astounding."

At the oncology systems unit, total inventory has been reduced 9 percent since 1988 while sales rose 72 percent. During this period, manufacturing costs declined by over 25 percent. The NMRI unit experienced similar excellent results. From 1985 to mid-1991, the average cumulative lead time for each product shrank from 260 days to seventy days, and manufacturing floor space dropped 46 percent. The cost of quality, which averaged 11.8 percent in fiscal 1990, dropped sharply to just 4 percent in August 1991.

> LESSON: Since most problems begin because companies lose their strategic focus, start by asking tough questions about what business you want to be in; then move to continuous improvement by empowering your employees, targeting customer satisfaction, and becoming a customer-pulled company.

Strike Quickly/Strike Boldly
TENNECO

"THE FIRST HUNDRED DAYS WERE A DEFINING MOMENT FOR US AT TENNECO—A TIME THAT SET THE STANDARD FOR HOW WE WILL WORK FROM NOW ON. COURAGEOUS. COMMITTED. RELENTLESS. TRUSTING AND RELYING ON EACH OTHER. FOCUSED ON RESULTS."

—MIKE WALSH, CHAIRMAN AND CEO (DIED 1994)

THE CHALLENGE

When Michael Walsh arrived at Tenneco in the fall of 1991, the company was like a giant ship afloat at sea without a clear sense of where it was headed or how it was going to get to wherever it was going. Yet there was no particular sense of crisis or urgency. Indeed, when Walsh came to the Drake Hotel in Chicago on September 4, 1991, it was supposed to be an informal meeting when he would be introduced for the first time to the presidents of the firm's seven divisions.

What he heard disturbed him deeply: the third-quarter operating loss at Tenneco's Case Corp. farm and construction equipment unit would be substantially larger than the $83 million forecast by securities analysts. As Walsh proceeded from this trouble area to other areas such as shipbuilding, auto parts, and natural gas, he began to understand why earnings had fallen three years in a row and why the company would be showing a net loss of $732 million that year.

Problems abounded. Inventories were bloated. Quality control was virtually nonexistent. Worst of all, nobody wanted to report the facts, only what they thought their superiors wanted to hear. And certainly, few were interested in thinking about what had to be done.

Walsh realized that he had to strike quickly and strike boldly—even though it was a month before he was to officially come aboard. And even then the board had decided that he should serve a seven-month apprenticeship as president before taking over as CEO because he had no experience in the company's main businesses.

THE RESPONSE

Title or no title, knowledge or no knowledge of the company's businesses, Walsh knew trouble when he saw it and he knew when action was required. "So we brought the key players into a room, closed the door, and said, 'Look, sports fans, we're facing a crisis. There's no way we're going to make that announcement that we're in a general financial crisis without also announcing a serious action plan. We have seventy-two hours.'" This may have been the first-ever casual corporate dinner that lasted three days.

Why a full three days? Walsh answered the question: "I arrived to find a big behemoth of the sort that tries two things on anyone who wants change: It waits you out or wears you out." Walsh himself almost fell victim. By the third night, he was so discouraged at the lack of progress, he phoned his wife and said, "Look, maybe we should just pull out of this." Her response was, "No. You got the job because there's trouble."

By the end of the third day, the group had committed to announce the "bad news" and the action plan the following day—a $2 billion restructuring plan that included asset sales, a dividend cut, and an equity infusion—all to be completed by the end of the year. And yes, the corporate staff was to be cut by one third.

How did Walsh feel about this bold move? "I was scared. For the first time in my life, I felt that everything I'd built was on the line—and that the balance might tip against me and Tenneco." Remarking on this period two years later at the company's Leadership and Planning Conference, Walsh put these first hundred days into perspective:

> Talk about teamwork! Everybody involved locked arms, and the program was executed almost flawlessly against what seemed to be insurmountable odds in a rotten environment. There were huge risks in that approach. But there was no other way to regain our credibility. Sure, we could have failed. It was clenched-teeth time for ninety days. Those values and qualities—risk taking, action, commitment, and competence—are the underpinnings of everything we're doing at Tenneco.

By New Year's day, Tenneco had sold almost $700 million in noncore assets, issued $500 million in new equity, cut expenses by $300 million, reduced capital spending by another $300 million, halved the dividend, taken major steps to address the pressing problems at Case, and announced a $0.5 billion write-off. It was a one-hundred-day blitz like few companies have every undertaken and achieved.

Much more could be said about these early steps. But equally fascinating and important are the longer-term steps that Walsh and Dana Mead, whom he brought on board as president and COO, have put in place to keep the transformation going at Tenneco. (Mead became the CEO in February 1994 and chairman in May 1994 after Walsh's death.)

There are certain key themes that Walsh stressed and Mead keeps emphasizing in speeches, interviews, and articles that account for the continuous shaking up taking place at Tenneco. The three major ones are: leadership, quality and results. We'll examine each in turn.

Walsh highlighted all three themes in his address to the November 1993 Leadership Conference. After reminding his corporate leaders what Tenneco's vision or ultimate goal is—becoming a truly world-class global industrial organization—he stressed that there are four basic things to build upon to have any hope of becoming world-class. After citing a competitive return to shareholders and serving customers well, his second point was the need for "leadership, management, and outstanding people." His argument was an "obvious" one, one that all too often gets lost:

> When you get by the rhetoric, and everybody uses pretty much the same words these days, ask yourself who does all this stuff? The answer is smart, highly committed people with a burning desire to win—what I call a kind of "clenched-teeth intensity." Fundamentally, these people are leaders and motivators—carriers of the torch rather than excuse-makers.

Leadership. Again, few people have stressed its critical importance better than Walsh, and importantly, we know that he practiced what he preached:

> In my judgment this whole thing comes down to one word, and that's leadership. I've been exposed to three companies: Cummins Engine, where I wasn't in charge, and Union Pacific and Tenneco, where I have been. And while you can talk about tools and techniques—and they're terribly important, whether they are quality processes or reducing the levels of organization or communication techniques—those are only tools and techniques. At the end of the day what it comes down to is relentless leadership from the top, in which the CEO makes himself or herself personally vulnerable at more points than you can keep track of.

A good leader can spot other people who will make good leaders. Noted Walsh:

> You've got to be very good at picking people you can trust—and getting them to share the load. I spend half my time on people and processes. Unless you get the people and the relationships between them straight, you aren't going anywhere. The engine of Tenneco's transformation consists of our six operating division presidents and a small but superior corporate staff.

Walsh certainly intended to go somewhere, as by 1994, four of the six operating company heads and all but one member of the corporate headquarters senior staff were new.

The third point in his speech was that companies must build processes that leverage leadership management, and here he was thinking of the company's many quality processes among others. Walsh told his key leaders: "We simply have to raise our sight as an organization, and quality is the principal tool for doing that." In recent years, Tenneco has launched a number of quality management initiatives. According to Walsh, quality initiatives have broad benefits that extend far beyond top-quality products, as the Tenneco quality management systems "focus the entire corporation on critical goals. They link Tenneco together as an organization despite our diversity by giving us a common approach to managing businesses and a common language to communicate plans and results."

Finally, Walsh emphasized: "Perhaps the most important characteristic of a world-class organization and one we have been working on the hardest, is results. Spell it: R-E-S-U-L-T-S. World-class companies produce results consistently and without fail." And just to make sure that everyone knew where Tenneco stood, after citing all the wonderful results of the previous two years, and where it had to go, he immediately followed with, "At Tenneco, the fact is that we still sometimes talk a better game than we play."

Walsh understood the meaning of results:

We should talk, too, about what being results-oriented really means, and what it doesn't mean. I've had some feedback that I'm excessive in my demand for results. Well, I am relentless about results because that's where winners focus —and I intend for this company to be a winner. No apologies for that.

But hear me: I don't demand results at any cost. There is no trade-off between results and ethical behavior. Between results and the health and safety of our employees. Between results and quality. We do what's right, and we play by the rules. But you need to know that another of the rules is that you hit your numbers. There is no contradiction between winning and playing by the rules.

Dana Mead points to an interesting analogy:

An essential prerequisite for consistently delivering results is an organization's ability to see change coming and adapt to it before the competition. The trick is to make your business think like a fighter pilot: observe, orient, decide, act, and do so quickly enough to preempt an adversary's move or to meet a change in the environment.

And when I talk about quickness, I'm including speed of decision making, not just implementation. Fast-response companies manage their decision cycles as rigorously as they do their manufacturing or marketing processes.

At the November 1993 Leadership Conference, President Dana Mead followed Walsh's address. Mead himself is the type of leader and motivator that Walsh so admired. In his speech, he highlighted the three key parameters for describing and reaching world-class status for Tenneco:

- deciding what is essential to your business's success and determining what must be done to achieve leadership in each essential area
- having a "balanced attack"—excellence in only one area isn't world-class
- setting "stretch" objectives.

He later went on to present a "stretch" objective to those assembled: obtain productivity improvements of at least 6 percent annually and as much as 10 percent to hit world-class. "I'm talking about every activity of the company."

Mead's motto—"plan deliberately; execute violently"—gives context to his relentless belief that the intensity of effort expended during the earlier crises must not let up.

THE RESULTS

What can a company with transformation on its mind achieve in less than three years? Despite flat-to-declining revenues, operating income, excluding restructuring charges, rose more than 300 percent from 1991 to 1993. Earnings per share, excluding restructuring charges, showed over a four-dollar improvement. Through the first half of 1994, earnings per share from continuing operations had increased at least 47 percent for nine consecutive quarters, excluding restructuring charges, in quarter-over-quarter comparisons. The stock price went from a low of $27 a share in late 1991 to around $50 a share in early 1994—an 87 percent increase. The market value of the company increased by about $4 billion from September of 1991 through the first half of 1994. Total debt was reduced by $4.7 billion from September 1991 through June 1994.

Another major turnaround story is the Case subsidiary. "Worth nothing" in 1992, according to an industry analyst, Tenneco was able to make an initial public offering of 35 percent of this subsidiary in early 1994. Case's "renaissance," as Mead calls it, enabled it to come back from an operating loss of $1.05 billion in 1992 to an operating income of $82 million in 1993. During the first half of 1994, Case earned $192 million.

Walsh had a balanced view in looking at the company's overall results: "The fact is that we are winning, and it is a lot more fun than losing" he told the company's leaders in November 1993. Around the same time, he told *Fortune*, "We're halfway home at best."

[
LESSON: When trouble abounds, strike quickly and boldly—then stress leadership, quality, and results in order to become a world-class company over the long haul.
]

WE'D LIKE TO HEAR FROM YOU

Our plan is to continue focusing on outstanding, cutting-edge business success stories. We hope to disseminate them in future books, reports, and newsletters, as well as videos and CD-ROMS.

To stay abreast of all the most exciting and creative initiatives taking place in American business, we ask you to let us know about your own company's success story. Remember, it can involve the whole company or just one part of it, such as an individual plant or subsidiary.

If you would like information regarding additional materials highlighting business stories, or would like to contact either of us for speaking engagements, please write us at the address below. We of course would love to hear your comments on this book and ways that we can make future business success stories even more useful to you.

Making It in America
Jerry Jasinowski and Robert Hamrin
1331-A Pennsylvania Avenue, NW
Suite 447
Washington, DC 20004

NOTES

Throughout the book, direct quotes from people employed at one of the fifty companies featured in the book and not included in the notes below can be attributed to an interview with them by the authors.

INTRODUCTION

Page

19 *"If your change"*: Noel Tichy and Stratford Sherman, *Control Your Destiny or Someone Else Will* (New York: Doubleday, 1993).

1. SUNRISE FOR MANUFACTURING

Page

24 *"Not only the wealth"*: Alexander Hamilton, *Report on Manufactures,* submitted to Congress December 5, 1791.

24 *"The most important"*: Peter F. Drucker, "Secrets of the U.S. Export Boom, *Wall Street Journal,* August 1, 1991.

26 *"A tendency to view"*: David Cantor, "Manufacturing Industry: Its Impact on the Economy," Congressional Research Service Report 93-370E, March 1993.

28 *"In 1980 America"*: William McWhirter, "Back on the Fast-Track," *Time,* December 13, 1993, 65.

31 **A 1993 study**: McKinsey Global Institute, "Manufacturing Productivity" (Washington, D.C.: McKinsey Global Institute, 1993).

2. TEN PATHS TO SUCCESS

Page

33   *"We got better":* in interview with Jerry Jasinowski.

33   *"Leaders at all levels":* Tom Peters, *The Tom Peters Seminar* (New York: Vintage, 1994), 271.

38   *"Most of our":* "Service Is Everybody's Business," *Fortune,* June 27, 1994, 60.

38   *"We have killed":* Michael A. Verespej, "Maverick Remakes Old-Line Steel," *Industry Week,* January 21, 1991, 30.

41   *"Every line of":* David Altany, "Newton's Son" *Industry Week,* April 1, 1991, 32.

42   *"Maybe we need":* in interview with Jerry Jasinowski.

43   *"If you really":* Jerry Bowles and Joshua Hammond, *Beyond Quality* (New York: Putnam, 1991), 56.

43   *"TQM works because":* "TQM—A Path to the Future," *Tooling and Production,* July 1993, 5.

45   *"There's a good":* "Special Report—The Environment," 3M internal publication, July 1991, 10.

46   *"Every organization has":* Peter Drucker, "The New Society of Organizations," *Harvard Business Review,* September–October 1992, 98.

47   *"You are all leaders":* Dana Mead, "The Leadership Challenge of Becoming World-Class," in Tenneco Inc. Executive Speech Series, 11–12.

3. EMPOWER EMPLOYEES

Page

52   *"We're not focusing":* "Evolving Self-Directed Teams at Abbott-Ashland," *Commitment Plus* (Schaumburg, Ill.: Quality and Productivity Management Association, September 1992).

53   *"When I first":* internal corporate memo of Wilson Sporting Goods.

53   *"Technique is important":* Tom Peters, *The Tom Peters Seminar* (New York: Vintage, 1994), 80.

55   *"It is not":* Norman Garrity, "People, Partnership, and Productivity," *PI Quality,* 4th quarter, 1991, 16.

64   *"It sounds syrupy":* Joani Nelson-Horchler, "The Magic of Herman Miller," *Industry Week,* February 18, 1991, 12.

69   *"The whole process":* all of Foley's statements are found in Herman Miller's newsletter *Connections,* March 1993, 2.

70   *"I use the word":* Stanley Gault, "Key to Business Success: Be Market Driven," speech at Timken Corporate Forum, Canton, Ohio, April 26, 1993.

72   *"The model has a":* URW International, internal document titled "A Generalized View of the URW/Goodyear Joint Process Model."

72   *"The Gadsden plant has been":* Cyndl Owens, "Goodyear CEO Says Gadsden Aids Team Effort," *Gadsden Times,* October 8, 1992.

72   *"We needed a tremendous":* Stanley Gault, "Leaders of Corporate Change," *Leadership '93.*

73 *"The significant achievement"*: Stanley Gault, speech before Goodyear's manufacturing directors, August 19, 1993.

74 *"During the past year"*: Gerhard Gschwandtner, "The Salesman Who Put the Go Back in Goodyear," *Personal Selling Power,* September 1992, 25.

74 *"We have had some success"*: Letter from James Jesse, URW Education Dept., July 29, 1993.

75 *"It has to start"*: The quotes by Ralph Stayer in this company write-up come from one of two sources: a phone interview between Stayer and Robert Hamrin; and from Ralph Stayer, "How I Learned to Let My Workers Lead," *Harvard Business Review,* November–December 1990.

77 *"These are line"*: quoted in James R. Healy, "U.S. Steel Learns from Experience," *USA Today,* April 10, 1992.

78 *"We'd have instances"*: Ibid.

78 *"I would say"*: quoted in Jonathan R. Hicks, "An Industrial Comeback Story: U.S. Is Competing Again in Steel," *New York Times,* March 31, 1992, A19.

4. TRAIN AND RETRAIN WORKERS

Page

82 *"otherwise you'll just"*: quoted in *Manufacturing Issues* (Chicago: Grant Thornton, Fall 1992), 5.

89 *"Educating employees is"*: from correspondence with Chaparral Steel.

91 *"We have expanded"*: David Churchill and Bill Burzynski, "More Training with Fewer Dollars," *Technical and Skills Training,* August–September 1991, p. 1.

91 *"CR Industries has simply"*: Ibid., p. 2.

93 *"As a business"*: Michael Bates, "Developing Employee Skills as a Business Strategy," Annual Meeting of the Association for Managing Technology, November 18–21, 1992.

94 *"If we continue"*: Joseph McKenna, "Fred Remmele's Investment, Bill Saul's Crusade," *Industry Week,* November 2, 1992.

94 *"Do we worry"*: Ibid.

94 *"Apprenticeship doesn't cost"*: Ibid.

94 *"As people go"*: "Training," *Minnesota Tooling and Machining Association Journal,* April 1993, 22.

95 *"We took their"*: Chapter 5, "Small Company Solutions," internal corporate training document, 20.

95 *"We have a very"*: Ibid.

97 *"The fact that"*: "Training," 23.

97 *"My experience has"*: McKenna, "Fred Remmele's Investment."

97 *"Training and development"*: "Training," 23.

98 *"I had to be"*: Wally Kniceley and Bob Gowatch, "Expanding Employee Involvement," *Sharing Our Pride* (UAW-Ford publication, Winter 1991), 14.

102 *"I believe the creation"*: Gary B. Hansen, "An Outsider's Appraisal," *From Vision to Reality* (UAW-Ford), 2.

5. REWARD GOOD PERFORMANCE

Page

114 *"Productivity used to be"*: Rick Wartzman, "A Whirlpool Factory Raises Productivity—And Pay of Workers," *The Wall Street Journal,* May 4, 1992.

115 *"If your machine"*: Ibid.

117 *"In 1985, we still"*: "Oregon Steel Mills," *Profile* (Washington, D.C.: The Employee Stock Ownership Association).

117 *"Mistrust and anger"*: Ibid.

118 *"Under the old"*: Ibid.

119 *"This was always"*: John Case, "Collective Effort," *Inc.,* January 1992, 38.

122 *"If the company"*: Thomas Rohan, "Maverick Remakes Old-Line Steel," *Industry Week,* January 21, 1991, 30.

6. EXCEED CUSTOMER EXPECTATIONS

Page

128 *"We've given everyone"*: "The Search for the Organization of Tomorrow," *Fortune,* May 18, 1992, 97.

129 *"They do it"*: Tom Peters, *The Tom Peters Seminar* (New York: Vintage, 1994), 45.

130 *"He asked me"*: Stephanie Anderson Forest, "Customers 'Must Be Pleased, Not Just Satisfied,' " *Business Week,* August 3, 1992, 52.

138 *"We had delivery"*: Patrick Oster, "Muscling in Overseas," *Washington Post,* January 26, 1992, H4.

142 *"We charged them"*: Michael A. Verespej, "Mort Mandel: When Old Is New And Not Old Fashioned," *Industry Week,* March 1, 1993, 23.

142 *"throughout our history"*: Ibid.

143 *"You can learn"*: Ibid., 24.

144 *"Our three core"*: Ibid., 26.

145 *"We created a vision"*: Joseph McKenna, "America's Most Admired CEOs," *Industry Week,* December 6, 1993, 27.

146 *"We were being wiped"*: quoted in Robert Heller, *The Super Chiefs* (New York: Dutton, 1992), 297–98.

148 *"We are living proof"*: Kate Ballen, "America's Most Admired Corporations," *Fortune,* February 10, 1992, 77.

149 *"We want the customer"*: Robert Howard, "The CEO as Organization Architect," *Harvard Business Review,* September–October 1992, 113.

150 *"I am changing"*: Ron Zemke with Dick Schaff, *The Service Edge* (New York: Plume, 1990), 505.

151 *"In the 1980s"*: Howard, "The CEO as Organization Architect," 108.

151 *"We've given everyone"*: "The Search for the Organization of Tomorrow," *Fortune,* May 18, 1992, 97.

152 *"The Xerox success"*: interview with Jerry Jasinowski.

7. ENVISION NEW PRODUCTS AND MARKETS

Page

154 *"What should I"*: David Sheff, *Game Over: How Nintendo Zapped an American Industry, Captured Your Dollars, and Enslaved Your Child* (New York: Random House, 1993), 21.

154 *"Speed in new"*: Boston Consulting Group, *International New Product Development Survey* (Boston: Boston Consulting Group, May 1993).

156 *"People never believe"*: Robert Levering and Milton Moskowitz, *The 100 Best Companies to Work for in America* (New York: Doubleday, 1993), 287.

157 *"An ordinary man"*: Sheff, *Game Over,* 38.

157 *"The key to"*: Brenton R. Schlender, "How Sony Keeps the Magic Going," *Fortune,* February 24, 1992, 77.

165 *"Our success is based"*: "Is Miscrosoft Too Powerful?" *Business Week,* March 1, 1993, 83–84.

166 *"There is very little"*: Levering and Moskowitz, *The 100 Best Companies,* 288.

170 *"We structured Thermo Electron"*: David Altany, "Newton's Son," *Industry Week,* April 1, 1991, 32.

170 *"Every line of"*: Ibid.

171 *"It is very"*: Ibid.

173 *"We have adopted"*: Levering and Moskowitz, *The 100 Best Companies,* 339.

173 *"We feel that if"*: Ibid., 338.

174 *"Everyone works very"*: Ibid., 340.

174 *"We're always folding"*: Joseph Weber, "A Big Company That Works," *Business Week,* May 4, 1992, 132.

8. GO GLOBAL

Page

178 *"To be competitive"*: quoted in *Manufacturing Issues* (Chicago: Grant Thornton, Spring 1992), 5.

191 *"Most people who"*: Andrew Tanzer, "Just Get Out and Sell," *Forbes,* September 28, 1992, 72.

194 *"Our underlying strategy"*: Andrea Knox, "Air Products' European Strategy: Invest, Invest, Invest Some More," *Journal of Commerce,* June 11, 1992.

196 *"Our strategic reasoning"*: Dexter Baker, "The Ultimate Test," *Directors and Boards,* Fall 1992, 10.

196 *"The point is"*: Ibid.

198 *"There is a bias"*: all quotes by Donald Moses came in an interview with Robert Hamrin.

201 *"Our whole key"*: in a memo to the authors.

202 *"Not all of"*: Ibid.

9. PURSUE TOTAL QUALITY

Page

220 *"Quality improvement goals"*: address by William J. Hudson at Global Planning Meeting, Munich, Germany, November 9, 1992, 9–10.

221 *"Quality is no"*: "Global Talk: AMP's CEO Speaks Out," *Electronic Buyers News,* February 15, 1993, 39.

221 *"If you really"*: Jerry Bowles and Joshua Hammond, *Beyond Quality* (New York: Putnam, 1991), 56.

222 *"Some people say"*: "The Myth of Unskilled Workers—Zen and the Art of Training," internal AMP paper, 5.

222 *"From the beginning"*: Jerry Bowles, "Planning for Excellence at AMP," *Fortune,* September 20, 1993.

223 *"I sometimes felt"*: Jerry Bowles, "Quality '92, Leading the World-Class Company" (advertisement), *Fortune.*

225 *"The Best-Cost"*: Charles F. Knight, "Emerson Electric: Consistent Profits, Consistently," *Harvard Business Review,* January–February, 1992, 61.

226 *"One final, basic"*: Ibid., 70.

227 *"The pressure of the"*: Seth Lubove, "It Ain't Broke, but Fix It Anyway," *Forbes,* August 1, 1994, 58.

228 *"You almost have"*: Michael A. Verespej, "The Self-Education of Bruce Hamilton," *Industry Week,* April 1, 1991, 22.

229 *"Somebody who becomes"*: John H. Sheridan, "Careers on the Line," *Industry Week,* September 16, 1991, 29.

229 *"Until The Goal"*: Martha E. Mangelsdorf, "What Chief Executives Read," *Inc.,* September 1990, 78.

230 *"Maybe you should"*: Verespej, "The Self-Education of Bruce Hamilton," 16.

230 *"Change is the"*: Sheridan, "Careers on the Line," 30.

231 *"This is not"*: Verespej, "The Self-Education of Bruce Hamilton," 18.

232 *"The biggest obstacle"*: in correspondence with the authors.

233 *"I believe TQM"*: "TQM—A Path to the Future," *Tooling and Production,* July 1993, 5.

234 *"Perhaps the most"*: in correspondence with the authors.

10. ACHIEVE ENVIRONMENTAL EXCELLENCE

Page

235 *"Environmental protection makes"*: "Eco-92, The Earth Summit" (advertising supplement), *Washington Post,* May 26, 1992, A10.

236 *"We don't see"*: "Special Report—The Environment," 3M internal publication, July 1991, 10.

238 *"With every year"*: John H. Sheridan, "Attacking Wastes," *Industry Week,* February 17, 1992, 45.

240 *"It's only in"*: "Special Report—The Environment," 7.

248 *"Our waste minimization"*: "Cooper Recycles Wastes," Cooper Tire and Rubber Co. internal document, 1.

249 *"We have just"*: in correspondence from the company.
250 *"We are here"*: from speech at Monsanto Pledge Award ceremony, June 13, 1993.
252 *"At Dow we are committed"*: "Eco-92," A10.
252 *"We have a"*: from correspondence with the company.
253 *"Wherever you have"*: Ibid.
254 *"The question isn't"*: Emily T. Smith, "Growth vs. Environment," *Business Week,* May 11, 1992, 75.
254 *"Our company recently"*: "Eco-92," A10.
255 *"If you have"*: Sheridan, "Attacking Wastes," 45.
255 *"Environmental management is"*: John H. Sheridan, "Industry's Talent for Solutions," *Industry Week,* January 4, 1993.
256 *"could pull from"*: Ibid.

11. INCREASE SPEED AND AGILITY

Page

259 *"puts it all together"*: Paul Swamidass, "Technology on the Factory Floor —II: 1994," National Association of Manufacturers, August 1994.
261 *"We've spent seven"*: John H. Sheridan, "Agile Manufacturing," *Industry Week,* April 19, 1993, 38.
268 *"I've said it"*: "Allen-Bradley Horizons," 1992, No. 1, 3.
273 *"We are selling"*: Sheridan, "Agile Manufacturing," 38.
274 *"What the customer"*: from correspondence with the company.
274 *"We've spent seven"*: Sheridan, "Agile Manufacturing," 38.
275 *"Each morning the"*: Thomas M. Rohan, "Factories of the Future," special section, *Industry Week,* March 21, 1988, 42.
277 *"It's a great time"*: from correspondence with the company.
278 *"You've heard of"*: Michael Meyer, "Here's a 'Virtual' Model for America's Industrial Giants," *Newsweek,* August 23, 1993, 40.
279 *"What we do"*: Charles Burck, "The Real World of the Entrepreneur," *Fortune,* April 5, 1993, 80.
280 *"Your employee is"*: Burck, "The Real World," 79–80.
280 *"Suppose the company"*: Edward O. Welles, "Built on Speed," *Inc.,* October 1992, 84.
282 *"CIM has been"*: Janet Endrijonas, "Automation Revisited: CIM Keeps the Music Playing," *Managing Automation,* December 1992, 54.
283 *"CIM means never"*: Ibid., 53.
284 *"Obviously, implementing a true"*: Ibid.

12. SHAKE UP THE ORGANIZATION

Page

285 *"There will never"*: David Kirkpatrick, "The Revolution at Compaq Computer," *Fortune,* December 14, 1992, 88.
285 *"If your change"*: Noel Tichy and Stratford Sherman, *Control Your Destiny or Someone Else Will* (New York: Doubleday, 1993).

286 *"People think the"*: Tom Peters, *The Tom Peters Seminar* (New York: Vintage, 1994), 57.

287 *"The action plan"*: Mike Walsh, "The Processes and Principles of Tenneco," 1992, 6–7.

288 *"Most importantly, we had"*: Eckhard Pfeiffer, "My Turning Point," manuscript for *Audacity* magazine.

290 *"This is a personal"*: Dana Mead, "The Leadership Challenge of Becoming World Class," in Tenneco Inc. Executive Speech Series, 11–12.

292 *"In retrospect, getting out"*: "Defining Intel: 25 Years/25 Events," Intel 1993, 23.

296 *"We had to commit"*: Ibid., 24.

301 *"One of our"*: Ibid., 32.

301 *"Today, some people"*: Ibid.

302 *"Today, the customer"*: Pfeiffer, "My Turning Point."

303 *"From our start-up"*: prepared text of Benjamin M. Rosen before the House Subcommittee on Telecommunications and Finance, April 21, 1993, 5.

304 *"I met with"*: Pfeiffer, "My Turning Point."

305 *"communication was our"*: Ibid., 4–5.

307 *"keep your vision"*: Eckhard Pfeiffer, "Strategies for a Shifting Industry," remarks to the Personal Computer Outlook Conference, December 7, 1992, 7.

307 *"In the two years"*: Stephanie Loree, "How Compaq Keeps the Magic Going," *Fortune,* February 21, 1994, 90.

308 *"The only way"*: Thomas A. Stewart, "Welcome to the Revolution," *Fortune,* December 13, 1993, 96.

309 *"it was equally"*: Lutz speech, 2.

309 *"Lee Iacocca laid the"*: Jerry Flint, "Volume Be Damned," *Forbes,* April 12, 1993, 52.

310 *"We don't have"*: Ibid.

311 *"I submit that"*: Lutz speech, 3.

313 *"Design can add"*: James Bennet, "The Designers Who Saved Chrysler," *New York Times,* January 30, 1994.

314 *"The company's production"*: "Developing a World-Class Manufacturing Strategy" (New York: Business International Corp., 1992), 52.

315 *"Varian had trouble"*: John Teresko, America's Best Plants," *Industry Week,* October 19, 1992, 56.

316 *"The journey toward"*: "Developing a World-Class Manufacturing Strategy," 127.

317 *"I am now"*: Teresko, "America's Best Plants," 55.

317 *"the sheer speed"*: Ibid., 56.

317 *"We were substituting"*: "Developing a World-Class Manufacturing Strategy," 29.

318 *"The challenge for"*: Ibid., 55.

319 *"The first hundred days"*: Walsh, "The Processes and Principles of Tenneco," 6–7.

320 *"So we brought"*: "A Master Class in Radical Change," *Fortune,* December 13, 1993.

320 *"I arrived to find"*: Robert Johnson, "Tenneco Hired a CEO from Outside, and He Is Refocusing the Firm," *Wall Street Journal,* March 29, 1993.

321 *"I was scared"*: "A Master Class in Radical Change," 90.

321 *"Talk about teamwork!"*: Mike Walsh, "Better, Faster, Smarter," in Tenneco Inc. Executive Speech series, 9.

322 *"When you get"*: Ibid., 2.

322 *"In my judgment"*: "Leaders of Corporate Change," *Fortune,* December 14, 1992, 108.

322 *"You've got to"*: "A Master Class in Radical Change," 90.

323 *"We simply have to"*: Walsh, "The Processes and Principles of Tenneco," 13.

323 *"focus the entire"*: Mike Walsh, "Quality Management at Tenneco," internal document, January 1993, 2.

323 *"Perhaps the most"*: Ibid.

323 *"We should talk"*: Walsh, "The Processes and Principles of Tenneco," 10–11.

323 *"An essential prerequisite"*: Mead, "The Leadership Challenge," 2.

325 *"The fact is"*: Walsh, "Quality Management at Tenneco," 1.

325 *"We're halfway home"*: "A Master Class in Radical Change," 90.

INDEX

accidents, industrial, 62
Action Centers, 230
action required (AR), 300
Advanced Cleaning Systems, 253
Advanced Consumer Technology, 168
Advanced Technology Group (ATG), 168
Advil, 177
aerospace industry, 30, 31
AFL-CIO, 148
Agan, Robert, 43, 232
Ahrens, Larry, 277
Air Products and Chemicals, 194–98
  Asian market of, 180, 196, 197
  European market of, 179, 195, 197
  global approach of, 41, 179–80, 181, 194–98
  Latin American market of, 196–97
Aleksick, Linda, 211, 216
Allaire, Paul, 128, 149, 151
Allen, Paul, 166
Allen-Bradley, 262–72
  "boot camps" at, 260, 266–67
  CIM operations and, 259
  electronics manufacturing strategy facility of, 45–46, 260, 262–72
  Industrial Control Group of, 262, 263
  teamwork at, 263–64, 269–71
  technological systems at, 259, 260, 262–72
  training at, 265–68, 272
  World Contractor Facility of, 266, 270
All Product Excellence (APEX), 78

American Home Products, 177
American Motors, 311
AMF, 147
AMP, 220–25
  Integrated Circuit Connector Products division of, 221
  morale at, 223
  Plan for Excellence of, 208, 221
  product quality of, 16, 43, 208, 220–225
Anderson, Rick, 111
Apple Computer, 139, 307, 308
apprenticeships, 80–81, 93–94, 97, 98, 100–101
Aqueous Clean-In-Place (ACIP), 44, 236, 250–51
Armada computer server, 306
assembly lines, 111, 276
"Assignment, The," 216
ATMs, 174
AT&T, 206, 224, 264
ATZ Products, 174
automatic call distribution system, 135, 138
automation, 82, 174, 264, 268, 282, 296
Automation Technologies, 268
automobile industry, 20, 27, 28–29, 77, 79, 201
  in Japan, 28, 98, 309
"Avenues of Growth," 99–100, 102
Axiss, 199

"back-to-basics" movement, 14, 17
Badger Meter, 259–60
Baker, Dexter, 41, 194, 196

Malcolm Baldrige National Quality
    Award, 152, 206, 207, 208, 214,
    221, 257, 267, 287, 288, 317
Baldwin, David, 52
Bank of America, 279–80
banking, 188, 279–80
Barrett, Craig, 289, 292, 293, 294, 295–
    296, 297
Barten, Patty, 210
Bates, Michael, 93, 94, 95, 97
Beals, Vaughn, 146
benchmarking, 150–51, 213, 220,
    292
Berlin, Lee, 178
Carl Bertelsmann Prize, 68
Best-Cost Producer Strategy, 43, 225
"Best Small Companies to Work For,
    The," 54–55
Bethlehem Steel, 123
bicycles, 42, 180, 181, 191–93
Blaise, Ann, 103, 110, 113–14
blueprints, 59, 86
Boeing, 60, 179
Boklund, Tom, 104–5, 117
Bolles, Ted, 245–46
Bonfoey, Bill, 115
bonuses, 37, 104–14, 122, 124, 214,
    281, 300
Boston Consulting Group, 154–55
Bowling, Adam, 95, 96
Bringer, Robert, 239–44, 246, 247
Buetow, Richard, 209, 211–12, 214,
    215, 218–19
"Built on Speed," 279
Burgum, Doug, 127–28, 132, 133–35
Burzynski, Bill, 91–92
business:
    renaissance of, 18, 20, 21, 23, 25, 29,
        51
    small, 21, 42, 54–55
    values of, 17–18
    see also corporations
Business America, 257
Business Roundtable, 219
Buyers Laboratory, 152
Buzzelli, David, 253, 254

Caldwell, Philip, 98–99
Cameron, Russell, 273
Campbell, Kerm, 68, 69
Canapik, Bob, 110, 113
Canion, Rod, 303
Cannondale, 191–94
    European market of, 42
    foreign sales of, 181

    global approach of, 178, 179, 191–94
    Japanese market of, 180, 181, 192–93
Canon, 128
Cantor, David, 26–27
capital expenditures, 222, 226, 298–99,
    321
Carpenter, John, 296
Carroll, Chuck, 160, 161, 162
"cart machine," 174
Cassell-Fix, Marti, 173–74
Castaing, François, 311–12
Caterpillar, 87, 179
Cause-and-Effect Diagram with the
    Addition of Cards (CEDAC), 230
CD players, 200
CD-ROM, 168
Challenge '95 program, 243, 247
Chandler, Rick, 212–13, 216–17
Chaparral Steel, training programs of,
    28, 36, 82, 83, 89–91
chemical industry, 31
Chevron, 236
chief executive officers (CEOs):
    customer satisfaction and, 130, 143–
        144, 145
    employee relations with, 35, 67, 75–
        77
    global strategy of, 165–69, 190, 202
    product innovation and, 161, 162,
        164
    training and, 36, 84, 85
China, People's Republic of, 168, 179,
    180, 182, 189, 196
chlorofluorocarbons, 271
Chrysler, 73, 79, 308–14
    comebacks of, 13–14, 28–29, 287,
        289, 308–14
    cost reduction by, 309, 310–11, 313–
        314
    customer service of, 310
    employee empowerment at, 13–14,
        35, 287–88, 308, 311, 312
    infrastructure of, 309–13
    Japanese competition of, 309, 314
    market share of, 310, 314
    product line of, 311, 312–14
    profits of, 313–14
    stock of, 289, 313
    teamwork in, 311–12, 314
    unions and, 312
Churchill, David, 91–92
Circuit Board Design Systems (CBDS),
    283
circuit boards, 265, 268, 271, 283
Cizik, Bob, 42

Clapper, Jim, 241, 242, 244
Clean Air Act Amendments (1990), 241
clothes dryers, 227
Coag, 245
Commercial News USA, 180, 201
community colleges, 36
Compaq Computer, 302–8
  alliances formed by, 306–7
  communication in, 305–6
  customer services of, 302, 303, 306, 308
  goals of, 286, 290
  Independent Business Unit of, 305
  layoffs at, 303
  manufacturing process of, 306–8
  market share of, 303, 304, 307
  product development at, 288
  product line of, 303, 304–8
  sales of, 286
  turnaround of, 285, 288, 289, 302–8
competence, 66
competition:
  benchmarking and, 150–51, 213, 220, 292
  downsizing and, 25
  employee, 111, 114
  global, 15, 18, 19, 20, 28–29, 30, 31–32, 47, 178–202
  Japanese, 19, 28, 29, 128, 145, 146, 147–48, 149, 150, 178, 232, 291–292, 309, 314
  quality and, 184, 223–24, 225, 232
  surpassing of, 15, 47
  technology and, 275–76, 291–92, 314
Competitors' War Fair, 159
Component of the Year (C.O.T.Y.) Award, 200
computer-aided design (CAD), 45, 46, 258–59, 261, 273–75, 283
Computer-Assisted Three-Dimensional Interactive Applications (CATIA), 283
computer-integrated manufacturing (CIM), 45, 46, 259, 260, 262–72, 282–84, 314
ComputerLand, 279–80
computer numerically controlled (CNC) tools, 232, 274
computers:
  accounting software for, 133–38
  architecture of, 297
  communications packages for, 135–136, 138
  distributors of, 131–40, 278–82
  industry for, 29, 30, 31, 41, 46, 139–140, 150–51, 168, 180
  memory upgrades for, 278, 279–80, 281
  microprocessors for, 29, 30, 288, 291, 293, 294, 296, 298, 299, 301
  office, 41, 141, 182, 184–89, 283, 306, 307, 308
  open systems for, 183–86, 189
  personal (PCs), 140, 141, 286–87, 294, 299, 300–308
  software for, 133–38, 140, 167–69, 207
  workstations for, 41, 182, 184–89, 283, 306, 307, 308
Congressional Research Service, 26–27
Consumer Electronics Show (1988), 199
contact lenses, 176
Contractor Performance Certification Program, 148
"convenantal" relationships, 67, 68
Cooper Tire & Rubber, 237, 238, 248–250
Corning, 35, 55, 233
corporations:
  bureaucracy in, 19, 171, 285–86
  core values of, 143–44, 175
  culture of, 72, 87, 98–99, 120, 143–144, 149, 155, 158–63, 171, 175, 240, 311
  decentralization in, 175, 177
  global approach for, 178–202
  goals of, 72–73, 81–82, 105, 162, 180, 182–83, 286–87, 290
  organization of, *see* organization, corporate
  partnerships for, 183, 186–89, 191, 227–28
  "perfect," 208, 209–10, 219
  restructuring of, 226, 287
  survival of, 75, 105, 215, 291
  turnaround of, 13–14, 28–29, 39, 101–2, 285–325
  "virtual," 261, 278–82
  see also individual corporations
corrosion control, 201
Countryman, J. R., 71
Cox, Jeff, 229, 231
creative freedom, 156–57
Creative Writer, 168
CR Industries, 91–92
  awards received by, 92
  training programs of, 17, 36, 82, 91–92

cryogenic products, 195, 198
Customer One program, 288, 313
customers, 127–53
    complaints by, 140–41, 152
    employee empowerment and, 77–79
    employees focused on, 39, 43, 127–
        128, 129, 153, 316
    expectations of, 38–39, 43, 47, 127–
        153
    forced registration of, 134–35, 138
    guaranteed response time for, 135,
        138
    loyalty of, 148, 206
    personalized needs of, 130, 139–40,
        146, 149, 232–34
    quality and, 206, 211, 213, 216–18,
        221, 222, 224, 225, 232–34
    sales vs. service and, 140, 150, 152
    satisfaction of, 22, 33, 38–42, 77–79,
        128, 129, 130, 138–45, 146, 149–
        153, 233, 264, 286
    service charges for, 135, 138, 142
    services for, 38, 39, 127–28, 129,
        131–38, 140, 142, 145–49, 150,
        152, 291, 294, 299, 302, 303, 306,
        308, 310, 316, 317
    telephone assistance for, 134–38
    tracking and measuring systems on,
        39, 129–30, 131–32, 134–36, 138,
        139

Daly, Kevin, 173
Dataquest, 152, 291
Davis, Don, 268
Deavenport, Earnie, 255, 256
John Deere, 92
deindustrialization, 25
Dell, Michael, 127, 130, 139, 140, 141
Dell Computer, 138–42, 307
    customer relations of, 39, 130, 138–
        142
    "Dell Vision" of, 140
    "Hour of Horror" at, 140–41
Demers, Roger, 132, 133, 135, 137
Deming Prize, 150
Dempsey, Tim, 138
DePree, D. J., 66, 67
DePree, Max, 65, 66, 67
De Schutter, Richard U., 250
DeSimone, L. D., 45, 242
Dham, Vinod, 290, 293, 295, 297, 298,
    299
Digital Equipment, 268
digital signal processing system, 174
direct sales, 27, 141, 180, 192, 194

dividends, 144, 177, 321
Dodge Intrepid, 313
Dodge Neon, 313, 314
Dodge Ram, 314
Dodge Stealth, 313
Dodge Viper, 312, 313
Doherty, John, 124
Dolezal, Tom, 94
dollar, value of, 31–32
DOS applications, 137, 140, 169
Dow Chemical, 235, 236, 237, 238,
    252–55
downsizing, 20, 25–26
Drucker, Peter, 24, 46
Dugan, Allan, 152
Duignan, Henry, 273, 274
Dwyer, Tim, 187, 188, 189
dynamic random access memory
    (DRAM), 286, 288, 292–93, 295
Dynamics system, 135–36

Eastman Chemical, 237, 255–57
Eastman Kodak, 256
Eaton, Robert, 28, 47, 309, 310, 312
Education, Development and Training
    Program (EDTP), 99–102
Education and Training Assistance Plan
    (ETAP), 99–100
Eggert, Glenn, 262–63
Ehrbar, Al, 32
electronic connector devices, 220,
    223–24
electronics, solid-state, 263, 265, 271
E-mail, 140, 168, 183
"embedded learning," 216
Emerson Electric, 43, 209, 225–28
employee involvement (EI) plans, 57,
    101
employees, 51–124
    absenteeism of, 62, 68, 84, 88, 113
    as "associates," 70
    benefits of, 87–89, 106, 109–11
    blue-collar, 288
    "boot camps" for, 260, 266–67
    CEOs and, 35, 67, 75–77
    communication with, 53–54, 305–6
    competition among, 111, 114
    creativity of, 16, 22, 25, 33, 34–37, 40
    as customer-focused, 39, 43, 127–28,
        129, 153, 316
    decision-making by, 59, 64, 69, 96,
        234, 277, 300, 323
    educational background of, 210–11
    empowerment of, 13–14, 16, 34–35,
        47, 51–79, 177, 207, 220, 221–22,

223, 263–64, 269–71, 287–88, 291,
    300, 308, 311, 312, 314
environmental issues and, 236–37,
    238, 244–45, 248, 249
as "environmental managers," 236–
    237, 248
financial incentives for, 37, 103, 107,
    108, 110, 118–19, 122–23
gainsharing by, 37, 104, 114–16,
    122–24, 312
hiring of, 61
inspections by, 59–60
layoffs of, 56, 71, 74, 85, 98, 111, 280,
    303
management relations with, 19, 34,
    35, 54, 57, 58, 64, 67, 68, 91, 108,
    111–12, 114, 115, 117
merit ratings for, 109, 111
morale of, 56–57, 72, 74, 84–85, 88,
    115, 212–13, 223
older, 112–13, 119, 266, 270
as owners, 37, 103–5, 117–19, 121
performance of, 34–35, 37, 56, 62,
    96, 103–24, 214, 226–27
personal growth of, 22, 36, 83, 100
quality control and, 52–53, 55, 56,
    59, 66, 87, 90, 96, 105–6, 112–13,
    116, 153, 207, 208, 213–18, 229–
    230
stock owned by, 37, 85, 87, 104–5,
    106, 116, 119–21, 123
tardiness of, 84
training by, 17, 36, 92
turnover of, 68, 88, 113
white-collar, 81, 288
workplace quality and, 59, 62–63
employee stock ownership plans
    (ESOP), 37, 85, 87, 104–5, 106,
    116, 119–21, 123
energy consumption, 73–74, 170
Engineering Education Program, 222
engineers, 59, 222, 234, 268, 269, 298
Entertainers Team, 218
entrepreneurship, 17, 28, 81, 110, 171,
    188
environmental issues, 44–45, 235–57
    cleaning processes and, 44, 236,
        250–51
    economic impact of, 235–36
    efficiency and, 240
    employee involvement in, 236–37,
        238, 244–45, 248, 249
    goals and, 240–44, 247, 248, 253
    government regulation and, 239,
        240, 241, 253, 254

job appraisals and, 237, 255
    management and, 246
    product development and, 163, 164
    programs for, 44, 236–48, 252–55
    quality and, 240, 246, 257
    research on, 237, 243, 245–46, 248,
        256, 257
    sustainable growth and, 246–47, 254
    technology and, 250–51, 271
    see also pollution
Environmental Protection Agency, 239,
    254
equity, 66, 171, 321
erasable, programmable read-only
    memory (EPROM), 292, 295
Erdle, Dennis, 133
Erickson, Shelly, 83–84, 97
Error-Free Team, 218
Ethicon, 177
European Common Market, 179, 195
Evans, Dale, 82
EVCO Plastics, 82
Everett, Nick, 262, 263
Excellence in Quality Improvement
    competition, 221–22
"Excellent Company Study, The," 133
Executive Development Center, 101
Express Manufacturing, 280

factories:
    focused, 95, 96, 276
    headquarters vs., 211–13
    housekeeping in, 59, 61, 254
    integrated, 262, 269
Fashner, Jeff, 57
Featherstone, Harry, 36, 82–88
Ferox, 195
fiber-optics communications, 30
Field, John, 265, 266–67, 268, 271–72
film, 254–55, 256
Fine Artist, 168
Fisher, George, 219
Foley, Dennis, 69
Food and Drug Administration (FDA),
    251
Ford Motor Company, 98–102, 224
    awards given by, 52, 73, 79, 92
    layoffs at, 98
    sales of, 28, 98
    Sharonville, Ohio plant of, 82, 83,
        101, 102
    training programs of, 78, 82, 83, 98–
        102
    unions at, 98, 99, 100–101, 102
Ford Taurus, 28

Ford-UAW National Joint
  Apprenticeship Committee, 100–101
Fortune, 30, 157, 164, 307, 325
Fortune 500, 42, 65, 141, 172
Forward, Gordon, 82, 89
486 chip, 288, 290, 297, 298
Franks, Steve, 211
Frost, Carl, 66
Frost, Robert, 23
Fujitsu, 184, 185
Fuji Xerox, 150
"future-tecture" team, 151

gainsharing plans, 37, 104, 114–16,
  122–24, 312
Gale, Tom, 313
Galvin, Bob, 36, 207, 213–14, 215
Garrity, Norm, 35, 55
gas, industrial, 196–97
Gates, Bill, 40, 165–69
Gault, Stanley, 39–40, 70, 72–73, 74,
  158, 162, 165
Gavoor, Mark, 77
General Electric (GE), 19, 224, 285–286
General Motors (GM), 56, 73, 79, 92
George, Tommy, 218
Germain, Jack, 213
Germany, 28, 30, 31, 81, 178
Goal, The (Goldratt and Cox), 229, 231
Goldratt, Eliyahu, 229, 231
Goldsmith, James, 70
Goodyear Tire & Rubber, 70–74
  Gadsden, Ala., plant of, 70, 71–74
  Lawton, Okla., plant of, 70–71, 72,
    73
  morale at, 72, 74
  training programs of, 71
  unions at, 54, 71, 72, 73, 74
"gotta units," 129
Grandaw, Diana, 265–66
Great Plains Software, 131–38
  customer relations of, 38, 39, 127–
    128, 129, 131–38
  factory outlet mall (FOM) of, 133
  inside system of, 132–33, 136–37,
    138
  Letter Lane of, 137
  million statement of, 132, 138
  outside system of, 134–36, 138
  teamwork at, 132, 136–37
  tracking and measurement system
    of, 129–30, 131–32, 134–36, 138
Great Plains University, 136

Gross Domestic Product (GDP), 26, 27
Grove, Andrew, 17, 47, 286, 289, 291,
  292, 296, 300, 301

Haines, Earl, 161
Hamilton, Alexander, 24
Hamilton, Bruce, 228, 229, 230, 231
Hammel, Sandi, 269
Hansen, Gary, 102
Hanson, Larry, 266, 267, 269, 270–71
Hardinge Brothers, 43, 208, 232–34
Harley-Davidson, 145–49
  customer relations of, 39, 128, 145–
    149
  Japanese competition of, 128, 145,
    146, 147–48
  management of, 145, 146, 147
  market share of, 145, 147–48
  quality control at, 130–31, 145, 146–
    147
  turnaround of, 128, 145, 146–48
Hart, Peter, 20
Harvard Business Review, 226
Hastings, Don, 107, 109, 111, 112
Hatsopoulos, George, 41, 170–71
Hawley, Darrin, 132, 136, 137
health insurance, 111
Hewlett-Packard, 268
Honda, 28, 147–48
Honda Accord, 28
Hong Kong, 182, 187, 189–90
"Hottest Entrepreneurs in America,
  The," 81
Houseman, John, 107
Hudson, William J., 220, 221–23
"human" capital, 36
Hunt, Michele, 65

Iacocca, Lee, 14, 47, 308–10, 312
IBM, 139, 141, 169, 224, 279, 283, 307,
  308
Ibuka, Masaru, 157
Idea Club, 67–68
improvement:
  continuous, 22, 23, 33, 39, 42–47,
    130–31, 205–34, 247
  self-, 22, 36, 83, 100
Inc., 54, 81, 279, 281
Incentive Management system, 104,
  107, 108, 112
industrial revolution, 18
industry:
  comeback of, 13–16, 24, 27–29
  downsizing of, 20, 25–26
  icons of, 56, 146

media coverage of, 25
see also manufacturing; *specific
    industries*
Industry Week, 62, 157, 262, 307
inflation, 162
Information Exchange, 169
Information Highway, 166, 167, 168,
    301
INFRA Group, 196–97
innovation:
    culture for, 39–41, 158–63
    fundamental values vs., 17
    leadership and, 23, 47, 285–325
In Search of Excellence, 133
Integrated Quality Systems, 177
Intel, 29, 140, 290–302
    benchmarking by, 292
    customer services of, 291, 294, 299,
        302
    design projects at, 297–98
    employee empowerment at, 291, 300
    fabs (fabrication facilities) of, 290,
        295, 299
    Japanese competition of, 291–92
    manufacturing process of, 293–96,
        302
    market share of, 291–92, 300–301
    paranoid attitude at, 290–91
    product development at, 288, 289,
        292–99
    sales of, 286, 291–92
    training programs of, 291
    turnaround of, 286, 290–302
    values of, 293–94, 302
interest rates, 31
inventory:
    just-in-time, 278, 280
    management of, 315
    reduction of, 60, 271
investment:
    foreign, 41, 181, 186, 194, 197–98
    in quality, 206, 207
    return on (ROI), 121, 123, 228
    in training, 36, 85, 94, 96
investment capital, 46, 123, 176, 191–
    192, 228
Ishikawa, Kaoru, 205
ISO 9000 series, 226
ISO 9001 series, 87
Itoh, C., 188
Iverson, Ken, 122

Jacobson, Allen, 241
Japan:
    automobile industry in, 28, 98, 309
    competition from, 19, 28, 29, 128,
        145, 146, 147–48, 149, 150, 178,
        232, 291–92, 309, 314
    computer industry in, 41, 168, 180
    foreign exports of, 31
    markets in, 41, 42, 180, 181, 182, 184,
        185, 187–89, 192–93, 196, 199,
        200
    productivity in, 30
    quality control in, 205, 214, 221, 232
    semiconductor industry in, 29
    steel industry in, 28
Japanese Jazz Lover's Award, 200
Jeep Grand Cherokee, 312, 314
Jiang Zemin, 168
job appraisals, 237, 255
job creation, 25–26, 27
Jobs, Steve, 127
Johnson Controls, 38
Johnson & Johnson, 174–77
    decentralization in, 175, 177
    product development at, 156, 157,
        174–77
    stock of, 177
    subsidiaries of, 176, 177
Johnson & Johnson Medical, 177
Johnsonville Foods, 75–77
    employee empowerment at, 16, 35,
        75–77
just-in-time (JIT) production, 46, 97,
    148, 228, 258, 259, 260, 278, 318

kaizen, 205
kanban, 228
K-cars, 313
Keep America Beautiful Recycling
    Award, 257
Keyes, James, 38
Kingston Technology, 46, 259, 260, 261,
    278–82
Kleckner, K. B., 73
Knight, Charles, 209, 225, 226, 227
Kolias, Gus, 306
Koppy, Mike, 97
Korea, 182, 196

Labor Department, U.S., 108
landfills, 248, 249, 254, 256
Lange, John, 160, 162
Larsen, Ralph, 156, 174, 175
latex, 254
lawyers, patent, 207
leadership:
    convictions and, 86, 188
    goals for, 72–73, 286–87

leadership: (cont.)
    innovation and, 23, 47, 285–325
    management and, 65, 75–76
    quality and, 207, 230
    roving, 67
    vision for, 16, 18–19
Leadership Is an Art (DePree), 65
Leadership Through Quality strategy, 150
Levy, Richard, 288, 317
LH cars, 313, 314
Lichtinger, Dave, 53, 56–63
Licking River Films Center, 254–55
Life/Education Planning Program, 100
Lincoln, James F., 107, 108
Lincoln, John C., 107
"Lincoln buck," 108
Lincoln Electric, 106–14
    advisory board of, 111–12, 113
    board of directors of, 107, 109
    bonus system at, 37, 104–14
    lack of benefits at, 106, 109, 110–11
    piecework system at, 104, 106, 107, 108–14
    productivity at, 109–10, 113, 114
Lindsly, Jim, 238, 252, 253, 255
Little Roughnecks, 163
Lord Corp., 55–64
    awards given to, 62
    employee empowerment at, 53, 54, 55–64
    employee-management relations in, 19, 35, 54, 57, 58, 64
    morale at, 56–57, 84
    teamwork at, 60–62, 63, 64
lot size, 60
lunch kits, litterless, 164
Lutz, Bob, 309, 310, 311, 312

McCabe, Pat, 163
McCaw, 168
McCready, David, 201, 202
McCullough, Gerry, 249–50
McGhee, Beverly, 211
machine tools, 232–34
machinists, 93, 94, 97
McInnes, Harold, 43, 221
Macintosh computers, 135, 137
McKinsey, 31, 133
McKnight, William, 240
McNealy, Scott, 180, 182, 184–88, 190
management:
    apprenticeships and, 36, 97
    customer satisfaction and, 143, 151
    employee empowerment and, 51–52

    employee relations with, 19, 34, 35, 54, 57, 58, 64, 67, 68, 91, 108, 111–112, 114, 115, 117
    environmental issues and, 246
    family-style, 261, 280
    hierarchical, 287–88
    leadership and, 65, 75–76
    micro-, 212
    "open book," 54
    over-, 59, 60, 212
    participative, 64, 66, 68
    quality and, 211–13, 214, 220, 223, 224, 227, 233
    technology and, 287–88, 300, 316
Mandel, Mort, 38, 129, 130, 142–44
manufacturing:
    comeback of, 15–16, 19–20, 24–32
    continuous flow, 260, 275–78
    "death" of, 19, 26, 30, 32, 84, 106
    economic impact of, 26–27
    flexible, 259–60, 273–75, 276, 277, 278, 296
    foreign exports and, 24–25, 26, 31–32
    "magic multiplier" of, 26–27
    processes of, 306–8
    setup time in, 59, 62, 228, 231
    unit-labor costs in, 32
    see also production
manufacturing resource planning (MRP), 224, 232, 282, 283
Manufacturing Skills Inventory System, 222
markets:
    Asian, 180, 196, 197
    capitalization of, 123
    creation of, 22, 33, 39–41, 154–77
    European, 42, 179, 195, 197
    global, 16, 38, 41–42, 81, 179–80, 181, 194–98, 223, 235, 322, 323, 324, 325
    Japanese, 41, 42, 180, 181, 182, 184, 185, 187–89, 192–93, 196, 199, 200
    Latin America, 196–97
    mass, 39
    opening of, 219
    research on, 134–35
    share of, 28, 47, 128, 145, 147–48, 149, 152, 154, 190, 285, 291–92, 300–301, 303, 304, 307, 310, 314
Mark of Excellence Award, 73, 79, 92
Marley, James, 221, 223
Marmon Group, 33
Marohn, Bill, 116

Martinez, Jamie, 211
Martynuik, Basyl, 210–11
Mattison, Gary, 160
"Maximize Human Resource
    Capabilities," 73
Mead, Dana, 47, 289–90, 321, 324
"mechanical integration," 264
medical instruments, 30
Mercorella, Phil, 64
Merisel, 140
merit ratings, 109, 111
meter housings, 276
Mexico, 196–97
microprocessors, 29, 30, 288, 291, 293,
    294, 296, 298, 299, 301
Microsoft, 165–70, 306
    Consumer Software Division of, 168
    as high-tech company, 56, 166–69
    insecurity at, 166–67
    product development at, 40, 156,
        157, 165–70
    stock of, 166
Microsoft Office, 167–68
Microsoft Research, 168
Microsoft at Work, 167
Herman Miller Inc. (HMI), 64–69
    awards given to, 68
    employee empowerment at, 54, 64–
        69
    employee-management relations at,
        67, 68
    Ethospace line of, 65, 68
    teamwork at, 67, 68–69
    vision statement of, 65
Milwaukee School of Engineering, 260,
    267, 268
mini-MBAs, 86
minimills, 27, 28, 82, 89, 90, 117, 122,
    123
Mississippi State University, 284
Mitsubishi, 139
Mobile Telecommunication
    Technologies, 168
Montgomery, Joseph, 178, 191–92, 193
Montgomery, Scott, 191, 192, 193
Moore, Gordon, 292
Morgan, Stanley, 29
Moses, Donald Wadia, 198, 199
Motorola, 35, 36, 207–20, 264
    benchmarking in, 213, 220
    cellular infrastructure manufacturing
        facility of, 210, 212, 215
    Communications Segment of, 219
    factory vs. headquarters of, 211–13
    General Systems Sector of, 219

Government and Systems
    Technology Group of, 219
Manufacturing Education Group of,
    216
morale at, 212–13
"perfect company" goal of, 208,
    209–10, 219
quality control at, 42–43, 207–20
sales of, 210, 219
Semiconductor Products Sector of,
    218, 219
teamwork at, 207, 208, 211, 216–18,
    220
training programs of, 207, 210–11,
    220
turnaround of, 213–15
Motorola Philippines Inc. (MPI), 218
Motorola University, 215
Murgatroyd, Larry, 88

Nakanishi, 199
Napolitano, Pat, 119
National Association of Suggestion
    Systems, 68
NEC, 29
Nintendo, 154, 156–57
Nippondenso, 264
Nippon Steel, 196
Nippon Telegraph and Telephone, 168
NML, 218
Nokia Corp., 218
notebooks, computer, 140, 141
Notes, 169
"not invented here" (NIH) attitude, 161
Novell, 306
nuclear magnetic resonance
    instruments (NMRI), 318, 319
Nucor, 122–24
    gainsharing plan at, 104, 122–24
    productivity at, 37, 103
    teamwork at, 122–24

Object Linking and Embedding (OLE),
    168
Odetics, 40, 157, 173–74
Odex 1 robot, 174
Ohno, Taiichi, 205
Oregon Steel Mills, 117–19
    employee ownership of, 37, 103–5,
        117–19
    productivity at, 37, 117, 118
    stock of, 118
organization, corporate:
    disruption of, 17, 19, 22, 23, 33–34,
        46–47, 258, 285–325

organization, corporate: (*cont.*)
  horizontal, 128, 151, 152
  models of, 45
O'Rourke, Tracy, 47, 286, 287, 288,
  314–19
Osten, Brenda, 132

pagers, 218
Partners in CIM Award, 268
partnerships, joint, 183, 186–89, 191,
  227–28
PCs Limited, 139
Peavey, Hartley, 284
Peavey, Melia, 284
Peavey Electronics, 259, 260, 282–84
Pennington, Hillary, 81
pensions, 113
Pentium chip, 288, 289, 290, 294, 297,
  298
Perry, Russ, 318
Personal Development Assistance
  (PDA), 100
Peters, Tom, 33, 53, 129
Tom Peters Group, 33
Pfeiffer, Eckhard, 47, 286–87, 302–8
pharmaceutical industry, 30, 31, 44,
  250–51
Phillips, Debbie, 19, 55, 57, 61, 63
phones, cellular, 168, 218
photocopiers, 149–52
phototonics, 246
piecework, 104, 106, 107, 108–14
Pilliod, Charles, Jr., 70–71
Pittman, Harry, 98
Plastic Recycling Research Center, 256
Poland, 195
pollution:
  air, 241–43, 245, 247
  control equipment for, 241
  corporate, 235–57
  holistic prevention of, 246
polyester plastic (PET), 255
Popoff, Frank, 235, 252, 254
Porcellato, Larry, 162
postindustrial society, 25
J. D. Power, 28, 141
Premier Industrial, 142–45
  core values of, 143–44
  customer relations of, 38, 39, 128,
    129, 130, 142–45
  stock of, 144
Presario computer, 307
Price-Waterhouse, 80
PrimeComputer, 187
Pritzker, Robert, 33

production:
  agility and speed of, 45–46, 47, 232–
    234, 258–84, 287, 318
  capacity for, 53, 264, 277, 319
  cycle time for, 45, 62, 148, 212, 214,
    315
  factors of, 264–65
  in Japan, 30
  just-in-time (JIT), 46, 97, 148, 228,
    258, 259, 260, 278, 318
  lead time in, 276
  lean, 312
  over-, 229
  technology for, 30–31, 45–46, 211
  total seamless flow in, 262
  volume of, 224
productivity:
  economic impact of, 27, 32
  employee empowerment and, 59,
    60, 62, 73, 76, 79
  growth of, 19, 24, 30, 31–32
  performance and, 109–10, 113, 114,
    116
  technology and, 258
  training and, 35–36, 82–83, 102
products:
  breakthrough, 156
  cost of, 13–14, 43, 47, 68, 71, 112,
    152, 209, 225–26, 287, 304, 309
  customized, 45, 157, 273–75, 277,
    279–80
  damage to, 52–53
  defects in, 87, 96, 184, 207, 209, 210,
    211, 213–14, 218–19, 227, 228
  design of, 219, 264–65, 271, 283,
    297–98
  details of, 39, 130, 160, 165
  development of, 39–40, 41, 44, 45,
    155–77, 234, 273–75, 286, 288,
    289, 292–99, 312–14
  "gray," 163
  ideas for, 155, 157, 158, 161–62, 165
  improvement of, 52, 156
  intermediate, 27
  introduction of, 271, 281, 294
  life cycle of, 243, 264, 283
  lines of, 303, 304–8, 311, 312–14
  multiple distributors of, 183, 186–89,
    199, 200, 201–2
  new, 39–41, 47, 154–77, 184, 227,
    264, 271, 287, 288, 307, 308, 309
  price of, 96, 219, 220
  reinvention of, 155, 158, 159–60, 165
  rejects of, 84, 218, 271
  second-sourcing of, 296

testing of, 218
trends for, 159, 162–63, 165
value-added, 186, 276
virtual, 46, 259, 260–61, 273–75
profits:
employee ownership and, 121
global competition and, 182, 193
product development and, 165,
169
quality and, 206, 225, 227
technology and, 298, 309, 313–14
ProShare, 300
P7 chip, 297
P6 chip, 289, 297
Putnam, Malcolm, 117

QE Award, 79
Q1 Award, 52, 79, 92, 102
Quad/Graphics, 286
Quadracci, Harry, 286
quality, 205–34
benchmarking and, 150–51, 213,
220, 292
competition and, 184, 223–24, 225,
232
cost and, 209, 225–26
customers and, 206, 211, 213, 216–
218, 221, 222, 224, 225, 232–34
efficiency and, 205
employee concern for, 52–53, 55,
56, 59, 66, 87, 90, 96, 105–6, 112–
113, 116, 153, 207, 208, 213–18,
229–30
employee empowerment and, 220,
221–22, 223
environmental issues and, 240, 246,
257
goals for, 15, 16, 20, 42–43, 44, 76,
105–6, 116, 150, 213–15, 220, 232,
320, 323
ideas for, 230–31
investment in, 206, 207
leadership and, 207, 230
management and, 211–13, 214, 220,
223, 224, 227, 233
matrix for, 223
media coverage of, 206
prices and, 220
profits and, 206, 225, 227
sales and, 210, 219, 223, 227–28
standards for, 42–43, 87, 96, 130–31,
145, 146–47, 152, 205–20, 221,
227, 232, 257, 267, 287, 288, 317
success and, 218–20, 223–24
suppliers and, 206–7, 214, 215, 221

teamwork and, 207, 208, 211, 216–
218, 220
technology and, 211, 226, 232–34,
258, 275–76, 314
total, 30, 42–43, 47, 92, 205–34, 246,
258
training and, 207, 210–11, 214, 215–
216, 220, 222, 229–30, 233

radiology equipment, 317–18
Raduchel, Bill, 178, 183, 185
raw materials, 27
recorders, time-lapse, 174
Recycle America, 256–57
recycling programs, 249, 256–57
Reflexite, 37, 104, 105, 119–21
Remmele, Fred, 81
Remmele Engineering, 93–98
teamwork at, 95, 102
training programs of, 81, 82, 83–84,
93–98
remote-I/O units, 271
research and development (R&D):
customer satisfaction and, 146
on environmental issues, 237, 243,
245–46, 248, 256, 257
investment in, 176
market, 134–35
sales and, 121
for technology, 31, 44, 171, 298, 302,
305
respirator masks, 244
Responsible Care Program, 247
retirement, 119
return on assets (ROA), 150
rework, 87, 96
RISC workstations, 182
robotics, 174, 282, 296
Rockwell International, 264
Rodgers, Mike, 100
Roebuck, Joe, 183, 187, 189–90
Rogers, Mike, 57–59
Rooney, Pat, 248
Rose, Jack, 85–88
Rosen, Benjamin, 285, 303, 304
Ross Controls, 273–75
technological advances at, 259, 260–
261, 273–75
training at, 260–61
virtual products by, 46, 259, 260–61,
273–75
Rowland, Hugh, 119, 120
Rubbermaid, 158–65
Home Products Division of, 160,
162, 163

Rubbermaid (*cont.*)
  innovative attitude of, 158–63
  product development at, 39–40,
    155–56, 157, 158–65
  Specialty Products Division of, 160,
    161, 163
  teamwork at, 158, 159, 162, 163–64
  trends spotted by, 159, 162–63, 165
Ruby team, 305
Russell, Chet, 37, 103, 118
Rust Belt, 19, 20, 84, 106, 262
Rust Evader, 41, 179, 180–81, 201–2

sabbaticals, industrial, 90
sales:
  commissions for, 280
  direct, 27, 141, 180, 192, 194
  product development and, 162, 286
  quality and, 210, 219, 223, 227–28
  research and, 121
  service vs., 140, 150, 152
Saul, Bill, 94, 97
Save Money and Reduce Toxics
    (SMART), 236
Scanlon Plan, 66
Schmitt, Wolf, 159, 160, 161, 162–63,
    164, 165
scrap:
  cost of, 62
  reduction of, 96, 271
Searle, 44, 236, 250–51
Sears, 227
semiconductor industry, 20, 27, 29,
    290, 291–92, 301
Senate Education Committee, 88
Seremban, 218
servers, computer, 141
service sector, 16, 20, 26, 27
setups, 59, 62, 228, 231
Shell, Andrew, 245
Shilter, Ray, 277
Shingo Award, 206, 231
Shut-up Team, 218
sick days, 88, 110–11
sign language, 88
Singapore, 189
Sirko, Joe, 105, 112–13
Six-Sigma status, 87, 96, 207, 209, 210,
    213–14, 218, 227
"Six Sigma Mechanical Design
    Tolerancing," 213
Slutzky, Joel, 173
Smedley, Mike, 56, 57, 61
software, 133–38, 140, 167–69, 207
solvents, 245–46, 250–51, 253

Sony, 157, 264
Southern Alleghenies Regional
    Development and Planning
    Association, 201
space exploration, 30
"spin-out" strategy, 156, 171, 172
Spoonholtz, Lloyd, 114, 115
Statistical Process Control (SPC), 95,
    112
Stayer, Ralph, 35, 75–76
Steelcase, 52–53
steel industry, 20, 27–28, 52, 77–79, 82,
    89, 90, 117, 122, 123
Stewart, Tom, 30
stocks:
  dividends from, 144, 177, 321
  employee ownership of, 37, 85, 87,
    104–5, 106, 116, 119–21, 123
stress, 58, 110
Stump, Tim, 244
success:
  counterintuitive measures for, 17,
    182–84, 185, 191
  examples of, 13–17, 21–23, 29
  human achievement and, 18–19, 22
  paths to, 21–23, 33–47
  quality and, 218–20, 223–24
  synergism in, 23, 295
  technology and, 271–72, 277, 306–7
Sun, David, 278–81
Sun Microsystems, 182–91
  foreign sales of, 181
  global approach of, 178, 179, 180
  Japanese market of, 41, 42, 180, 182,
    184, 185, 187–89
  New World Tours of, 190
  open systems developed by, 183,
    184, 185–86, 189
  partnership model of, 183, 186–89,
    191
Superfund, 253
"sweating the details," 160

tape products, 241–42
Team Viper, 312
teamwork:
  employee empowerment and, 35,
    53, 263–64, 269–71
  for product development, 158, 159,
    162, 163–64, 173–74, 177
  quality and, 207, 208, 211, 216–18,
    220
  self-directed, 60–62, 63, 64, 95
  technology and, 263–64, 269–71,
    276–77, 321

training and, 59–69, 82, 83, 95, 102,
    122–24, 132, 136–37, 158, 159,
    162, 163–64, 207, 208, 211, 216–
    218, 220, 311–12, 314
technology, 258–84
    competition and, 275–76, 291–92,
        314
    core, 171
    demand-flow, 318
    digital, 199–200, 259, 282
    efficiency-enhancing, 42, 240, 259
    energy-conservation, 73–74, 170
    environment and, 250–51, 271
    "hard," 45–46
    improvement of, 22, 259–61, 273–75
    information, 39, 129–30
    management and, 287–88, 300, 316
    organizational change and, 258
    process, 289, 293–96, 302
    production, 30–31, 45–46, 211
    productivity and, 258
    profits and, 298, 309, 313–14
    quality and, 211, 226, 232–34, 258,
        275–76, 314
    research for, 31, 44, 171, 298, 302, 305
    "soft," 46
    success and, 271–72, 277, 306–7
    suppliers and, 268, 278–82, 305, 306,
        312
    systems for, 259, 260, 262–72
    teamwork and, 263–64, 269–71, 276–
        277, 321
    training and, 82, 88, 260–61, 262, 265–
        268, 272, 273, 284, 312, 313, 316
Teerlink, Richard, 145, 148
Tele-Communication, 168
Teledesic, 168
Tenneco, 319–25
    action plan of, 287, 321–24
    earnings of, 324–25
    global market of, 16, 322, 323, 324,
        325
    leadership of, 289–90, 321–22, 324
    quality control at, 320, 323
    stock of, 321, 322, 324
    subsidiary of, 320, 324–25
    turnaround of, 287, 319–25
thermal oxidizers, 241
Thermedics, 171
Thermo Electron, 170–72
    product development at, 40, 41, 156,
        170–72
    "spin-out" strategy of, 156, 171, 172
    stock of, 171
"things gone right" (TGR), 206

"things gone wrong" (TGW), 206
Thomas, Tom, 139
Thompson, Charlie, 229
386 chip, 288, 289, 296
3M, 119–20, 239–48
    Central Research of, 245–46
    environmental programs of, 44, 236,
        237, 238, 239–48
    Operations Committee of, 241, 243
    product development at, 44, 45, 155
    waste reduction by, 236, 244, 248–
        250, 251, 252–55
    Year 2000 goals of, 243, 247
3P (Pollution Prevention Pays), 44, 236,
    239–48
3P+ (Pollution Prevention Plus), 236,
    240, 242–43, 244, 246–47
Tiger software, 169
T-1 communications, 283
toothbrush holders, 161
Toshiba, 29, 185, 188
Total Customer Satisfaction (TCS)
        Worldwide Team Competition,
        217–18
Total Employee Involvement (TEI),
    230, 231
total quality management (TQM), 30,
    42–43, 47, 92, 205–34, 246, 258
toxic release inventory (TRI), 253
training, 80–102
    CEOs and, 36, 84, 85
    comprehensive, 36, 83–84, 89, 102
    continuous, 97, 211
    corporate goals achieved by, 81–82
    downsizing and, 25
    efficiency and, 80
    by employees, 17, 36, 92
    investment in, 36, 85, 94, 96
    math, 95, 267
    productivity and, 35–36, 82–83, 102
    programs for, 17, 28, 36, 71, 81–100,
        207, 210–11, 220, 260–61, 265–68,
        272, 291
    quality and, 207, 210–11, 214, 215–
        216, 220, 222, 229–30, 233
    re-, 101
    skills acquired in, 59–62, 86–87, 94
    survival and, 35, 87
    teamwork and, 59–69, 82, 83, 95,
        102, 122–24, 132, 136–37, 158,
        159, 162, 163–64, 207, 208, 211,
        216–18, 220, 311–12, 314
    technology and, 82, 88, 260–61, 262,
        265–68, 272, 273, 284, 312, 313,
        316

trust, 35, 53, 58, 64, 95, 322
Tu, John, 278–81
"12 Objectives for Managing Goodyear Successfully in the '90s, The" (Gault), 72–73
286 chip, 298
Tylenol, 176–77

Understanding Six Sigma, 214
unemployment, 20, 25–26, 56, 71, 74, 85, 98, 108, 111, 280, 303
unions, labor, 54, 71–74, 77, 78, 98–102, 148, 277, 312
United Electric Controls, 43, 208, 228–231
United Nations, 239
United Rubber Workers, 72, 74
United States Surgical, 176
Universal Instruments, 268
University of Tennessee, 256, 257
UNIX workstations, 186
Ursprung, Cecil, 120
U.S.:
    budget deficit of, 31
    economy of, 18, 26–27, 30, 71, 80, 106, 309
    foreign trade of, 19
    global competition for, 15, 18, 19, 20, 28–29, 30, 31–32, 47, 178–202
    Gross Domestic Product (GDP) of, 26, 27
    standard of living in, 27
USX (US Steel), 77–79, 123
    customer services of, 77–79
    employee empowerment at, 52
    Gary, Ind., plant of, 28, 52, 77–79
    as industrial icon, 56
    unions at, 54, 77, 78

Valued Ideas Program, 230
Varian Associates, 314–19
    customer services of, 316, 317
    employee empowerment at, 288, 314
    focus of, 315–16
    oncology systems unit of, 317, 319
    Operation Excellence of, 315–19
    turnaround of, 286, 289, 314–19
VAX systems, 268
Velte, David, 52
Vistakon, 176
vocational schools, 93
Volvo, 68, 88

Wadia Digital, 41, 179, 180, 181, 198–200
Wagner, Harold, 194
Walker, Mauro, 211
Wall Street Journal, 31, 32, 262
Walsh, Bernard, 176
Walsh, Mike, 23, 287, 319–25
waste disposers, 227
Waste Reduction Always Pays (WRAP), 236, 252–55
Welch, Jack, 19, 285–86
Whirlpool, 114–16
    gainsharing plan at, 37, 104, 114–16
    quality control at, 105–6, 116
Whobrey, Rodger, 282, 283
wholesale distribution, 194
Wiley, Helen, 100
Will-Burt, 84–89
    layoffs at, 85
    morale of, 84–85, 88
    sales of, 87
    training programs of, 82, 83, 84–89
Williams, Jackie, 118–19
Williams, Samantha, 53
Wilson Sporting Goods, 53
Windows applications, 135, 137, 140, 167, 169
Windows NT, 167
Winterbotham, Jim, 57, 61–62
WMX, 256
Wood, John, 171
Word program, 166–67
work process standards (WPS), 92
workstations, computer, 41, 182, 184–189, 283, 306, 307, 308
World Class Competitor Award, 73
World Class Manufacturing University, 177
World Economic Forum, 20

Xerox, 149–53
    Customer Satisfaction Measurement System of, 129, 150–52
    customer services of, 39, 128, 129, 130, 149–53
    Japanese competition of, 149, 150
    market share of, 149, 152
    quality control at, 150
    turnaround of, 128, 149–52
X-ray film, 256

Yamauchi, Hiroshi, 154, 156–57
Yokai, Gunpei, 154
Younkin, Jim, 317